Naval Campaigns of the Civil War

by PAUL CALORE

D0562314

McFarland & Company, Inc., Publishers
Jefferson, North Carolina, and London

Library of Congress Cataloguing-in-Publication Data

Calore, Paul, 1938–
    Naval campaigns of the Civil War / by Paul Calore.
        p.   cm.
    Includes bibliographical references and index.
    ISBN 0-7864-1217-8 (softcover : 50# alkaline paper) ∞
    1. United States — History — Civil War, 1861–1865 — Naval operations.
    I. Title.
    E591 .C26   2002
    973.7'5 — dc21   2001051196

British Library cataloguing data are available

Manufactured in the United States of America

Cover image ©2001 Corbis Images

McFarland & Company, Inc., Publishers
    Box 611, Jefferson, North Carolina 28640
        www.mcfarlandpub.com

Contents

List of Maps

Preface

Books on the Union and Confederate navies, particularly those written about their history, development, and battles, are conspicuously few in number. Long the unknown participants in the conflict, or at best the least celebrated, the naval arm of the Civil War was unwittingly consigned to the gray area of our nation's history.

To some extent the responsibility for this exclusion can be placed squarely on the lack of accurate and well-documented accounts by the writers of that period. While the land battles were abundantly detailed in newspaper accounts, reports, magazines, journals, diaries, and in many other forms, naval battles and the saga of their commanders were somewhat cursorily embraced.

Reporters, photographers, and artists traveled extensively with the armies, capturing every detail of each victory, the dejection of each defeat, and the personalities of the generals that commanded the field. The armies provided the action and the bloodshed, the devastation and the best news, the stories that would sell newspapers and magazines.

This book, however, reminds us all that the Civil War wasn't just about the bloodshed of infantry forces, but also about the anguish suffered by their counterparts in the navy. It was, in reality, a team effort, particularly for the Union, where the ultimate success of the infantry owed a great deal to the victories and support of the U.S. Navy. Without this support, Union ground troops almost certainly would have had to wage a longer fight with thousands of additional casualties.

On the other hand, it was extremely difficult for anyone — other than the participants themselves — to accurately record the events of a battle on the rivers or at sea. Space onboard ship was at a premium. The crews, numbering up to several hundred on most ships, were tightly packed into cramped quarters along with ammunition, supplies, food, and all the other resources that made the expedition self-sufficient away from their home port. In fact,

Secretary of the Navy Gideon Welles issued orders that prohibited reporters from traveling along with the Union ships and even for his officers to speak with the press about naval matters.

Consequently, with the exception perhaps of the voluminous Official Record, for today's writers, research material on the Civil War navies is relatively scarce, and what there is of it must be examined quite carefully. My challenge, therefore, considering the limited amount of first-hand information at one's fingertips, was to crosscheck and verify nearly every fact of the struggle against many other sources to ensure that one participant's ego, another's failing memory, or the wide diversity of views did not compromise the accuracy of the book.

Crammed into close quarters, subsisting on meager rations, and enduring hardships unthinkable in present day terms, this Civil War story recounts the heroic — and sometimes the tragic — efforts made by the commanders and their crews in over fifty naval encounters. Most were small and obscure in the context of the rebellion, others well known or recognized only by name. Beginning with the events leading up to the war, and a brief history of the Union and Confederate navies, I tried to relate not only the enormity of their missions, but also their remarkable achievements, the successes that gave birth to our modern navy.

In writing this book I established two goals. The first was to bring to life the gamut of naval action from the historic fight between the *Monitor* and the *Merrimack* in Hampton Roads, and the bloody gunboat clashes on the western rivers, to the stubborn Confederate resistance against the Union fleet in Charleston Harbor, and Farragut's famous battle in Mobile Bay. At the same time I wanted to convey an insight into the enormous effort confronting the Union to blockade Southern ports, the ensuing struggle to overcome the challenges of blockade-runners, and the terror unleashed by Confederate commerce-raiders.

My second goal was to describe the Union and Confederate navies, and each of their major campaigns, in a text that was clear and concise, while at the same time simple but accurate, and in a book that was as instructive and enjoyable to read as it had been for me to write. Although broad in its scope, and succinct in its style, this work has, I believe, achieved both of these goals.

Naval Campaigns of the Civil War should be assessed as an introductory reader, an account intended to establish a foundation upon which the Civil War enthusiasts can build. With a renewed interest in Civil War navies, my desire is simply to motivate and encourage the reader to embark on a mission for further study, so as to gain a more comprehensive knowledge of the role our navies played in our nation's bloodiest war.

Twelve maps are included, as well as a glossary to clarify a number of Civil War and naval terms used in the text.

Combining the use of this book with my earlier title, *Land Campaigns of the Civil War* (McFarland, 2000), the reader may better understand the entire scope of our nation's bloodiest struggle.

1

Prelude to War: December 1860–March 1861

The resounding beat of a military band filled the railroad depot on December 18, 1860. It was a crisp and clear Tuesday afternoon, and the echoing throb of the drums and brass could be heard throughout the city. With a population of 40,000, Charleston was a thriving seaport. Her waterfront constantly bustled with activity as black laborers toiled among the cotton-laden ships tied up at her piers, and on any given day her refined Southern ladies could be seen strolling along the Battery. Attracted by the band music, a crowd grew, and soon the depot took on a boisterous and festive air.

One hundred seventy delegates were arriving in Charleston that day. They were the men chosen by the various districts of South Carolina to decide the fate of their state and the future of the Union. The delegates had previously convened at the Baptist Church in Columbia on the 17th but, owing to an outbreak of smallpox in the city, chose to relocate their deliberations to Charleston. Before adjourning in Columbia, however, this assemblage of South Carolina's finest, including five former governors, voted to appoint a select committee to draw up an ordinance of secession.

That afternoon in Charleston, with a contingent of military cadets to escort them to Institute Hall, the delegates were convinced in their hearts that the Southern people were fed up with federal rule, and discontented with Northern hostile rhetoric against their "peculiar institution." They were equally convinced that Lincoln's presidential victory and his refusal to allow the South to extend slavery to the territories had deprived them of their constitutional right to further their institution, their prosperity, and their heritage, and had brought them to this historic gathering. Secession was the only option left to take, and they were the instruments to carry out that decision. South Carolina would lead the way and the other Southern states would follow.

At Institute Hall that Tuesday, the delegates listened to impassioned speeches, endless motions, and mundane reports. Towards the end of the day a vote was taken and it was agreed by most of those present that the next meeting would be held at St. Andrew's Hall. With today's business attended to, the meeting adjourned.

Two days later, December 20, the delegates met at St. Andrew's Hall to hear the report from the chairman of the Committee to Prepare an Ordinance of Secession. Anticipation was high that morning as the chairman took his place at the podium. The tension was unmistakably outlined on the faces of the delegates sitting in the hall, now uncharacteristically silent. The endless speeches, reports, motions, and committee meetings were all mere dressing. This was the moment they were waiting for and the only reason they were there. As the speaker began his address, everyone listened intently. The chairman's presentation was short and to the point as he outlined the result of the committee's deliberations, a resolution that read:

"We, the people of the State of South Carolina, in Convention assembled, do declare and ordain, and it is hereby declared and ordained, that the Ordinance adopted by us in Convention on the twenty-third day of May, in the year of our Lord one thousand seven hundred and eighty-eight, whereby the Constitution of the United States was ratified, and also, all Acts and parts of Acts, of the General Assembly of this State, ratifying amendments of the said Constitution, are hereby repealed; and that the union now subsisting between South Carolina and other States, under the name of 'The United States of America,' is hereby dissolved."

In this political forum, the resolution represented a rare piece of legislation that required no debate. This was the message the delegates expected to hear, and they wasted little time in casting their votes. Although a few may have been apprehensive about the uncertainty of the future, their minds were virtually made up, and, in fact, the resolution was carried 169 to 0. A motion was made to meet again that night for the formal signing ceremony. Agreeing to the motion, the delegates adjourned.

That evening St. Andrew's Hall, hereafter called Secession Hall, was a bedlam of cheering and chattering, and at times on the verge of unbridled chaos. The public was invited to witness this moment in their history, and it seemed like half the city was there at St. Andrew's clamoring for a better vantage point to observe the signing. In addition to the convention president and the members of the delegation, also on hand to view the proceedings were the members of the South Carolina Senate as well as the House of Representatives. Called in turn, it took just two hours for the delegates to sign the parchment that officially severed the bonds between South Carolina and the rest of the Union. South Carolina, declared the convention president, was now an "Independent Commonwealth," and how the people rejoiced.

The city of Charleston was dressed up in colorful bunting, and the streets took on an air of gala celebration. Besides the customary parade of military companies, there were bonfires, salvos of artillery by the Citadel cadets, music, and fireworks. People gathered in the streets waving palmetto flags and even banners of their own design. Many others, also caught up in the excitement of the moment, ran ecstatic through the streets cheering and dancing. One *New York Times* reporter who was on the scene would write, "The city was alive with pleasurable excitement."

Similar expressions of joy were also evident in most other major cities of the Deep South, such as Montgomery, Mobile, Wilmington, and New Orleans, where parades, gun salutes, and speeches created an air of wild jubilance, unwittingly premature in the face of darker events looming just over the horizon. The border states of Maryland, Kentucky, Delaware, and Missouri, however, would reserve their enthusiasm over secession and would take a wait and see attitude.

Northern reaction to South Carolina's secession was one of incredulous disbelief, and, to the ears of Southern listeners, expressed in their usual arrogant and flippant manner. Most Northerners refused to take the matter too seriously, believing that South Carolina was acting like a "spoilt child wandering from the fold of a paternal government." Even the Union newspapers appeared somewhat unconcerned. Initially, several Northern newspapers had for the most part accepted secession as a matter of principle. Three days earlier, the *New York Tribune* printed an article that stated, "If the Declaration of Independence justified the secession of three million of Colonists in 1776, we do not see why it should not JUSTIFY the secession of five million of Southerners in 1861." The *New York Herald* also acquiesced on the matter of secession, saying, "Each State is organized as a complete government, possessing the right to break the tie of the Confederation. Coercion, if it were possible, is out of the question." Several months later, however, in May 1861, the *Tribune* would write, "But, nevertheless, we mean to conquer them [the Confederate States], not merely to defeat, but to conquer, to subjugate them.... The whole coast of the South, from the Delaware to the Rio Grande, must be a solitude."

Southern newspapers, on the other hand, like the *Charleston Mercury*, voiced the sentiments of most South Carolinians on the perceived intent of Northern abolitionists in the Republican Party by writing, "The ruin of the South, by the emancipation of her slaves, is not like the ruin of any other people. It is not a mere loss of liberty ... but it is the loss of liberty, property, home, country — everything that makes life worth living."

In a bid to explain their actions to the Northern people, South Carolina declared that the free states of the North had "… assumed the right of deciding upon the propriety of our domestic institutions; and have denied the rights of property established in fifteen of the States and recognized by the Constitution; they have denounced as sinful the institution of Slavery; they have permitted the open establishment among them of societies, whose avowed object is to disturb the peace and to eloign the property of the citizens of other States. They have encouraged and assisted thousands of our slaves to leave their homes; and those who remain, have been incited by emissaries, books, and pictures, to servile insurrection. For twenty-five years this agitation has been steadily increasing, until it has now secured to its aid the power of the common Government…. A geographical line has been drawn across the Union, and all the States north of that line have united in the election of a man to the high office of President of the United States whose opinions and purposes are hostile to Slavery … and that a war must be waged against Slavery until it shall cease throughout the United States. The guarantees of the Constitution will then no longer exist; the equal rights of the States will be lost. The slave-holding states will no longer have the power of self-government, or self-protection, and the Federal Government will have become their enemy."

President James Buchanan had a different view of secession, however, as he stated in his final address to Congress on December 4. In the president's opinion, the Union was not "a mere voluntary association of States, to be dissolved at pleasure by any one of the contracting parties…." He also insisted that the founding fathers "never intended to implant in its bosom the seeds of its own destruction, nor were they guilty of the absurdity of providing for its own dissolution." In addition, the president's position on slavery was that it was a moral and political evil, and that slavery in the territories was one to be settled by judicial means. He endorsed the principle of non-interference by Congress regarding slavery in the territories, and denounced abolitionists.

Having created a sovereign state, the seriousness of their action was only beginning to be understood along with its inherent responsibilities. On December 22, 1860, the delegates met again, this time to consider the forts that were built to protect the city of Charleston. Although still under federal control, the forts were now within the jurisdiction of South Carolina and considered a threat to their sovereignty. The federal fortifications guarded the entrance to Charleston Harbor as well as the approach to the city of Charleston. They were Fort Moultrie, garrisoned by a small contingent of Union troops under Maj. Robert Anderson, and Castle Pinckney, a modest stone fort under the watch of one Union ordnance sergeant acting as caretaker. There was also Fort Johnson on James Island, which the Union had abandoned, and Fort Sumter, an unfinished fortress being built on a small man-made island in Charleston Harbor and named after Thomas Sumter, a Revolutionary War patriot.

In early December South Carolina's congressional delegation in Washington were convinced that the U.S. Government would yield to the principles of state sovereignty when their state officially seceded and therefore would acquiesce to the transfer of the forts into their possession. To preclude the possibility of trouble, they thought it best to get a heads up on the situation now, so that the transfer of the forts would occur smoothly and without problems later on. The only fair way, they agreed, was to meet with the president before South Carolina voted to secede, and hopefully come to some amiable understanding on the issue. In this context most of the congressmen met with President Buchanan on December 8 to discuss documenting an agreement on this matter that would be acceptable to all concerned. The result of this meeting was a statement, signed by five of the congressmen, outlining what they understood to be a consensus that neither side would attack, fire on, or reinforce any fort in and around Charleston Harbor before the convention committed itself. The statement concluded, "... and we hope and believe not until an offer has been made through an accredited Representative to negotiate for an amicable arrangement of all matters between State and Federal government, provided that no reinforcements shall be sent into those Forts & *their relative military status remains as at present* [italics added]." President Buchanan, on the other hand, did not exactly agree with the wording of this statement and felt he was under no obligation to support it, especially once South Carolina voted to secede.

The convention delegates, however, meeting on December 22, convened with the erroneous perception that a tentative agreement had been reached with President Buchanan on the matter of transferring the forts. With this understanding, they voted to send a three-member commission to Washington to negotiate further the timely transfer of the federal property to South Carolina.

Major Anderson, meanwhile, increasingly concerned over the threats from hostile citizens nearby, decided to evacuate Fort Moultrie and to move his entire command across the harbor to Fort Sumter. A 35-year veteran from Kentucky, and loyal to the core, Anderson considered Fort Moultrie too small, too old, and, considering the times, extremely unsafe. Surrounded by a stone wall and shifting sand dunes, the approximately two acres within contained a number of wooden buildings and about 55 guns. Anderson knew it was only a matter of time before the South Carolinians asserted their claim on the old fort. None of the guns protected the approaches to the rear, which was entirely exposed to the surrounding heights of Charleston and where Anderson expected an attack to occur. Another consideration was that the guns were all mounted in the open. Since the design of the fort afforded no protection at all for his artillerists manning these guns, Anderson felt compelled to evacuate immediately. Before leaving, however, the men spiked the guns and set fire to the carriages.

In the deepening shadows of sunset, on the evening of December 26, Anderson and his 65 regulars quietly trekked a quarter of a mile through the small town of Moultrieville to the nearby coastline. Luckily, the streets were abandoned. It was siesta time and the Charleston militia were still taking their afternoon naps. Not seeing a soul, they located their hidden boats bobbing by the seawall, quickly stowed their baggage, and began rowing the one-mile across the harbor to Fort Sumter. Within minutes, the light of a secessionist guard-boat was seen cutting through the gathering darkness. Spotting one of Anderson's small crafts, the intruding sentry, manned by troops of the Washington Light Infantry, stopped alongside and inspected the shadowy inhabitants in the waning light. Anderson had already opened his coat to conceal his brass military buttons and had also ordered his men to cover the muskets with their coats. Seeing nothing to arouse their suspicions, the Southerners assumed the Union troops were workmen from the fort and resumed their patrol. The Union men continued on and soon would occupy Fort Sumter, a fortress four times the size of Fort Moultrie.

When the people of Charleston awoke to see the Stars and Stripes fluttering over "their" fort, reaction was swift. The three-member commission, already in Washington, met President Buchanan on December 28 and angrily denounced the invasion of Fort Sumter and insisted that he honor his earlier agreement by ordering Anderson to leave the fort immediately. Buchanan's response was that since South Carolina seceded from the Union he was under no obligation to honor any agreement. On that note, the testy and somewhat heated meeting quickly ended, and Major Anderson remained at Fort Sumter.

Shortly afterwards, a copy of the Ordinance of Secession was delivered to the president, along with a stern letter from the commissioners concerning the breakdown of negotiations and the takeover of Fort Sumter. The letter stated, in part, "Until those circumstances are explained in a manner which relieves us of all doubt as to the spirit in which these negotiations shall be conducted, we are forced to suspend all discussions as to any arrangements by which our mutual interests might be amicably adjusted. And in conclusion, we would urge upon you the immediate withdrawal of the troops from the harbor of Charleston. Under present circumstances they are a standing menace which renders negotiation impossible, and, as our recent experience shows, threatens speedily to bring to a bloody issue questions which ought to be settled with temperance and judgement." The angry protests from the Southern commissioners proved to be somewhat hypocritical when Buchanan found out later that South Carolina had already seized Castle Pinckney, Fort Moultrie, and every other federal property within its borders except Fort Sumter. Buchanan scoffed at this letter and chose to ignore it.

By December, the Buchanan administration appeared to be falling apart. Southern members of his Cabinet had resigned to render their support and allegiance to their home states in this growing crisis, while others quit, supposedly over policy disagreements, particularly on how to handle the growing problem in Charleston Harbor. Confronted with these resignations and the subsequent Cabinet reshuffling, Buchanan was forced to replace his secretary of the treasury — twice, the secretary of state, the secretary of war, the secretary of the interior, and the attorney general. The breakup of the Cabinet, however, was a blessing in disguise. Buchanan had found it extremely difficult to obtain sound advice from advisers that were themselves divided. Now with a more Unionist persuasion, the Cabinet was set to delve into a crisis unique in American history.

Informed of the dire straits in which Major Anderson and his men found themselves, on or about December 31, Buchanan had finally made up his mind to send a relief ship to Fort Sumter carrying troops and provisions. This decision was agonizingly difficult to reach and was made after hours of heated debate with his new Cabinet, as well as with Gen. Winfield Scott, commander and general-in-chief of the Union army and Buchanan's military advisor. The 74-year-old general, overweight and failing, was the commander and hero in the war with Mexico in 1847, and was a presidential candidate in 1852. As early as October of 1860 the general had predicted an "early act of rashness preliminary to secession," and had recommended strengthening or installing garrisons at Forts Jackson and St. Philip at New Orleans, Morgan in Mobile Bay, Pensacola and McRee in Florida, Pulaski below Savannah, Moultrie and Sumter in Charleston Harbor, and Monroe in Hampton Roads. This was all well and good; however, at the time the army lacked the manpower and the material resources for such an ambitious effort, and so the matter was dropped as impractical. Unable to keep up with the demands of a more modern army in a more modern war, Scott would be forced to retire within the year.

Spurred into action by Buchanan's decision, Secretary of the Navy Isaac Toucey ordered the commandant of the Norfolk Naval Yard, across from Norfolk, Virginia, to prepare the steam sloop USS *Brooklyn* for service. At the same time, General Scott wired the commanding officer at Fort Monroe, instructing him to form an infantry force of 200 regular troops, armed and provisioned for 90 days, to be ready to board the *Brooklyn* when she arrived.

Secretary Toucey selected the *Brooklyn* because she was one of the latest warships of the day. Not yet three years old, the screw-driven sloop-of-war could boast of firepower from nothing less than twenty 9-inch Dahlgren smoothbores, two 100-pdr. Parrots, two 60-pdr. rifles, and one howitzer. Awe inspiring, she was a force to be reckoned with indeed.

On January 3, 1861, the *Brooklyn*, loaded with provisions, arms, and ammunition, was anchored off the coast of Fort Monroe, prepared to embark on her mission to Charleston Harbor. Within hours of sailing, President Buchanan notified her captain that his orders were canceled and to await further instructions on the deployment of his ship. Buchanan was persuaded to modify his plans after being advised that the *Brooklyn's* draft was too deep and there was a fear she might run aground in Charleston Harbor. Also, General Scott convinced the president that in all likelihood the mission was no longer a secret to the authorities in Charleston. Instead of using a powerful warship, Scott suggested, they should attempt the relief effort with a much faster vessel capable of slipping into the harbor and to the fort before anyone was the wiser. Selected for the mission was the side-wheel merchant steamer *Star of the West*. Her shallow draft made her more suitable for this expedition, and because she was unarmed she would appear to be less threatening.

The *Brooklyn*, on the other hand, with about 100 troops aboard, was redirected to Pensacola Bay to head off what the administration presumed was another potential crisis. In anticipation of problems from the imminent secession of Florida, the *Brooklyn* was dispatched to Fort Pickens, located at the entrance to Pensacola Bay, where she would report to Capt. Henry A. Adams, naval commander in the Gulf, aboard the USS *Sabine*.

In addition to Fort Sumter, Pickens was one of the few remaining forts between Charleston and Mexico still under federal control. The others, also in Florida, were Fort Barrancas and Fort McRee, also in Pensacola Bay, and Fort Taylor and Fort Jefferson, the latter two located in the Florida Keys.

In December, while secession fever was gripping the headlines, Secretary Toucey thought it prudent to alert the commandant of the Pensacola Navy Yard to be "... vigilant to protect the public property." Toucey's warning proved to be not only wise but also extremely timely, because on January 12, 1861, two days after Florida seceded, several hundred secessionists stormed the Pensacola Navy Yard, also referred to as the Warrington Navy Yard, and demanded its surrender. Without a shot fired in self-defense, however, the commandant, septuagenarian Capt. James Armstrong, timidly capitulated when the Southerners overwhelmed the base and hauled down the American flag.

Encouraged by their quick success, the emboldened Southerners went on to seize both Fort McRee and Fort Barrancas, located only a few miles away.

Earlier, at Fort Barrancas, Lt. Adam J. Slemmer had a sense that the

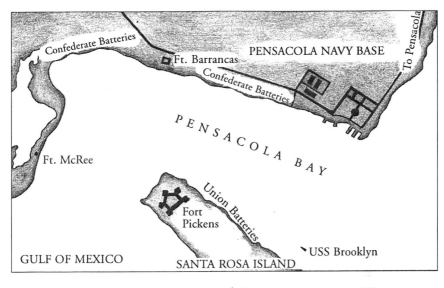

Confederate Batteries

Ft. Barrancas

PENSACOLA NAVY BASE

To Pensacola

Confederate Batteries

P E N S A C O L A   B A Y

Ft. McRee

Union Batteries

Fort Pickens

GULF OF MEXICO

SANTA ROSA ISLAND

USS Brooklyn

Pensacola Bay

rumors and Southern threats to attack the Union forts were real and not to be taken lightly. Also realizing the vulnerability of his command, prior to the raid on the Pensacola Navy Yard, he ordered his men to evacuate to a fortification he considered more secure. Finding himself in somewhat similar circumstances to Major Anderson at Charleston, on January 10 Slemmer moved his entire garrison to Fort Pickens.

Built among the sand dunes on Santa Rosa Island, Fort Pickens guarded the entrance to Pensacola Bay. Abandoned since the Mexican War, the fort was grossly neglected and found to be in a decayed and run-down condition. The garrison was loaded aboard several small boats, along with provisions, field artillery, and ammunition, and towed the two miles or so across the bay by the USS *Wyandotte*.

Furious over Slemmer's bold move, the governors of Florida and Alabama threatened to attack the fort. They demanded the surrender of Fort Pickens not once but on three occasions, on January 12, 15, and 18. The young lieutenant, reflecting his bravado and his naïveté, made it clear to the Southern authorities that he would not give up the fort without a fight.

Although he was still in a tenuous position at best, Slemmer had over 50 guns primed for battle, enough supplies to last several months, and a modest contingent of 80 men, including a number of sailors that managed to flee the Navy Yard during the January 12 raid. The garrison was not a threatening force, however, against the 800 to 900 Southerners gathered across the bay preparing to carry out the governor's threat.

As the *Brooklyn* was steaming south to Fort Pickens with the troops and supplies, Sen. Stephen R. Mallory of Florida (soon to be Jefferson Davis' secretary of the navy) was in Washington negotiating a deal with President Buchanan. The deal struck was simple: If Fort Pickens wasn't reinforced, there would be no attack. Consequently, on January 30, orders from the Navy Department were delivered by the USS *Crusader* to Captain Adams to keep the troops aboard the *Brooklyn* unless the fort was attacked or under immediate threat of attack.

The troops on board the *Brooklyn* arrived in Pensacola Bay on February 9. Without orders to the contrary, they and their immediate commander, Capt. Israel Vogdes, had little choice but to wait aboard the ship for further instructions.

With his term over in March, many considered Buchanan's deal with Mallory nothing more than a delaying tactic. The lame-duck president felt the troublesome issues emanating from secession were the direct result of Lincoln's political policies, certainly not anything he was responsible for.

The *Star of the West*, in the meantime, now stocked up with provisions, supplies, and 250 troops from the 9th U.S. Infantry, sailed out from Governors Island in New York Harbor on January 5.

The secrecy of this clandestine mission was uncovered, as General Scott had predicted. There was evidence that Buchanan's secretary of the interior, a Mississippian, was the source of the leaks to Charleston just before he resigned. But even so, it is highly probable that if the leaks hadn't occurred, the mission would have been exposed anyway. When the administration in Washington attempted to notify Major Anderson of the planned relief expedition, the letter was sent through normal postal channels through Charleston. Since the post offices were seized along with the other federal buildings, there is little doubt the letter was intercepted. At any rate, the officials in Charleston knew it and duly notified Governor Francis Pickens. Even the newspapers picked up the story, which, oddly enough, is how Major Anderson was informed.

Arriving at 1:30 a.m. in the pitch-black morning of January 9, the *Star of the West* gingerly crept towards Charleston Harbor. At the first rays of dawn, and now moving at full steam, she crossed the outer bar of the main channel and soon attracted the attention of the cadets from the Citadel, South Carolina's military college, manning the Confederate batteries hidden among the sand dunes on Morris Island. Suddenly, an explosion broke the early morning stillness. A single warning shot from Morris Island arched slowly across the bow of the *Star of the West* and splashed harmlessly in the channel. Belowdecks the anxious troops sat quietly in the humid darkness and waited nervously for the next and perhaps fatal shots. The unarmed vessel continued on its forward movement when in rapid succession the hidden battery opened a barrage of missiles. Of the 17 shots fired by the cadets, two struck aft, one near the rudder, the other about two feet above the water line. Suffering only minor damage, the ship continued on its forward course but now found herself in range of the artillery on Fort Moultrie, which also proceeded to fire on the unarmed craft. Recognizing the danger of passing by the closer and more heavily armed fort, the captain prudently lowered the U.S. flag, ordered the ship around, and, at full steam, fled down the channel out of range and back to New York.

The repulse of the *Star of the West* was hailed as a confirmation of Southern determination and of the integrity of its independence. The local newspaper, the *Charleston Mercury*, exulted with banner headlines on the South Carolina victory: "The haughty echo of her cannon has reverberated through every hamlet of the North. And if blood they want, blood they shall have. For, by God of our Fathers, the soil of South Carolina shall be free!"

Over the next several weeks the legislatures of six additional states from the Deep South also elected to secede. Together with South Carolina, they voted to meet in convention at Montgomery, Alabama, to form a separate and independent Union of their own. Mississippi seceded on January 9, Florida on the 10th, Alabama on the 11th, Georgia on January 19, Louisiana on January 26, and Texas on February 1. Seven states had now left the Union, and there was no way of turning back.

On February 4, 38 delegates, learned and honorable men from six of the seceded states, met at Montgomery. (Texas had seceded only three days earlier, too late to send delegates.) Their task was to create a new constitution for a new government, and to select the people who would implement it. The goal set by the delegates was to accomplish this feat before the new Lincoln administration took over in four weeks. Laboring under extreme pressure, in only five days the delegates were able to forge together a provisional constitution, based mostly on the U.S. version, and to elect a provisional president and vice-president. The Constitution for the Provisional Government of the Confederate States of America was adopted on February 8. The following day the delegation elected Jefferson Davis president.

Born on June 3, 1808, in Christian County, Kentucky, Jefferson Davis was educated at Transylvania University in Kentucky, followed by four years at the U.S. Military Academy. Following his graduation from the Academy in 1828, Davis served in the Black Hawk Indian War in 1832 but resigned his commission three years later and married the daughter of Colonel Zachary Taylor, who would go on to be the 12th president of the U.S. His young wife died three months into their marriage, at which time Davis settled down in Mississippi and spent the next decade as a planter. In 1845 Davis' life was reborn. Not only did he remarry that year but also his intense preoccupation

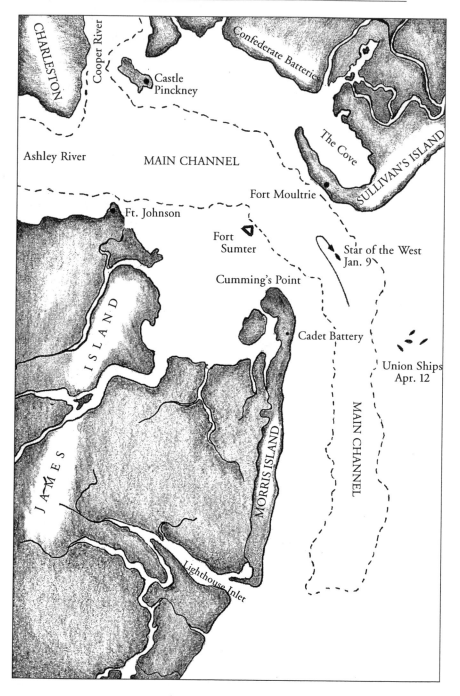

Charleston Harbor — 1861

with politics won him a seat in the U.S. House of Representatives as a Democratic congressman from Mississippi. The following year he left politics to take a command in the Mexican War, was wounded, and returned to Washington in 1847, this time as a U.S. senator. Franklin Pierce, the new president in 1853, offered Davis the position of secretary of war in his administration, which he readily accepted; and four years later he returned to the U.S. Senate, remaining until 1861. When Mississippi seceded, Davis announced his resignation and went home to support the Southern cause. As a Southern senator, Davis was a staunch advocate of states' rights and gained the reputation as the leading spokesman for the Southern point of view.

Elected vice-president was Alexander H. Stephens of Georgia. A diminutive, frail man, Stephens had served in Congress with Lincoln and was a staunch fighter for States Rights.

On February 18, on the steps of the Alabama State capitol at Montgomery, Davis was sworn in as Provisional President of the Confederate States of America, to serve a six-year term. His inauguration as elected president would be held on February 22, 1862. Also taking the oath of office that morning was Vice-President Stephens.

Davis insisted in his address that the founding fathers had established a constitution designed to foster specific principles, and that, "... when, in the judgement of the sovereign States now composing this Confederacy, it had been perverted from the purposes for which it was ordained, and had ceased to answer the ends for which it was established, a peaceful appeal to the ballot-box declared that so far as they were concerned, the government created by that compact should cease to exist." He also emphasized that secession illustrated "... the American idea that governments rest upon the consent of the governed, and that it is the right of the people to alter or abolish governments whenever they become destructive of the ends for which they were established."

A new nation was born, with Montgomery as its capital.

To his wife Varina, Davis would later write, "Upon my weary heart was showered smiles, plaudits and flowers; but, beyond them, I saw troubles and thorns innumerable. We are without machinery, without means, and threatened by a powerful opposition; but I do not despond, and will not shrink from the task imposed upon me."

In Charleston, Gen. Pierre G. T. Beauregard, a Mississippian and former gunnery student of Major Anderson's at West Point, was busy coordinating the placement of ordnance and troops in the batteries that nearly surrounded Fort Sumter. These included the batteries on Morris, James, and Sullivan's Island, Fort Moultrie, Castle Pinckney, a floating battery in Charleston Harbor, and the Cumming's Point battery. The positioning of the batteries was extremely critical. Besides ensuring that Fort Sumter was within their range, the batteries were also tasked with sealing off the harbor from Union incursion.

President Davis selected General Beauregard personally for this command, the first of the new Confederacy. On March 3 the general was ordered to Charleston to represent the Confederate Government, which had now taken control of the growing crisis there. In charge of the artillery and several thousand troops, Beauregard was certain that he would be fully prepared to meet the challenge if force became necessary.

Major Anderson, on the other hand, was by now well aware of the political incident his occupation of Fort Sumter had triggered, and the danger in which he and his men found themselves. Following the failure of the Union relief expedition, Major Anderson and his troops began to shore up the defenses of Fort Sumter in anticipation of an attack. They mounted guns, bricked up embrasures, stacked sandbags, secured the approaches to the fort with wire traps, and constructed a cheval-de-frise. The entire effort would take over three months to complete. Anderson's food supply, however, was limited. Now that the city of Charleston no longer provided provisions to the fort, he knew something had to be done politically before his men starved. Taking stock of his food inventory, Anderson had already informed his superiors that, at the extreme, he could probably hold out until April 15. At that point his plan was to evacuate the fort.

Until then, Anderson and Beauregard could do nothing but stand by while their governments tried to figure out what to do next.

In Washington, meanwhile, on a cold but sunny March 4, Abraham Lincoln took his oath of office. Administered by Chief Justice Roger Taney beneath the unfinished dome of the nation's capitol, Lincoln was sworn in as the sixteenth President of the United States. Earlier that day, in the U.S. Senate chamber, Vice-President Hannibal Hamlin was also sworn in.

In his inaugural address, Lincoln reminded the country that, "... no State upon its own mere motion can lawfully get out of the Union; that resolves and ordinances to that effect are legally void, and that acts of violence within any State or States against the authority of the United States are insurrectionary or revolutionary, according to circumstances." Furthermore, as the leader of the country he had a solemn oath to "preserve, protect, and defend it."

Tucked within his address was also a veiled threat to the states of the South that he, as President of the United States, was constitutionally bound to "hold, occupy, and possess the property and places belonging to the Government...."

With that said, the new administration had drawn its line in the sand.

2

The Opening Salvo: March–April 1861

In a primitive dirt-floor log cabin near Hodgenville, Kentucky, Abraham Lincoln was born on February 12, 1809. Abe's father, Thomas, succumbing to his pioneering spirit, sold the homestead for 10 barrels of whiskey and twenty dollars when Abe was seven years old and moved the Lincoln family to Spencer County, Indiana. Three years later, following the death of Abe's mother, Nancy Hanks, his father married an old friend and widow from Hodgenville, Sarah Bush Johnston, who had three children of her own. Including Abe, his sister Sarah, who was two years older, and an orphaned cousin, the Lincoln household now stood at eight, all crowded into one tiny cabin.

Whenever the weather permitted, or when he could be spared from his chores, young Abe attended a small, windowless log schoolhouse, walking there through the woods with his sister by his side. In the Lincoln household, where the labors of homesteading took priority over "book learnin'," in aggregate, his formal schooling amounted to about one year. Despite the brevity of his education, little Abe was eager to learn, and by applying himself in his studies he managed to read and write. In fact, reading books became a passion for him and a welcome diversion from the thankless toils expected from a young farm boy in the early nineteenth century.

Nearly six feet tall when he was fifteen, the young lad considered himself extremely fortunate that his size and strength could earn him a little money by cutting and selling wood, and later by ferrying customers across the Ohio River. Nevertheless, Abe grew tired of hard labor. His goals were much loftier, and so he began to search for a way to secure a better future. His chance came in 1831, at 22 years of age, when he seized an opportunity to strike out on his own by transporting farm produce to New Orleans aboard his homemade flatboat. Following the success of this venture, Abe accepted employment in New Salem, Illinois, on the Sangamon River, running the local store and gristmill, serving as its postmaster, and even worked for a time as a surveyor.

In 1834, while still living in New Salem, Lincoln won a seat in the Illinois legislature, then at Vandalia, serving in that capacity for two terms. Although Lincoln never received a formal education, during this period of his life he spent many hours studying law by reading school books borrowed from a lawyer friend. After submitting the required papers testifying to his moral character, as was the custom in 1837, he received his license to practice his new vocation. Excited yet apprehensive, the new attorney rode a borrowed horse into Springfield, only 20 miles from Vandalia, and launched a new career.

After several years of courtship, in November 1842 the 33-year-old lawyer married Mary Todd, a 21-year-old socialite from Kentucky who was living with her sister in Springfield. Lincoln opened a Springfield law firm two years later with his partner William H. Herndon. Enjoying a comfortable income, the young couple soon bought a new house for $1,500, where they raised four boys, although only one, Robert Todd Lincoln, lived to adulthood.

Despite his love for practicing law, Lincoln longed to return to politics, especially to represent his constituents in Washington. His opportunity came in 1846 when he represented the Whig Party in the Illinois seventh district congressional race. Winning two-thirds of the vote, Lincoln was elected to a two-year term in the House of Representatives as a new member of the 30th Congress. His exposure to the heart-wrenching sights of the slavery business in the nation's capital taught him a great deal about the terrible treatment of slaves and the appalling practice of slave auctions.

Following his terms as congressman, Lincoln returned to Springfield where he continued his law practice. Although the Lincoln-Herndon partnership thrived, Lincoln found it very difficult to sit idly by as his country struggled with the immense problems of the times. Predictably, Lincoln was drawn back to the political arena in 1854 when the spread of slavery to the territories, an issue he had profound ideas against, was being hotly debated. Two years later the newly formed Republican Party nominated him to represent Illinois in the U.S. Senate, a seat held by incumbent Stephen A. Douglas. Abe lost that hotly contested election to Douglas, but his performance in the 1858 campaign debates won him national recognition. The following year Lincoln barnstormed the country, speaking throughout the Midwest, New York, and New England. So impressive was his potential that he was being discussed as a possible candidate for the upcoming presidential election.

In 1860, after winning 17 of the 33 states, and with 40 percent of the popular vote, Lincoln won the presidential election. For the new president the victory was bittersweet. Although he rejoiced in his success, he knew his success also won him the unenviable task of leading a country teetering on the brink of war.

On the first morning of his presidency, Lincoln arrived at his office and immediately confronted a constitutional crisis, as well as developing incidents in Charleston Harbor and Pensacola Bay, any one of which could lead to civil war. Seven states had seceded from the Union, and secessionists had seized all federal property within each one of them, such as arsenals, forts, office buildings, post offices, and custom houses. Even the U.S. Mint in New Orleans was taken over by the secessionists and over $500,000 in coin was transferred to the Louisiana treasury. Of the remaining forts still under the control of U.S. military forces, only two, Sumter in Charleston Harbor, South Carolina, and Pickens in Pensacola Bay, Florida, were under a direct threat of Confederate attack.

The War Department's first order of business, therefore, was to order an investigation into the situation at Fort Pickens. For nearly two months Union troops had languished aboard the *Brooklyn*, anchored a half-mile or so off the Santa Rosa coastline. From their inquiries, the new administration soon discovered the deal made in January between Florida Sen. Stephen R. Mallory, now the Confederate Secretary of the Navy, and President Buchanan that prohibited the troops from going ashore unless Fort Pickens was attacked or was under threat of attack.

Incensed over this revelation, on March 12 the navy war office sent the USS *Mohawk* on an urgent run to Pensacola Bay. Aboard the *Mohawk* were new orders, signed by the assistant adjutant general of the army, that directed Capt. Israel Vogdes, commander of the troops aboard the *Brooklyn*, to land his men at the first opportunity and reinforce Fort Pickens. The senior naval commander in Pensacola Bay, however, Capt. Henry A. Adams, saw the army instructions and promptly informed Washington that he would not allow them to be carried out. As far as he was concerned, the orders of January 30 from the Navy Department took precedent, and until the navy sent new orders to the contrary, the troops would stay put. Somewhat frustrated over this seemingly mere technicality, on April 6 Secretary of the Navy Gideon Welles immediately forwarded revised orders to Captain Adams. They were delivered personally via rail by navy courier Lt. John L. Worden, who would soon command the ironclad USS *Monitor* in her epic battle with the CSS *Virginia*, the first engagement ever between two iron ships.

While the War Department was sorting out matters in Pensacola Bay, Lincoln's attention was primarily focused on Fort Sumter. Should the fort merely be handed over to South Carolina and thereby give credibility to this whole secessionist movement, or should an attempt be made to reinforce it and risk a civil war? To Lincoln, the pledge he made in his inaugural speech to protect all government property was one he took seriously and one he felt he had to carry out, even if it meant using military force.

In a letter sent to Lincoln on March 12, however, General Scott thought the use of military force was out of the question. The navy was incapable of such a feat, he told the president, and the army would require about 25,000 men. Scott was quite emphatic that he not only lacked sufficient quantities of troops, but, even if he did have the manpower, he realistically wouldn't have the time to train, equip, and field them. Certainly not by April 15, the date Major Anderson predicted his food would run out and he would evacuate the fort, anyway.

Most of the Cabinet, including Secretary of War Simon Cameron and Secretary of the Navy Gideon Welles, agreed with General Scott and favored abandoning the fort. But on March 28 General Scott went even further. He opined that the evacuation of Fort Sumter as well as Fort Pickens "would instantly soothe and give confidence to the eight remaining slave-holding States, and render their cordial adherence to the Union perpetual" and that "the giving up of Forts Sumter and Pickens may be best justified by the hope that we should thereby recover the State to which they geographically belong by the liberality of the act, besides retaining the eight doubtful states." Coming from the president's military advisor, it was a startling political analysis. That evening, President Lincoln, somewhat distressed over this revelation, disclosed Scott's recommendation to the Cabinet at a rare late night emergency meeting. Once Lincoln convinced the Cabinet that Scott's rationale for abandoning the two forts was not really based on military considerations but was politically motivated, the Cabinet reversed itself and agreed to support the president.

During these trying times, questions of true loyalty were always raised when Southern-born officers gave even the slightest appearances of favoring their home state. In this circumstance, no matter how false the perception really was, to some in military and government circles, General Scott's allegiance was suspect, not merely because he was a Virginian but also because of his opposition to reinforcing the forts, and, as stated in his letter, his willingness to give them up. Now questioning Scott's credibility, the following day the Cabinet agreed with the president that an attempt to reinforce Fort Sumter was not only necessary but should be done immediately. But the question was, how to do it?

The answer came from a textile businessman from Massachusetts, Gustavus V. Fox, a former officer in the navy who was also the brother-in-law of

Lincoln's postmaster general, Montgomery Blair. Considering the number of high-ranking army and naval personnel at his beck and call, to an outside observer, a U.S. President that considered and approved a military plan proposed by a civilian was certainly something quite novel indeed. But a novel problem sometimes required novel solutions, and this would be the first of many.

Fox's ideas for the relief of Fort Sumter had been previously relayed to the president at one of Lincoln's Cabinet meetings. Lincoln though it was a good plan, and the Cabinet liked it too. A 40-year-old Annapolis graduate and veteran of 15 years in the navy, Fox thought it best to ferry troops and provisions to the entrance of Charleston Harbor aboard transports. Warships would escort the troop carriers and would also provide protection for the small flotilla. The supplies and troops would then be transferred to smaller vessels outside the bar and, in the middle of the night, towed by tugboats in a mad dash to the fort.

Since the *Star of the West* fiasco, the consensus was that the Confederates, to prevent another such attempt, may have placed obstructions in the channel of Charleston Harbor and increased their battery defenses along the shorelines. Based on these assumptions, there was much concern over the increased risk facing the tow-boats and their launches, given the fact that once past the obstructions Fox would still have to pass by the Confederate batteries at Cumming's Point and the batteries on Sullivan's Island as well. General Scott disapproved the scheme, and many others were also concerned, that is, except Gustavus V. Fox, who remained confident in his plan and in the ultimate success of the mission. Shortly afterwards, Fox was summoned to the White House to brief the president on his plan.

When Lincoln gave the order to proceed with the relief effort, he set in motion a sudden flurry of activity from the White House, the Army, and the Department of the Navy.

Fox received his orders on April 4 with authority from Secretary of War Cameron to board the supplies and troops the army would furnish, on a transport, and to proceed to Fort Sumter. Promptly leaving Washington for New York, Fox chartered the large civilian steamer *Baltic* as a troop transport and secured the use of three tugs, *Uncle Ben*, *Yankee*, and the *Freeborn*. At the same time, Secretary of the Navy Gideon Welles began making arrangements for the preparations of the warships. They were the 16-gun steam side-wheeler *Powhatan*, the mission flagship, commanded by Capt. Samuel Mercer; the *Pocahontas*, a 5-gun steam sloop under Capt. J. P. Gillis; and the 8-gun screw sloop *Pawnee*, skippered by Cmdr. Stephen C. Rowan.

A considerable amount of scrambling was necessary, however, to get the *Powhatan* prepared for this mission. She had just been decommissioned on

March 28 at the Brooklyn Navy Yard and her crew placed in a standby status. Secretary Welles had ordered the decommissioning to put the *Powhatan* into dry-dock for badly needed repairs. Persuaded that the *Powhatan* was the ideal ship for the Sumter expedition, he sent a telegram to the commander of the navy yard, Commodore Samuel L. Breese, rescinding the order. Breese was also instructed to prepare the ship for her departure to Fort Sumter. Complying with the Secretary's wishes, the Commandant ordered all transfers and leaves cancelled and the crew recalled back to the ship.

Also on hand would be the revenue cutter *Harriet Lane*. Furnished by the Treasury Department, the 7-gun steamer was named after President Buchanan's niece, who was also his official hostess, and was the largest cutter in the U.S. Revenue Marine, the forerunner of the U.S. Coast Guard.

There was one problem, however. Several ranking naval officers believed the fleet would never arrive in time to save Major Anderson before he surrendered the fort on April 15, and for this reason they turned down the offer to command the fleet. Without a military commander to coordinate the mission, Fox would have to direct the expedition himself.

As the relief effort evolved in Washington, however, a bizarre episode began to play out concerning the use of the USS *Powhatan* and the controversy it caused between the secretary of state and the secretary of the navy.

While Secretary Welles was busy working on plans to relieve Fort Sumter, Secretary of State William H. Seward, on his own initiative, was delving into matters not officially assigned to his office, specifically organizing a clandestine expedition to reinforce Fort Pickens.

Secretary Seward thought Lincoln, being new to executive politics, was incompetent and still green in higher governmental affairs. His opinion was that Lincoln had "no system, no relative ideas, no conception of his situation, and little application to great ideas." Under the influence of this philosophy, Seward believed that he alone was more qualified, and consequently better able, to resolve these very urgent matters. After all, he reasoned, wasn't he the front-runner for the presidential nomination that Lincoln eventually received? And besides, he had his own agenda, which he thought best served the country. In his opinion, Fort Sumter should be given up, that it was much too close to Washington and wasn't worth going to war over. Instead, he felt it was in the country's best interest to reinforce Fort Pickens, and if the Confederacy resisted that effort, then that's where the war should begin.

Therefore, to make sure his own agenda was pursued to the letter, Seward took command of the effort personally. In his mind, the timing couldn't have been better. As far as he knew, with the existing naval presence in Pensacola Bay, an expedition to Fort Pickens was never contemplated by the navy or, for that matter, even discussed by Secretary Welles. Seizing this opportunity to insure that no one interfered with his plan, Seward would also strive to gain the president's agreement on the need for secrecy. Lincoln's pledge would guarantee that Welles remained out of the loop.

He was so confident that his plans would succeed that Seward even began leaking information to Southern authorities and the press that Fort Sumter would be abandoned. Even when the Confederate officials he met with appeared confused over the conflict of information they were receiving, Seward reassured them of the imminent evacuation of the fort in Charleston Harbor.

To assist him in carrying out his operation, on March 31 Seward enlisted the help of two military officers, Army Capt. Montgomery C. Meigs and Navy Lt. David D. Porter. Called to Seward's office early that morning, the three men discussed a plan for the relief of Fort Pickens, a plan the president was scheduled to review later that day. The choice of Meigs and Porter wasn't exactly a random selection for Seward. Both men were close acquaintances and had become, like Seward, highly critical of the president. They had often discussed their ideas on reinforcing Fort Pickens and even for winning back the Pensacola Naval Yard. With their plans in hand, that evening Seward, Porter, and Meigs gathered in Lincoln's office and outlined their ideas to the president.

The mission plan called for the *Atlantic*, a large steam transport, to ferry 600 men, artillery, and supplies to the entrance of Fort Pickens. A warship would serve as an escort to deter Confederate interference. Lincoln liked the plan and approved it.

Seward also selected the warship that would accompany the *Atlantic*; she was the USS *Powhatan*. Sporting ten 9-inch Dahlgrens, one 11-inch pivot gun, and five 12-pdrs., it was the very same ship Secretary Welles assigned to Fox's fleet and was now being prepared to embark for Fort Sumter. In addition to choosing the *Powhatan*, Seward even picked the naval officer who would command the vessel, Lt. David D. Porter. Coming from a family rich in naval tradition, he was the son of Capt. David Porter, a much-respected commander in the early nineteenth century navy, brother of William D. Porter, and stepbrother of David G. Farragut, both of whom were also serving in the Union navy.

Evidently, both Welles and Seward knew the *Powhatan* was in New York, but neither knew that, independently, each had issued different orders for the use of the same ship, at the same time and with different commanders.

Secretary Seward also spoke to Lincoln at length on the need for secrecy, telling the president that it was the only way the mission could be accomplished. In the back of Seward's mind was his belief that if the Navy Department was involved, "… the whole matter would be known to the

Confederates by being flashed across the wires an hour after Secretary Welles got an order to prepare the ship for sea...." After assuring Lincoln that he would "... make it all right with Mr. Welles," Lincoln agreed to the secrecy of the expedition.

To complete the plan, Seward got the president to routinely sign a stack of orders, one of which assigned Lieutenant Porter to command the *Powhatan*. Included in the stack as well were the orders to Commodore Breese directing him to provide arms and provisions to the *Powhatan* for this expedition, and supplementary instructions to Breese that stated, "She is bound on secret service, and you will under no circumstances communicate to the Navy Department the fact that she is fitting out."

All of this maneuvering was done behind Lincoln's back, as well as infringing on the duties of Secretary of War Simon Cameron and Secretary of the Navy Welles. Seward blatantly failed to follow the chain of command. Instead, he left both Cameron and Welles uninformed to accomplish his own agenda and to placate his huge ego. Only Secretary Cameron had the authority to coordinate the adoptions of military plans and to dispatch troops in support of that plan. Likewise, it was under the exclusive jurisdiction of the secretary of the navy to select the ships and their commanders for any mission. As Welles would later say about Porter, "As a lieutenant, he was entitled to no such command as the *Powhatan*, a fact of which Mr. Seward, who had little knowledge of details, was ignorant...."

At the navy yard, Capt. Andrew H. Foote, acting in place of Commodore Breese, who was on leave, was totally confused after receiving two different sets of orders for the same ship, one from the president and the other from Secretary Welles.

When Porter and Mercer arrived at the Brooklyn Navy Yard, a meeting was held between all parties concerned, including General Meigs, who had arrived to confirm Porter's orders. During the course of this meeting it was agreed that the president's order should prevail. It was at this point that Seward's "presidency" began to unravel. When Captain Mercer telegraphed Secretary Welles of the decision, the extremely irate Navy Secretary lost no time in confronting Seward, who by now also learned of the plans Welles had for the *Powhatan*. Fearing his own expedition was in peril, Seward angrily demanded that the navy call off the Sumter expedition immediately. After a heated argument between Seward and Welles, a meeting was quickly arranged to discuss the whole matter with the president. Highly disturbed over the mix-up, Lincoln agreed that the Sumter expedition had the priority and, accordingly, ordered Welles to send new orders to Captain Mercer reinstating his command to the *Powhatan*, and for Seward to notify Porter that his command was rescinded.

But Porter indignantly refused to honor Seward's directive because his original orders came from a higher authority, the president himself. With that said, Porter set his course for Fort Pickens and sailed the *Powhatan* out of port on April 6, replying, "I received my orders from the President and shall proceed and execute them." The *Atlantic*, meanwhile, had already departed earlier that day with the troops.

In actuality, the South was rather wary of Secretary Seward's comments on Fort Sumter and never really believed the information he was passing along. So, in spite of what the secretary of state may have said to Southern agents, Jefferson Davis was still preparing for a stand at the fort in Charleston Harbor.

As far as Seward's meddling was concerned, after the meeting in Lincoln's office, Secretary Welles gave Seward a proper dressing down by explaining to him, in a rather piqued manner, the different responsibilities of their respective offices. From that time on, Secretary Seward mended his ways. And because of Lincoln's unintentional complicity, Secretary Welles decided to overlook the whole sorry affair; and to Lieutenant Porter's relief and surprise, he remained in command of the *Powhatan*.

In Pensacola Bay, meanwhile, Lieutenant Worden had delivered Welles' message to Captain Adams on April 12. The following day the troops and supplies aboard the *Brooklyn* were brought ashore and Fort Pickens was finally reinforced.

Five days later the *Atlantic* also arrived with the troops Lincoln had sent down on March 31, and within hours the *Powhatan* dropped anchor in Pensacola Bay, her belly heavy with artillery.

Now under the command of 65-year-old Col. Harvey Brown, Fort Pickens was garrisoned with over one thousand troops and would no longer be a problem for the rest of the war. As for the *Brooklyn* and the *Powhatan*, they were subsequently assigned to patrol the waters at the mouth of the Mississippi River.

In the meantime, while Seward's surreptitious expedition to Fort Pickens was playing out, the effort to relieve Fort Sumter was moving forward in New York Harbor, where the launches, provisions, and troops were loaded on board the *Baltic*. When his preparations in New York were completed, Fox intended to rendezvous with the rest of his small fleet outside the entrance to Charleston Harbor (not knowing, of course, that the *Powhatan* had been diverted to Fort Pickens).

Fox, however, was disappointed that Lincoln had compromised his plan, a strategy that Fox sincerely believed would succeed the way it was originally designed. A major part of the scheme was to use darkness as a cover for a speedy run to the fort before the Southerners could react. The element of surprise was no longer needed now because Lincoln planned to inform

Governor Pickens that warships were going to the relief of Fort Sumter, and with orders to shoot if necessary.

The president's message to Pickens was quite simple: "... an attempt will be made to resupply Fort Sumter with provisions only; and that, if such attempt be not resisted, no effort to throw in men, or ammunition, will be made, without further notice, [except] in case of an attack on the Fort."

Lincoln was now putting his cards on the table. Not only was he calling their bluff, but he was also telling them to prepare to back up their words with action, that he was willing to go to war, but only if the South committed the first aggressive act. Of course, Pickens and most of the South would insist that Northern voters had already committed the first overt act last November. Be as it may, instead of a rescue operation, Fox was now being used as bait to test the Southern resolve for war.

Governor Pickens, on the other hand, still maintained his tough rhetoric that, "... nothing can prevent war except the acquiescence of the President of the United States in secession and his unalterable resolve not to attempt any reinforcement of the Southern forts."

Even before President Davis was informed of Lincoln's message, rumors of the impending naval expedition were filtering into the executive mansion in Montgomery. The Fort Sumter crisis not only placed Lincoln in a tenuous position, but it also had Jefferson Davis feeling the pressure from his constituents as well. On one side there were the hawks wishing to defend the new sovereignty of South Carolina no matter what the consequences, and on the other side there were the doves fearing a bloody civil war if Fort Sumter was fired upon.

The *Charleston Mercury* would print, "Border southern States will never join us until we have indicated our power to free ourselves — until we have proven that a garrison of seventy men cannot hold the portal of our commerce. Let us be ready for war...."

During a Cabinet meeting on April 9, Confederate Secretary of State Robert Toombs tried to persuade Davis against taking aggressive action against the fort or, for that matter, the U.S. Navy. Toombs would remark to Davis, "Mr. President, at this time it is suicide, murder, and will lose us every friend at the North. You will wantonly strike a hornet's nest which extends from mountain to ocean, and legions now quiet will swarm out and sting us to death. It is unnecessary; it puts us in the wrong; it is fatal."

As Secretary Toombs was speaking those very words, the *Baltic*, with Fox aboard, along with the launches, troops, and provisions, was steaming from New York for Charleston.

Davis listened politely to his secretary of state, but to his ears the words were not convincing. It was unconscionable to some that the citizens of

Charleston would fire on a fort originally constructed in Charleston Harbor to protect the very citizens set on destroying it and the men inside. All they had to do was merely wait until the Union troops exhausted their rations for them to surrender. The Confederate President, however, had already made up his mind. He wanted nothing better than to capture Fort Sumter, and he wanted to do that very badly. He didn't want the fort simply turned over to him. He wanted to take the fort by a sheer show of force against the U.S. Government. In this way he could show the other Southern states, as well as the world, that the Confederacy could indeed stand up for its principles and its ideals. He will show that good always conquers over evil.

On April 10, therefore, Davis made his decision, and through the Secretary of War, Leroy P. Walker, the following message was sent to General Beauregard in Charleston: "If you have no doubt of the authorized character of the agent who communicated to you the intention of the Washington Government to supply Fort Sumter by force you will at once demand its evacuation, and if this is refused proceed, in such manner as you may determine, to reduce it." The message was clear. In President Davis' mind, if the approaching fleet were somehow successful in re-supplying the fort with food and supplies, Major Anderson's stay at the fort could be extended indefinitely and deal a real blow to the young Confederacy. Davis wanted General Beauregard to settle the Fort Sumter issue now — before the Union relief effort arrived.

The following day three Confederate agents approached Fort Sumter under a white flag. With them was a written demand from General Beauregard for Major Anderson to surrender the fort immediately. Anderson refused. Early the next morning, the 12th, at 3:30 a.m., another attempt was made to persuade Anderson to evacuate the fort, and again Anderson refused. This time, however, the agents penned a message to Anderson, which read, "By authority of Brigadier-General Beauregard, commanding the Provisional Forces of the Confederate States, we have the honor to notify you that we will open the fire of his batteries on Fort Sumter in one hour from this time."

A man of his word, General Beauregard's artillery commenced fire on Fort Sumter at 4:30 a.m. on April 12.

Major Anderson's efforts to defend the fort and his men, although gallant and brave, were wholly ineffective. The Union firepower was no match against the Confederate barrage of shells and hot shot that rained down on them from an arc of hostile batteries. Capt. Abner Doubleday, a Union officer at the fort, described what he saw. "The scene at this time was really terrific. The roaring and crackling of the flames, the dense masses of whirling smoke, the bursting of the enemy's shells and our own which were exploding in the burning rooms, the crashing of the shot, and the sound of masonry falling in every direction, made the fort a pandemonium."

Also that morning the *Baltic* arrived outside the Charleston Harbor at 3 a.m., joining the *Pawnee* and the *Harriet Lane*. Severe seas had forced the *Pocahontas* and the smaller tugs to separate from each other, so their arrival would be delayed. As the three vessels tossed in the high winds and heavy seas waiting for the other ships, the reports of heavy artillery could be heard in the distance. Little did they know that the war had already begun.

Finally, in the early afternoon of April 13, only the *Pocahontas* arrived, and Fox was informed that the *Powhatan* had been diverted from the mission. A mix-up had occurred in Washington, he was told, and new orders now called for the *Powhatan* to steam towards Fort Pickens. Fox was devastated. His entire plan had unraveled. There could be no landing without the launches, which were on the *Powhatan*, or without the tugs, which also failed to arrive; and certainly without the protection of his powerful warship, the mission was impossible at best.

In a matter of hours, as Fox stood on the deck of the *Baltic*, his gaze transfixed on the burning fort in the distance, he knew his efforts to relieve Fort Sumter were over. Unable to see the American flag above the fort (the flagpole was struck by a direct hit), a bitterly disappointed Fox aborted the mission.

With his adopted fort totally destroyed by some three thousand shells, with no food left to eat, and with fire threatening the powder magazine, Major Anderson surrendered.

At Fort Sumter on April 14 the rays of the morning sun gave shocking evidence of the barrage that had devastated the fort and endangered the troops within. Once a new state-of-the art fortification, its solid brick walls, eight to twelve feet thick, were now horribly pockmarked and reduced to mounds of crumbling rubble.

That morning, to the strains of Yankee Doodle, he and his men marched out of the fort to a waiting ship, the Confederate steamer *Isabel*. Ironically, the draft of the *Baltic* was found to be too deep for a safe approach to Fort Sumter and she was forced to wait outside the harbor for the *Isabel*. As the Stars and Bars were being hoisted over the fort, Anderson and his men were transferred aboard the *Baltic* to join Fox for the trip north.

Later, Fox would say, "I had the mortification of witnessing the surrender of the Fort with no part of my proposed plan arrived. As for our expedition, somebody's influence has made it ridiculous...." However, President Lincoln didn't think it was so ridiculous. Admiring his courage and patriotism, the president appointed Fox the chief clerk of the navy on May 9, and on August 1 promoted him to be the first ever assistant secretary of the navy.

Governor Pickens was overjoyed at the Confederate victory. When informed of Anderson's surrender, he commented, "We have met them and we have conquered."

3

Virginia Secessionists — Wrath Unleashed: April 1861–March 1862

While Beauregard and Anderson were playing out their drama in Charleston Harbor, a less heralded but arguably more significant incident was beginning to heat up at the Norfolk Navy Yard, also referred to as the Gosport Navy Yard. Located on the Elizabeth River across from Norfolk, Virginia, it was — and still is — one of the largest naval base and ship repair facilities in the country. The naval base boasted of an enormous crane, one of only two granite dry docks known to exist, and a large arsenal housing a fortune in heavy ordnance and ammunition.

In the shipyard at the time were eleven vessels of various classes, all of them dismantled and in various stages of disrepair. They included the 120-gun *Pennsylvania*, now stripped of its weapons and being used as a receiving ship; 3-deckers *Columbus* and *Delaware*; as well as the *New York*, an abandoned hull still unfinished after 20 years. Also on hand were the frigates *Columbia* and *Raritan*, both seaworthy but in desperate condition; the *United States*, the oldest ship in the U.S. fleet; the 22-gun sloops-of-war *Germantown* and *Plymouth*; the dispatch boat or brig *Dolphin*; and a steam frigate warship, the USS *Merrimack*.

In early April of 1861, with threats of Virginia seceding from the Union flying fast and furious, the Lincoln Navy Department anticipated trouble around Norfolk and a possible attack on the navy yard from a band of highly vocal and extremely agitated Virginians. To Secretary Welles, immediate action was considered necessary in light of several reports that described the angry mood and extremely hostile tensions at the naval facility, as well as in the Portsmouth and Norfolk area, all of it directly aimed at the presence of the military personnel and naval vessels at the base.

The object of the navy's concern was one of the most awesome warships in the Union fleet, the five-year-old, 40-gun *Merrimack*. Now unarmed and dismantled, her condemned engines lay disassembled and wantonly strewn about the yard. To prevent this prized warship from possibly falling into Southern hands, an order was issued on April 10 to the Norfolk commander instructing him to "Prepare the *Merrimack* promptly for temporary service under steam alone...," and he was warned, "It is desirable that there should be no steps taken to give needless alarm."

Receiving this order was Capt. Charles S. McCauley, commander of the Norfolk Navy Yard and responsible for the 800 men and officers under his command. Sixty-eight years old and extremely loyal to his country, McCauley would find that the quickly evolving events were too much for him, and his actions over the next several days would highlight his total lack of sound judgment. A remnant of the old school, with over 50 years of service, his training and experience had not prepared him for the decisions he was expected to make during these volatile times. He not only failed to foresee the possible dangers ahead, but also had not prepared for the defense of his command or the plans for its evacuation. Many of McCauley's contemporaries, however, felt that this dereliction of duty was based, to a large extent, on McCauley's reliance on the advice of his subordinates, the Southern officers in his command in whom he had placed his trust.

Nevertheless, despite having orders in hand, McCauley balked on preparing the powerful warship for sailing. In his judgment, the launching of the 40-gun *Merrimack* in this tense climate would only provoke hostile reactions from the Virginia secessionists, particularly after he was ordered not "to give needless alarm." Under this rationale, McCauley ordered the work stopped.

In Washington the urgent priority placed on this matter was quite evident in the manner in which Secretary Welles tirelessly focused on implementing the rescue of the warship. On April 11 Welles dispatched Cmdr. James Alden to Norfolk. His orders were to take command of the *Merrimack* and to sail her out under full steam for Philadelphia. Welles also ordered the commander of the Brooklyn Navy Yard, Commodore Samuel L. Breese, to deliver a crew of 250 sailors to Norfolk. The following day Welles angrily reacted to McCauley's work stoppage by sending the navy's chief engineer to Norfolk to supervise the repair of the engines and to insure the ship was effectively seaworthy. Finally, on the 16th, Commander Hiram Paulding, an over-aged old salt, was also ordered to the navy yard to oversee the entire project and to expedite the removal of the *Merrimack* out of Norfolk.

In Virginia, meanwhile, events were spiraling out of control. The State

Convention at Richmond voted to join the Confederacy on April 17, and following this vote, Henry A. Wise, who was the governor of Virginia when abolitionist John Brown was sent to the gallows, and a truly dedicated secessionist, mobilized the militia for action against the Norfolk Navy Yard. Wise had already sent troops to seize Harpers Ferry several days earlier, actions the current governor, John Letcher, would belatedly approve.

Southern militia troops were soon dispersed on the banks of the Elizabeth River across from the naval base, and batteries established along the shoreline. In addition, fanatical secessionists, inspired by the fall of Fort Sumter and the Southern call to arms, were bent on preventing the warships from leaving Norfolk. To accomplish this, they sank several old hulks in the channel of the Elizabeth River in an effort to block the passage of the Union ships, albeit a largely misguided exercise.

On the 18th, with the work on the *Merrimack* finally completed, she was again rearmed, under full steam, and refitted for the passage to Philadelphia. Since the sailors from New York had not yet arrived, however, plans were quickly improvised to use a skeleton crew from the 30-gun *Cumberland* that had only recently been moored at the yard for repairs. At this point Captain McCauley interceded again. In his opinion the obstructions in the river would definitely impede the removal of the *Merrimack*; and so convinced was McCauley that the movement of the warship would be interpreted by the Virginians as an aggressive act, that he refused to allow the ship to leave the port. Instead, he ordered the *Merrimack* repositioned so her firepower could be used for the possible defense of the base.

Commander Paulding was back in Washington at this time conferring with naval officials. Outraged over this abrupt and unilateral decision, and with questions beginning to surface on McCauley's motives, Secretary Welles ordered Paulding to relieve McCauley as commander of the Norfolk Navy Yard, effective immediately.

Meanwhile, back at the shipyard, on April 19 McCauley decided he had had enough. He only had six naval officers left willing to join him in the defense of the navy yard, the rest being Southerners who had resigned the day before and gone home to join the Confederate movement. Practically his entire civilian workforce, all of them Southern sympathizers, had done likewise. Coupled with the fact that he could see the Confederate troops under Gen. William Taliaferro — and menacing batteries — gathering in force across the river, McCauley was sure he was about to be invaded. Therefore, to prevent the ships from being captured, he ordered them scuttled, all eleven of them, including the *Merrimack*.

Commander Paulding arrived back at the navy base around 8 p.m. on the 20th aboard the screw sloop *Pawnee*, along with about 350 soldiers from the 3rd Massachusetts Infantry Regiment. Too late to save the ships, he was appalled at what he saw. Assessing that his troops would be unable to hold off the Southern forces massing across the river, he had little choice now but to complete the job begun by McCauley. He ordered the buildings torched, the new granite dry dock destroyed, all ordnance spiked or thrown in the river, and the superstructure of the sunken ships set on fire. In the early morning hours of April 21, the machine and repair shops, five warehouses, the foundry, and the living quarters were set ablaze, while flammable fluids ignited the remains of the scuttled ships, and barrels of gun powder were set in place on the dry dock, its slow fuses to be lit as the evacuation was underway.

As the crackling flames and glowing embers illuminated the early morning darkness, the *Pawnee,* along with the *Cumberland,* slipped out into the river and sailed off towards Hampton Roads. Aboard the *Cumberland* stood McCauley, silently lost in thoughts of his lost command.

Moments after the federal evacuation the Southern soldiers entered the base and frantically extinguished the flames in an attempt to salvage as much as possible. At dawn the new Confederate commander of the navy yard, 65-year-old Capt. French Forrest, accompanied by several state officials, moved in to survey the damage and to claim their spoils. To their delight, although most of the ships were destroyed, the all-important dry dock was still intact (the barrels of gunpowder failed to explode). Most of the buildings survived also, as did much of the ammunition, various types of machinery, engines, construction materials, equipment stores, steel plates, and castings. They were especially pleased when over a thousand canons were found, 300 of which were new Dahlgrens of various caliber, many of which were salvaged from the river.

Over the next several years this loss of nearly twelve hundred pieces of artillery to the Confederacy would prove to be catastrophic to the Union side. Without the means to manufacture such an enormous quantity of heavy ordnance in the short term, the South hit the jackpot when they captured this cache of weapons at the outset. The confiscated guns would be used to arm numerous Confederate fortifications, killing thousands of Union troops throughout the four year war at such places as Hatteras Inlet, Roanoke Island, Port Royal, and New Orleans. In fact, many of these very pieces were recaptured at Forts Henry and Donelson, as well as at Island No. 10, Memphis, Vicksburg, Grand Gulf, Port Hudson, and even Manassas.

The submerged ships, some antiquated, all sodden and burned, were beyond salvage and probably not worth the time, effort, and the cost to recover them. On the other hand, one vessel stood out from all the rest and was examined with special interest. She was the USS *Merrimack.* In a matter of weeks the scuttled prize would be raised from her watery grave and brought back to life as the Confederate ironclad CSS *Virginia,* a reincarnation that would launch a whole new chapter in naval design and warfare.

With little fanfare, the *Pawnee* and the *Cumberland* arrived at the Washington Navy Yard on April 23; and with them came the news that, along with Pensacola, the Norfolk Navy Yard was now also in Confederate hands. (Both navy facilities would revert back to the Union in 1862 after being abandoned by the Confederates in May.)

Since the beginning of the year, Confederate forces had occupied, seized, or taken over nearly every Federal fort, camp, and arsenal located within the borders of the seceded states. The Pensacola Navy Yard in Florida, Fort Sumter in Charleston Harbor, South Carolina, and the Norfolk Navy Yard in Virginia were just three of the most significant ones. These were indeed major losses for the Union, and the war was just beginning.

When Virginia voted to secede on April 17 the news unleashed the pent-up rage and hostility of the local secessionists. Like a frenzied mob, within just a few short days the enmity between the two sides had played itself out not only at the Norfolk Navy Yard and at Harpers Ferry, but was now about to rear its ugly head along the shores of the Potomac River as well.

A vital water link between Washington and the outside world, the Potomac was, in fact, a super-highway over which hundreds of vessels traveled each day. Carrying passengers, produce, foreign goods, and a myriad of other materials and commodities, the commercial and private ships that plied this waterway were now feeling the wrath of the times.

Southern forces were gathering at various points along the Virginia shores of the lower Potomac with artillery and manpower in a brute show of force that threatened the safety of the United States capital. Furthermore, in early May the all-important rail depot and wharf at Aquia Creek, 45 miles south of Washington, was now also dotted with rifled batteries and earthworks, as was Mathias Point and Quantico. These hostile moves, under the direction of Capt. William F. Lynch, CSN, in turn fed a growing paranoia that had crept into the Lincoln administration. There were new anxieties that Confederate forces were attempting to isolate Washington, it being so close to the Southern side, by taking control of the Potomac River. These fears were motivated to some extent by recent events in Baltimore. There, irate city officials attempted to cut Washington off from the North to prevent the Union from transporting soldiers from the New England States through their fair city. This concern quickly escalated to a state of alert as Virginian forces, using artillery captured from the Norfolk Navy Yard, began firing at the passing ships. These blatant attacks interrupted traffic flow on the river, created heightened apprehension and anxiety among passengers who dared to run the batteries, and impeded routine commercial activity.

Once the Confederate batteries began firing on unarmed vessels, Lincoln felt compelled to counter this bold act of aggression. In response to these assaults, in May of 1861 the Union navy assembled a flotilla of small steamboats to patrol the Potomac. Lightly armed, the boats were ordered to cruise the river, keeping a watchful eye on the Confederate batteries lining the shore. Called the Potomac River Flotilla, it was under the command of Cmdr. James H. Ward, a 28-year veteran, and consisted of an old side-wheel steamer, the *Freeborn*, and two small tugs, the *Anacostia* and the *Resolute*.

To those critical of Secretary Welles, the fact that the Union government was able to muster only these three flimsy vessels for the war's first naval engagement was a sad commentary on the state of the naval forces at that time. This was made quite clear when it was pointed out that the vessels of the Potomac Flotilla were challenging large caliber Confederate ordnance arrayed along the riverbank with guns, the heaviest of which was only one 32-pdr.

In spite of this adversity, reacting to Confederate artillery action from the batteries at Alexandria (the most annoying of them all), on May 24 Union army troops were dispatched aboard the USS *Pawnee* to assist the flotilla, and assigned to clear the enemy batteries that flaunted their presence in sight of the U.S. capital. Commanded by Stephen C. Rowan, the *Pawnee* went on to capture a Confederate steamer outside Alexandria, the *Thomas Collyer*, on May 25; and, under threat of her devastating firepower, the Confederate troops wisely evacuated the city. For the first time in the war Union troops had landed on Confederate soil. The occupation of Alexandria not only eliminated the troublesome batteries but also provided a somewhat comforting buffer zone between Washington and the Confederate States.

The first combat fatality of the Civil War also occurred shortly after the Union troops landed on May 24. It came about when a 24-year-old Union army officer, Col. Elmer Ellsworth, was shot and killed in the stairway of a hotel by the owner for tearing down the Confederate flag from the roof of his building, the Marshall House. His brutal and irrational death, over what was perceived as such a relatively minor incident, captured the imagination of the Northern people. For the first time they understood the senseless tragedy of war and were shocked and saddened by it. So great was the impact of his death that flags flew at half-staff and his body lay in state in the East Room of the White House. In turn, the incident provoked a new wave of resentment towards the Confederate establishment and inspired a whole new round of enlistments.

Continuing on with their sweep of the Potomac shoreline, the flotilla was dispatched on May 31 to attack and destroy the enemy's battery at Aquia Creek. Aboard the *Freeborn*, a three-gun paddle-wheel steamer, Commander Ward ordered a concentrated shelling of the Confederate position. After two days of sporadic bombardment, now joined by the guns of the *Pawnee*, the Confederate forces withdrew from the artillery duel, briefly evacuating their batteries after torching the railroad pier and several adjoining buildings.

Several weeks later, however, on June 27, a Confederate sniper shot and killed Ward as he stood on deck directing the gunfire on Mathias Point. Union troops from the *Pawnee* were in the process of landing on the beach when a sizable force of Confederates suddenly advanced towards the Federal landing party. In the ensuing exchange of gunfire, Commander Ward was hit. With his death the flotilla commander now held the dubious distinction of being the first Union naval officer killed in the Civil War.

The small flotilla, although gallant in its intent, was unable to drive the Confederate troops from the southern edge of the river. In fact, it was on the Potomac that the Confederates scored their first naval capture. This occurred in June when a Confederate naval commander and several armed accomplices, posing as civilian passengers, boarded a small steamer, the *St. Nicholas*, and, when underway, took control of the ship. In reality, the capture of the *St. Nicholas* was only the first phase of a much larger scheme to seize their principal antagonizer, the USS *Pawnee*. But unable to locate the *Pawnee* (she had taken the men to Ward's funeral), the Southerners took the *St. Nicholas* and refitted it for use in the Confederate navy.

In October of 1861 Union fears were heightened anew when secret intelligence reached Union naval authorities that Southern troops were planning to cross the Potomac and invade the Northern side. Learning the identity and location of the rebel ship intended for use in this mission, the Confederate plan was quickly and soundly rebuffed when three boats were dispatched on a clandestine mission to intercept the enemy craft. Under the cover of darkness the commander of the Union raiding party boarded the ship and set her ablaze, totally destroying the schooner as she lay at anchor in Quantico Creek.

The Potomac Flotilla, now considerably larger (with ten additional vessels), continued to maintain its surveillance, mostly between the mouths of the Potomac and the Rappahannock Rivers. The flotilla kept a vigilant eye on the remaining Confederate batteries until they withdrew in March of 1862. Unable to carry out their sordid aims, the Southern artillerists finally withdrew their weapons from the shores of the Potomac and moved on to assist Gen. Robert E. Lee and the Army of Northern Virginia.

In spite of the Confederate withdrawal, the flotilla remained in place for most of the war. Occasionally intercepting ships trading in salt, a vital meat preservative in short supply in the South, the tiny fleet continued its daily patrols of the river to insure it remained opened to Northern shipping.

4

Presidential Posturing: April–May 1861

The dreadful news that Fort Sumter had fallen to the Confederate forces reached the White House on Sunday, April 14. Earlier that day Lincoln endeavored to maintain a sense of routine, an air of cool detachment from evolving events. In spite of his public demeanor, however, anxieties ran high that day as he waited for word from Charleston.

The president's reaction to the bad news was to immediately call for his Cabinet, and together they discussed the ramifications of this blow to federal authority. It's very likely they even discussed the steps Lincoln should take, not only to regain the confidence of the people in their government but also to assert the power of his office. In any event, the result of their meeting was quite evident the following day.

On Monday President Lincoln issued a proclamation that shook the South to its very core, and exacerbated the rush to war. Lincoln made an appeal to the governors of all the states for 75,000 volunteers to serve a 90-day term of enlistment. From December of 1860 to April 1861 Southern secessionists had seized dozens of federal forts and arsenals from South Carolina to Texas. Under Lincoln's proclamation, the volunteers would be assigned "... to repossess the forts, places, and property which have been seized from the Union...."

Lincoln's request was aimed not merely at the Northern states but even the Southern states that had not chosen to secede. In his proclamation Lincoln made his position crystal clear. The call for troops and the purpose of their enlistment left little doubt of his intentions in the coming weeks. The president's immediate aim was to take back the federal property now occupied by Confederate forces, but his ultimate goal was to reunite the Union — peacefully if possible, by force if necessary.

Lincoln also called for the members of both Houses of Congress to meet in special session on July 4 to "... consider and determine such measures, as, in their wisdom, the public safety, and interest may seem to demand."

In reality, Lincoln had no congressional authority to call for more troops, but, as he understood it, as Commander-in-Chief it was within his constitutional powers to do so. Congress was in recess during this time, and until they reconvened, Lincoln felt he was free to do as he chose for the good of the country. When Congress met in July they retroactively granted congressional authorization for all the president's actions. The legislators also authorized up to $250 million for the war effort and passed the first personal income tax levied on U.S. citizens to help pay for it.

It wasn't long before word reached the people in the Northern states that Fort Sumter had surrendered. Although initially saddened by the implications of such an incident, the emotional ground swell created a spontaneous outpouring of patriotism and loyalty for the Union. Suddenly, flags were displayed everywhere, as in storefront windows, from rooftops, and unfurled by excited demonstrators rallying in the streets and town squares. This display wasn't one of joy, but was instead a fervent statement of support for the Federal Government's right to expunge the forces that desecrated their flag.

Meanwhile, in Richmond, wild celebrations over the fall of Sumter were running rampant through the streets. News from Charleston had arrived in the Virginia capital on April 13, and as the word quickly spread, jubilant crowds rushed to the capitol building to exult in their victory. The city "... seemed to be perfectly frantic with delight. I never in all my life witnessed such excitement...," described a Virginian who participated in the festivities. "Everyone is in favor of secession." The same expression of unbridled excitement was quite evident in other major cities of the South as well. In cities such as Wilmington, Montgomery, and Nashville, processions and parades continually tramped up and down the streets. Militia bands tirelessly played "Dixie's Land" throughout the day, and there were endless speeches on every street corner calling for their states to join the secession movement. The *Times* of London reported that the Southern people could not contain themselves as they loudly rejoiced with "... flushed faces, wild eyes, screaming mouths, hurrahing for Jeff Davis and the Southern Confederacy."

All this partying would abruptly stop, however. In the midst of all the revelry the text of Lincoln's proclamation began to hit the headlines in the Southern newspapers. On hearing of Lincoln's call for volunteer troops, the Southerners were incensed, livid to think that the president had the audacity to ask them to send their own sons, brothers, and fathers to invade sister-states and fight against their own "kinfolk." They were repulsed and outrageously insulted at this blatant display of coercion. The governor of Virginia,

John Letcher, was asked to send three regiments of infantry. Until this moment he had been taking a wait and see attitude towards secession, but after Lincoln's proclamation, he called the state's secession convention to reconvene.

On April 16 Governor Letcher sent his reply to Lincoln, berating the president for his latest action. In the letter, Letcher wrote, "In reply to this communication, I have only to say that the militia of Virginia will not be furnished to the powers at Washington for any such use or purpose as they have in view. Your object is to subjugate the Southern States, and a requisition made upon me for such an object — an object, in my judgment, not within the purview of the Constitution or act of 1795 — will not be complied with. You have chosen to inaugurate civil war, and having done so, we will meet it in a spirit as determined as the Administration has exhibited towards the South."

The governors of Kentucky, North Carolina, Tennessee, Arkansas, and Missouri all sent similar sentiments. In fact, Lincoln's aggressive request to pit the Southern states against each other was enough to drive Virginia, Arkansas, Tennessee, and North Carolina out of the Union. Virginia went out on April 17, Arkansas on the 6th of May, North Carolina on the 20th, and Tennessee seceded on June 8. With Virginia now in the Confederacy, the Southern Congress accepted the invitation to move its capital to Richmond, the South's most industrialized city.

Towards the end of 1861, two additional Southern states, Missouri and Kentucky, were vying for Confederate recognition. Missouri was voted into the Confederacy on November 28. However, soon after the State seceded, the Confederate State government was evicted and a pro–Union legislature installed, ending Missouri's allegiance to the Southern cause. Kentucky ended its neutrality in September. Favoring not to secede, the "Bluegrass State" voted to side with the Union. However, in the southwest corner of Kentucky a small number of secessionists formed their own provisional government, which was admitted into the Confederacy on December 10.

Thirteen Southern states were voted into the Confederacy, but only eleven remained loyal to the cause. For this reason the Confederate battle-flag displayed thirteen stars, but in reality only eleven states actually fought under its colors.

Southern concerns were mixed over the prospects that secession would instigate an outbreak of hostilities. Some were convinced that Northerners were too timid to fight. "A lady's thimble will hold all the blood that will be shed" was one popular assessment on the severity of any conflict. Others, however, felt a bloody civil war was indeed inevitable, and were eager to fight, bound by a strong sense of duty to defend the honor of their birthplace.

While both presidents were men of measured and profound self-control, tension was rapidly intensified as each side counteracted the other, each weaving and maneuvering while equally steadfast in their political views. In the coming weeks the result of this presidential sparring provoked a series of proclamations and/or presidential orders from the White House in Washington and the Executive Mansion in Richmond.

When President Davis was given the news of Lincoln's proclamation, Davis responded by issuing one of his own on April 17. In it Davis appealed for owners of privately owned ships to apply for letters of marque, a license or permit sanctioned by the Confederate Government allowing privately owned ships to attack and capture U.S. merchant vessels at sea. In his appeal, Davis invited "all those who may desire, by service in private-armed vessels on the high seas, to aid this Government in resisting so wanton and wicked an aggression, to make application for commissions or letters of marquee and reprisal to be issued under the seal of these Confederate States." A form of legalized piracy, it was also called privateering, and was used previously by the U.S. with some success in the Revolutionary War, as well as the War of 1812. There were those who considered this move by Davis one of the worst decisions he made, because in the final analysis it forced Lincoln's hand, and the results would later prove to be disastrous.

Two days later Lincoln issued a second proclamation. To some, this was a response, and to others, retaliation to the Southern request for privateers. Lincoln called for a naval blockade of all Southern ports, from South Carolina to Mexico. (This would be amended on April 27 to include Virginia and North Carolina.) The proposed blockade would cover the coastlines of all the seceded states and would prohibit ships from entering or leaving their ports. The order was an ambitious one indeed, and one that reflected Gen. Winfield Scott's proposed "Anaconda Plan," a scheme to "envelope" the South with a blockade at sea and with offensive gunboats on the Mississippi.

President Davis, now the leader of a new country, was politically empowered to establish diplomatic ties with foreign countries. He was eager to fulfill his responsibility in this regard, particularly in those countries where he wanted to do business, like England and France. Furthermore, with purchasing agents dispatched to negotiate contracts for new ships for his embryonic navy, Davis understood fully that he would be well advised to get on good terms with their governments. What's more, since these countries were world leaders in shipbuilding and manufacturing of heavy ordnance, it became imperative that the Confederacy be recognized as an independent government.

With this in mind, Davis came up with a scheme that used his most lucrative cash crop to gain a degree of leverage for obtaining their cooperation. Southern politicians knew for some time that the English economy was largely dependent on its textile industry and, by implication, its enormous need for cotton imports from the Southern states. How would the British economy fare if its cotton imports stopped, and what would the English government do to preserve these imports? One Southern newspaper instructed its planters to "keep every bale of cotton on the plantation. Don't send a thread to New Orleans or Memphis till England and France have recognized the Confederacy — not one thread."

To force the issue, Davis ordered an embargo on all exports of cotton to England. With this move he hoped the shortage would strain the British economy to the point where it would persuade the British to formally recognize the Confederate government, and to insist that Lincoln lift the blockade. The Charleston newspapers agreed: "The cards are in our hands and we intend to play them out to the bankruptcy of every cotton factory in Great Britain and France for the acknowledgment of our independence."

As matters turned out, however, this maneuver was a huge miscalculation because not only did England not need the cotton to the extent predicted by Davis, but the Southern treasury loss millions of dollars in revenue from the unsold cotton. Actually, Davis was unaware that England not only had enough cotton reserves, but also could buy it elsewhere if necessary.

The Confederate plan for financing the war was through loans from citizens on bonds secured by Treasury Notes, and by the cash income from duties on exported cotton. In 1863, when Davis realized he desperately needed funds, the end result of his deception was painfully apparent. By that time the Union blockade had tightened sufficiently enough to limit the export of his mighty cash crop, and Davis found himself sorely pressed for capital.

Despite the attempts made by diplomatic missions for European support, England and France would remain neutral, both taking a wait and see attitude. England again specifically refused to intervene in the conflict in any way, shape, or form, instead acknowledging that to do so would probably hurt English interests more than the blockade would have.

In Washington the Lincoln administration soon realized that the quickly escalating crisis required more troops than originally requested. It also became quite apparent that a 90-day enlistment would be far too short a time to recruit and properly train, equip, and field the thousands of raw troops. With that in mind, on May 3 Lincoln announced his third proclamation, now calling for 42,000 more men to serve a three-year enlistment.

Of this number, 18,000 would be allocated to the naval forces, an arm of the military whose strength and experience was inversely proportional to the new mission it would soon undertake.

Three days later, on May 6, the Confederate Congress passed an act "recognizing the existence of war between the United States and the Confederate States of America."

5

The Union Navy:
April–December 1861

In the two decades prior to the Civil War, the U.S. Navy, largely the supporting arm of the military forces, maintained its traditional role as guardian of the commercial sea lanes and protector of U.S. property and interests abroad. The wooden fleet of that time was primarily circa 1820s. Although majestic and proud, they were also old and tired.

Owing to many years in a peacetime economy, congressional funding for building new warships was not a particularly high priority. Congressional leaders, especially those dealing with naval matters, lacked the vision and the proactive style necessary to insure the country possessed a strong and evolving naval force. Instead, they were noncommittal and were slow to recognize the importance of investing in a more modern naval fleet. This was also evident as late as March of 1861 when the House of Representatives was debating a naval appropriation bill. "I am tired," said a congressman from Illinois, "of appropriating money for the army and navy when, absolutely, they are of no use whatever ... I want to strike a blow at this whole naval expenditure and let the navy go out of existence." Indeed, despite the large output of new vessels of all types in the 1850s, the construction of new warships was carried out on a very modest scale. In addition, naval yards were being grossly neglected, dry docks were in disrepair, and many ships were carelessly laying about, inactive and literally rotting hulks. It came as no surprise, therefore, that when Lincoln called upon the U.S. Navy at the beginning of the war, only 42 active ships were in their inventory.

Nevertheless, Congress wasn't the only one at fault. A cadre of high-ranking naval officers, as well as government administrators in the Navy Department, was also guilty of being shortsighted and indifferent.

The naval officers, those that supposedly could see the big picture, were negligent in promoting and encouraging changes to the fleet they served with for so many years. The institutional lethargy prevalent at that time was far from being a product of battle fatigue, but was more a result of dull idleness. With the exception of minor skirmishes in the Mexican War, the navy had not fought in a major battle since the War of 1812. The aged commanders, trained and reared in a sailing ship era, were too entrenched in their time-honored routines and ultra-conservative mindset, which precluded any chance for rapid acceptance of new ideas and improved technology.

Since about 1840, newer technological advances, such as steam power, had revolutionized the ship propulsion system to the point where sailing ships were becoming more and more obsolete. Growing acceptance of steam power in commercial and foreign fleets brought on more radical changes in ship design, such as paddlewheels, screw propellers, and even twin-screws. The U.S. Navy administrators, however, ever mindful of the bottom line, half-heartedly consented to these changes but still preferred sail-driven vessels to steamers because they were more efficient and far cheaper to run than the modern steamers, which used the more expensive coal for power.

There was one exception, however, one which represented an early example of innovation in the American fleet. This was the USS *Michigan*. Launched in 1843, she was the first iron-hulled ship in the U.S. Navy. Ordered by Secretary of the Navy Abel P. Upshur, she was built "to ascertain the practicability and utility of building vessels, at least for harbor defense, of so cheap and indestructible a material." In addition to her sails, the side-wheeler was primarily powered by steam, only the second U.S. Navy vessel so designed. Overlooking the potentially superior innovations designed into the *Michigan*, the government continued to rely on the more traditional wooden ships to which it had grown so accustomed. Meanwhile, the iron-hulled *Michigan* spent the entire war patrolling the Great Lakes and guarding the Union prisoner of war camp at Johnson's Island in the harbor of Sandusky, Ohio, far from the real action. After the war, as the USS *Wolverine,* she served in the Pennsylvania Naval Militia and the U.S. Naval Reserve until 1923 when she was decommissioned. Corroding away on a sandbank in Erie Harbor, she was sold in 1948 and scrapped a year later. Only her bow and cutwater were saved and are on display in Erie.

Over time, the naval authorities accepted the new technology, but the transition appeared to be very slow and painful. Eventually, as steam engines gained approval, sail power became an auxiliary source of propulsion, and riggings were significantly modified to include only one mast fore and aft, and then spars were eliminated above the deck. Enormous improvements to naval ordnance were also introduced, such as rifling for greater accuracy, range, and penetration; guns designed with higher calibers; and the inclusion of breech-loaders.

Not only was most of the fleet aging, but so too were the commanders in charge of naval operations. At the beginning of the Civil War there were approximately fifteen hundred Union naval officers on duty, scores of them with many years in grade. Not having a retirement system, the only way to leave the service was to resign or die. This led to the inevitable top-heavy command structure and, with it, growing concerns on what to do with the most senior officers, who by tradition felt their seniority deserved them positions of command responsibility. Without question, this crowding at the top precipitated a trickle down effect of slow promotions for everyone else down the chain of command. For the younger junior officers, therefore, morale was quite low and invariably forced many capable and promising men to leave the navy for more lucrative and equally fulfilling occupations in other fields.

Although half-hearted attempts were made to organize some form of retirement procedure, the war only exacerbated the inherent difficulties of an unsatisfactory policy. Consequently, in 1862 Congress instituted a meaningful retirement system whereby naval personnel could leave the service at the age of 62, or with three-quarters of sea pay after 45 years of duty. To supplement the longstanding policies for promotions based on seniority, rules were also established to promote individuals for outstanding conduct during combat, and a new structure in officer grades and salary was passed, including a new grade for squadron commanders.

Prior to July 1862, a squadron commander usually held the rank of commodore and also enjoyed the lofty recognition as a flag officer. Congress now upgraded this position to rear admiral and, at the same time, maintained the designation of flag officer, titles frequently used interchangeably. Flag officers were allowed certain perks, one of which permitted them to identify the status of their rank and position by displaying a special flag or banner from the mast of their ship, which would now be called their flagship.

In descending order the new grades were: rear admiral, commodore, captain, commander, lieutenant commander, lieutenant, master, ensign, and cadet.

Officers on sea duty were paid according to a schedule granting rear admirals $5,000 a year; commodores, $4,000; captains, $3,500; and commanders, $2,800. The grade of the commanding officer was usually commensurate with the classification of his ship, which fell into one of four levels or rates. A commodore usually commanded a ship of the first rate; captains, the second rate; and third and fourth rate by commanders and lieutenant commanders, respectively. The pay for shore duty was usually 20 percent less.

To provide four years of intensive and dedicated training for career minded officers, an institution of higher learning was established at Annapolis, Maryland. President John Quincy Adams originally suggested the concept in 1825, but it wasn't until two decades later that Secretary of the Navy George Bancroft reintroduced the idea. As a result of Bancroft's prodding, and without congressional funding, in 1845 the Naval School was established at Fort Severn, renamed the U.S. Navy Academy, in 1850.

The cadets, or midshipmen as they were called, received their offshore training on the USS *Santee* and the USS *Constitution*, which, incidentally, was launched in 1797 and is still in commission today. Owing to Annapolis' close proximity to the South, and with increasing fears of Confederate attack, at the beginning of the war the Naval Academy staff, the corps of midshipmen, and the training ships were temporarily moved to Fort Adams in Newport, Rhode Island. They returned to Annapolis in September 1865.

Candidates to the academy had to be between 14 and 18 years of age, and required a congressional or presidential appointment. The Naval School began with about 50 midshipmen and seven instructors teaching such courses as seamanship, mathematics, geometry, navigation, gunnery and steam, chemistry, English, philosophy, and French. In July 1864 Congress recognized the existence of changing technology and the increased number of technically minded recruits by introducing the additional designation of cadet engineer. These students were placed in a two-year program in lieu of four years, and their training was specifically tailored so that upon graduation they would be commissioned as naval constructors or as civil steam engineers.

In the spring of 1861 a huge void in the officer ranks came about when approximately 370 U.S. naval officers resigned their commissions to support the Confederacy. This represented about 25 percent of the naval officers on the rolls at the time and was of grave concern to the Navy Department. Congress responded to this problem in July 1861 by authorizing an accelerated training schedule at the academy, so that in the first year of the war two classes were allowed to graduate earlier. Doing his part to alleviate this shortage, Secretary Welles began drawing from a vast pool of experienced veteran officers serving in the merchant marines. New regulations were instituted by Welles, which permitted temporary commissions to merchant marine officers who passed an examination designed to demonstrate their skill and expertise in a specific field.

On May 3, 1861, Lincoln called for 18,000 men to fill the ranks of the U.S. Navy and to serve terms from one to three years. Tours of duty varied considerably, depending on when and where one signed up. Since a firm policy on this matter had not been established, some men were signing up for a few months, while others for three years or even until the war was over. On August 5, however, Congress established the enlistment term at three years.

At that time the enlisted ranks numbered about 7,500 men, or "blue jackets" and "jack-tars," as they were called. Their grades ranged downward from line and staff petty officers, through the various classes of seamen and firemen, to coal heavers and boys, or "powder monkeys," young lads whose job it was to bring the powder cartridges from below.

As the war progressed and the fleet of ships grew larger, the existing supply of sailors fell far short of the growing demand. This shortage was tempered somewhat by utilizing scores of experienced sailors from the merchant marines, a practice comparable to the army's use of trained militia troops. Nevertheless, without a naval reserve to depend on, the lack of adequate manpower would continued to plague the navy throughout the war, which forced the service to institute more aggressive recruiting efforts. Eventually, over two-thirds of the enlisted ranks were made up of landsmen, inexperienced sailors on board ship for the first time. Despite a law prohibiting foreigners from serving on U.S. Navy ships, newly arrived immigrants made up the bulk of these new recruits — so much so that it was fairly common for crews to contain 25 to 30 different nationalities on board a single ship. One reason the navy did so poorly recruiting seamen was that no bounty, or enlistment bonus, was offered, as did the army. Congress corrected this inequity in July 1864 when enormous bonuses of $600 and $700 were offered. As for wages, seamen were paid $18 per month, landsmen received $12, and "boys" $8.

Unlike in the South, where it was considered "a white man's war," black sailors were accepted to serve aboard Union ships from the beginning. At first, only free blacks were routinely signed up, but when manpower shortages became acute, around September 1861, Secretary Welles allowed contrabands, or runaway slaves, to be enlisted as "boys" (and some later estimates stated that black sailors accounted for eight or nine percent of the navy). Eventually they served as firemen, coal heavers, and servants. Four of their number won the Medal of Honor, but, by regulation, they could hold no rank higher than petty officer.

Recruits were trained on a "receiving ship" for up to six weeks, the length of the training depending on the immediate need at the time. If an entire crew were needed, the training would obviously be longer than the training of an individual or two for immediate replacement duty. Generally, the training consisted of basic seamanship and gun and cutlass drills.

Each day began at approximately 5 a.m. when reveille sounded, at which time the ship was scrubbed down, the brass polished, and the sails firmly fixed. Breakfast was called at 8 a.m. followed by various battle-related drills, which began at 9:30 a.m. and was interrupted only by lunch at noon and dinner at 4:00 in the evening. Hammocks were in place for sleep at 8 p.m., except for those in the crew whose turn beckoned their presence on the eight to midnight watch, one of six continuously cycled four-hour watches.

Mealtimes were always a welcome break from the dreadful monotony of routine days at sea. The food served aboard ship was somewhat better fare than the infantry was used to eating and usually consisted of pork or beef, fresh fish, beans, peas, desiccated potatoes to prevent scurvy, dried fruit, butter, cheese, biscuits, and coffee or tea. Of course, this menu varied considerably under wartime conditions, when occasionally dinner for days on end consisted of pork and beans and hardtack, or just salt pork and coffee. Fishing was extremely popular and almost always helped supplement the diet, as did fowl, eggs, vegetables, or any other edibles brought on board from outside sources. For a time even liquor was permitted, until political pressure demanding sobriety aboard Union vessels forced its demise in July 1862. In spite of the ban, alcohol was frequently smuggled on board ship following shore leave. The officers, however, ate food prepared in their own galley, had their own steward, and were allowed to keep wine in their rooms. Overall, however, complaints about the navy mess were few.

The weekends, as in most military environments, were customarily reserved for washing and mending clothes, visiting the sutler, getting haircuts, writing letters, reading, religious services, and, of course, the dreaded Sunday morning inspections.

Combat action was not as frequent as it was in the army, nor as severe. This one factor made life in the navy a bit safer than crouching behind breastworks on the frontlines, or being in the advance of a formation charging across an open battlefield. This difference may account for the fact that while the Union army lost an estimated 380,000 soldiers, the navy placed her combat loss at about 2,110.

Living conditions were also better than life in the chaotic camps of the Union Army, with the possible exception of a hot and noisy ironclad warship where temperatures were frequently over a hundred degrees. On the other hand, to serve on board a navy ship, life was, in one word, strict. Without question, the restrictions of close quarters in a cramped ship mandated tough rules and harsh discipline. Some commanders were stricter than others, as observed one sailor serving on the flagship USS *Lackawanna*: "... the ordinary routine of ship life was rigidly observed on board, for we were flag-ship, and must set an example." Seamen were expected to live for months in confined quarters where bad ventilation was the norm. This unhealthy environment proved extremely conducive to the spread of disease and undoubtedly contributed to the approximately 2,800 naval personnel that died from various illnesses.

To most sailors, however, sea duty was considered dull and monotonous. They enjoyed playing cards, dominoes, checkers, chess, and singing, but the next liberty or shore leave was always in the back of their minds. Shore leave was granted only occasionally, and depended mostly on where the ship was located. For instance, the crew aboard a river gunboat seldom went ashore because of the ever-present hostile environment of bush- whackers and enemy raiding squads. Liberty for gunboat sailors had to wait until their boat pulled into a Union occupied town. Blockade crewmembers, on the other hand, went ashore every time their ship returned to base for supplies or repairs. One blue jacket explained it this way: "There were two bright points in our life to be kept well in view — one the chase after the blockade runner ... the other, an occasional visit to New Orleans for necessary repairs, and perchance to expend some of the money accumulated during months of hermitage as sea."

Although army and navy officers on both sides were allowed to resign their commissions anytime they saw fit, the enlisted men were not allowed to leave the service until their tour had expired. To do so would have been interpreted as desertion and subject to punishment, which in some cases would have been death. Be that as it may, the few Union sailors of Southern her- itage and Southern loyalties spent much of the war aboard ships assigned to duty on the high seas and away from the action at home.

The fact that the Confederates lacked anything remotely resembling a navy did not diminish the concerns the Union government had about its own naval readiness. One of the major problems confronting the Union was that their warships were much too big and much too heavy to enter most of the Southern ports, being designed primarily for use on the high seas and foreign stations. This single factor mandated that a massive shipbuilding effort was absolutely essential in order to rebuild the navy to a fighting force capable of carrying out its new mission in U.S. waters. Therefore, in the context of what was actually needed to fight this war, both sides began the conflict in search of an operational navy. The South had to build a defensive naval force from absolutely nothing, and the North had to rebuild her existing navy.

With over a million dollars in congressional funding now available, in 1861 the government was ready to take on the navy's massive expansion pro- gram. Luckily, the burden of accomplishing this gigantic effort fell on the shoulders of the ablest and most competent officer in the Lincoln adminis- tration, the 24th Secretary of the Navy, Gideon Welles.

Distinguished by a full white beard and brown wig, the 58-year-old Welles was an imposing character and was quite conspicuous in any crowd. Born a Connecticut Yankee in July 1802, Welles was an editor and part owner of the *Hartford Times* until 1836, and served as Hartford's postmaster until 1841. Welles spent a few years in State government before working for the U.S. Navy as Chief of the Bureau of Provisions and Clothing. Serving on its national committee, he also helped organize the new Republican Party in 1856, and was a member of the national executive committee from 1856 to

1864. At the 1860 Republican National Convention in Chicago, he was the chairman of the Connecticut State delegation and was instrumental in steering the votes and the nomination over to the lawyer and former congressman from Illinois.

Following Lincoln's election, Welles was selected as the navy secretary in March of 1861, despite little in the way of experience and background to support his appointment. His only naval expertise, as it were, came from his four-year stint as Chief of the Navy's Bureau of Provisions and Clothing. This office was given to him in 1845 for being an active campaigner during President Polk's run for office, a position ordinarily held by a high ranking naval officer. Following Welles' appointment as naval secretary, there was an instant uproar from those who were bypassed for this cabinet post and who considered themselves more qualified and more experienced. His critics were convinced that Welles lacked the experience, the political savvy, the executive ability, and the sound judgment for that high a position. Their lobbying efforts went largely unheeded, however, as almost immediately Welles proved to be one of the principal problem-solvers of the war and the one person Lincoln could rely on when the going got tough.

The responsibility for the day-to-day operations of the department fell upon the extremely able Gustavus V. Fox, the assistant secretary of the navy. President Lincoln appointed Fox on August 1, 1861, several months after his aborted expedition to relieve Fort Sumter. The position was a new one and Fox was the first to establish and implement its policies. With his appointment, Fox brought to the department something it always lacked, expert naval advice and assistance to the secretary. His naval experience and professionalism helped to provide the necessary coordination between each of the navy bureaus, and as a result a more efficient and responsive agency. A third administrator in the department was a Chief Clerk responsible for managing the navy's business operations.

Secretary Welles had surely not planned for the new responsibilities thrust upon him by Lincoln's April 19 proclamation, and his navy was caught somewhat unprepared. As war plans began to materialize, his department was faced with two major missions to accomplish. They were to organize and implement an effective blockade of the entire 3,550 miles of Confederate coastline, and to take control of the Mississippi River and its tributaries.

Fortunately for Welles, the North possessed an enormous potential for future shipbuilding production. At the beginning of 1861 the navy operated out of ten naval yards. They were at Annapolis, Boston, Mare Island in California, Pensacola, Philadelphia, Norfolk, Portsmouth in New Hampshire, Brooklyn, Washington, and Mount City in Illinois. The Norfolk Navy Yard, being the largest, was without question the superior of the ten yards. The number of foundries, rolling mills, machine shops, ordnance manufacturers, and engineering firms were more than adequate to launch the Navy Department's initial war efforts. Also, blessed with skilled labor, an abundance of raw materials, and a sprawling web of rail lines and rolling stock to construct and deliver the merchandise and supplies, the North, unlike their Southern cousins, had an enormous base upon which to expand.

To maintain the fleet's mission at home and abroad, the Navy Department was organized into departments or bureaus. On July 5, 1861, Congress reauthorized the bureaus, which included the Bureau of Yards and Docks, the Bureau of Equipment and Recruiting, the Bureau of Navigation, the Bureau of Ordnance, the Bureau of Construction and Repair, the Bureau of Steam Engineering, the Bureau of Provisions and Clothing, and the Bureau of Medicine and Surgery. A bureau chief, holding the rank of commodore, commanded each of these departments, and all reported to the assistant secretary of the navy.

At the outbreak of hostilities the mainstay of the U.S. fleet was six large screw frigates built in 1855 — the *Niagara, Roanoke, Colorado, Merrimack, Minnesota,* and *Wabash*— and 12 smaller sloop-of-war steamers built three years later, including the *Hartford, Brooklyn, Richmond, Iroquois, Dacotah,* and *Pawnee.* The U.S. fleet, compared to its more technologically advanced European counterparts, was ranked third in naval world power, behind England and France. By the end of 1861, however, the policies implemented by Secretary Welles had transformed the Union Navy into a first rate fighting force of over 260 vessels and about 22,000 seamen. At the conclusion of hostilities in 1865, Welles could proudly boast of his greatest achievement. The U.S. naval inventory had grown to a fleet of nearly 700 vessels, almost half of which were powered by steam. Of these, 200 were warships, including over 60 ironclads, and were manned by over 58,000 officers and seamen. U.S. naval power would now be ranked first in the world.

Although the Union Navy was a long way from what if would become, by the end of 1861 Old Glory flew over a navy that by anyone's standard was a far cry from what it used to be, and one that would prove to be enormously instrumental in the ultimate successful conclusion of the Civil War. Enforced with a growing fleet of heavily armed vessels, the warships of the U.S. Navy embarked on a new and exciting chapter in naval warfare.

6

Mallory Builds a Navy:
April–December 1861

The Southern states were primarily an agrarian society, a culture that achieved a tremendous degree of economic growth through marketing their cash crops, those grown in the millions of acres of rich and productive soil. They also enjoyed an enormous network of navigational rivers and superb harbors to move their products, and an immoral and divisive social system that incorporated forced labor to make it all work. As such, the aristocratic class in this society, specifically the planter-politicians who controlled the political and economic climate of the South, concerned themselves above all else with the lifeline of their existence. Their concerns revolved primarily around three interests. The first was the planting, harvesting, and processing of their cash crops — cotton, tobacco, rice, and sugar. The second was to insure that production kept pace with customer demand, both domestic and foreign; and the third was to realize greater and greater profits. Since the Southern planters relied on "outsiders" to ship their goods, the need for an infrastructure of maritime organizations wasn't of prime importance in the quest to maintain their Southern way of life. Even the enormous quantities of raw materials, assorted products, and luxury items that the South had to import was accomplished by ships not of Southern origin. It came as no surprise, therefore, that when the Confederate Navy was born, created by an act of Congress within weeks of Jefferson Davis' presidential oath, that it was a navy possessing neither a fleet of ships nor the crews to sail them.

Even before the outbreak of hostilities, however, a few ships did fall into the hands of the Southern states, primarily the unfortunate Union vessels found trapped in their harbors and rivers and immediately confiscated when the States seceded. For instance, shortly after Florida left the Union in January of 1861, the *Dana* was captured at St. Augustine, Florida, one of three coastal survey schooners taken by Southern forces. The Southerners also seized numerous revenue cutters, surveying ships, lighthouse tenders, river steamers, and just about anything else that could float. Most of these vessels were armed with small caliber guns, and operated in a State Navy to guard their rivers and harbors until they were transferred later to the Confederate Navy.

In New Orleans, for example, nearly a dozen boats of mixed character were either seized or bought outright. When refitted for military duty, these "warships" constituted the initial Confederate naval fleet on the lower Mississippi River. Even the *Star of the West*, of Fort Sumter fame, was captured in April off the coast of Texas while performing transport duty and sent to New Orleans to be used as a receiving ship. The only U.S. naval vessels inherited by the Confederacy were the scuttled warship USS *Merrimack* at the Norfolk Naval Yard and the 24-year-old side-wheel steamer *Fulton,* found in dry dock at the Warrington Navy Yard at Pensacola.

Nevertheless, despite these small gains in early 1861, the Confederacy was still forced to buy a number of second-hand boats, such as privately owned commercial steamers, ferryboats, passenger boats, barges, and flatboats. When guns were mounted and volunteer crews assembled, this makeshift and motley assemblage of floating craft was ready for action and represented the beginnings of the Confederate Navy. This "fleet" may not have been high-tech or equipped with great firepower, but in the reality of the times it was simply a matter of something was better than nothing.

Although some shipbuilding did occur in several coastal cities, such as Charleston, Wilmington, and New Orleans, the Confederacy not only lacked suitable ships but also the means to build the kind of fleet they envisioned to defend their waterways. Southern shipbuilders did not have the capabilities to maintain wartime production requirements, being so small, understaffed, under-equipped, and underfunded. Even if they had the capacity to take on this monumental effort, the South would still have had to import enormous quantities of practically all the raw materials necessary for building warships, except wood. Lumber was certainly plentiful in the South, but only for constructing wooden sailing warships.

Before long, the state-of-the-art fighting machine would be the steam-powered ironclad gunboat, a vessel especially favored not only for its impervious resistance to heavy ordnance, but also for its speed and maneuverability on winding rivers, something the South also had plenty of. But again the South came up short. Not only did the Confederacy lack sufficient quantities of mines to supply the iron ore, they also lacked an interconnecting system of railroad track and rolling stock adequate enough to deliver it. And with only a few smelters, and less then a half dozen rolling mills existing in the entire South to manufacture iron plate, the Confederacy was at a tremendous disadvantage.

For the production of heavy ordnance, the South did possess a premier foundry, the Tredegar Iron Works in Richmond. Together with the Bellona Foundry, also in Richmond, as well as a few other smaller plants in Georgia, Alabama, and North Carolina, the foundries worked full time, struggling to supply the Confederacy with iron plate, mostly from recycled railroad track, and ordnance throughout the war. There were also very few powder mills, only one cordage plant (in Petersburg, Virginia), and very little in the way of machinery for manufacturing steam engines, small arms, and ammunitions — or, for that matter, the skilled men to operate them. It was quite a bonanza, therefore, when the South captured the Norfolk Navy Yard and found itself in possession of enormous quantities of ammunition and heavy ordnance.

Ironically, the U.S. Government unwittingly found itself a principal supplier of weapons to the Confederacy. In addition to the cache of ordnance captured at Norfolk and the navy base at Pensacola, the seceded states also confiscated huge amounts of munitions and war materiel from the federal arsenals and forts they had seized before the war, as well as vast numbers of small arms and artillery that picked up from the battlefield during the conflict.

One problem always remained for the Confederacy, however, and that was the shortage of skilled labor in the civilian workforce. The scant supply of trained artisans, those that could build seaworthy vessels, reliable engines, and quality small arms, would plague the Confederacy throughout the war and was further compounded by the military's continuous demand for more and more recruits.

This labor shortage was especially critical in the need for experienced seamen. The navy had no sailors and virtually no skilled mechanics to speak of at the beginning of the war, although when the Norfolk Naval Yard surrendered in April 1861, a number of Union naval officers resigned their commissions to join the Confederacy. Most of the Union's Southern officers received telegraphed appeals from the Confederate government urging them to switch sides; many were unable to contemplate the terrible thought of fighting against their own kin or against their home state. Like most young Southern men answering the call to defend their homeland, they possessed a profound sense of duty to their new country, their state, and the honor of their family name. The contagious spread of resignations by Southern U.S. naval officers continued throughout the Union Navy until about 370 had gone south. Included in this number were such notables as Raphael Semmes, soon to be one of the Confederacy's most prolific commerce-raiders; John M. Brooke, who would go on to design the ironclad CSS *Virginia* (*Merrimack*); and Flag Officer Franklin Buchanan, the future skipper of the *Virginia*. In the end, the resignations represented about 25 percent of the Union officer ranks and ultimately formed the nucleus of the Confederate naval officer corps. In fact, since there were more officers than ships to assign them to, many were forced to man batteries or were detailed to the army until naval assignments became available.

A year later, as the number of naval vessels increased, the Confederate government began to recognize the need to expand the rolls of the naval officer pool. The result of this new legislative effort saw Congress, in April of 1862, authorizing the creation of over 300 new officer positions, ranging through the entire grade spectrum, from admirals down to first lieutenants and masters. A revised chain of command structure was also established listing an admiral as the most senior rank, followed by commodore, captain, commander, first lieutenant, second lieutenant, master, and passed midshipman. A new salary range was also set at this time, granting about $200 per year for a seaman to $6,000 for each of the four new admirals.

Despite the number of Union officers joining the Confederate Navy, the Richmond administration also recognized that the day-to-day operations of a wartime navy, whether at sea or on shore, would need more officers over the long term.

Originally decreed under the Congressional Act of March 16, 1861, the Secretary of the Navy established a Naval Academy on March 23, 1863. Somewhat modeled after the Union version, the academy was organized by Lt. William H. Parker, a former Union officer and top cadet in his class at Annapolis. Applicants had to be appointed by the Confederate legislature and be between 14 and 18 years of age, after which they were placed in classes usually averaging about 60 students. A well-rounded curriculum of studies was offered on board ship as well as in the classroom on shore. Shipboard training was held on the ten-gun steamer CSS *Patrick Henry*. Especially equipped with a mast and a full set of sails, the ship was located in the James River near Drewry's Bluff, 12 miles south of Richmond. While one class of cadets were training at sea, another group of about the same number would be ashore receiving classroom studies. This arrangement would continue for six months, after which they would switch places for another six months. Anywhere from nine to thirteen instructors taught classes in astronomy, navigation, seamanship, naval tactics, naval gunnery, swordsmanship, surveying, mathematics, algebra, physics, French and Spanish, English grammar, geography, history, artillery, and infantry tactics.

In 1864 the Confederate midshipmen enjoyed one advantage not in the training program of their Union counterparts. The cadets were able to get hands-on, actual battle experience. The Union's Army of the James was fairly active at that point in the war in and around the James River area. Consequently, with the South experiencing manpower shortages, the cadets were frequently used to occupy the batteries along the shores at Drewry's Bluff, or to serve aboard ships of the James River Squadron.

After the Confederate Government fled from Richmond in 1865, the Confederate Naval Academy was mustered out of existence without ever graduating a single cadet. A number of midshipmen, however, were tasked with carrying out their final assignment. They were ordered to escort the Confederate archives and bullion, worth a half million dollars in gold and silver, from Richmond to Danville, Virginia. The cadets arrived in Danville on the fifth of April, finding no one there with the authority to accept the treasured possessions. When information was received that President Davis was traveling to Charleston, South Carolina, via Charlotte, the train immediately headed for a rendezvous with the fallen leader. A short time after pulling into Charlotte, however, it was discovered that Davis wasn't there either. Moving on south, the train stopped at Chester, South Carolina, on April 12. Transferring the boxes onto wagon trains, the midshipmen journeyed to Newberry, South Carolina, where they reloaded the bullion and archives on another train and traveled westward, this time to Abbeville, South Carolina, arriving on April 26. Davis and his staff arrived on May 2. After relinquishing the government property in Abbeville, the midshipmen were given $40 apiece in gold to pay for the trip home.

By the end of 1864, Confederate officers on active duty peaked at about 1,600; but for the Confederacy, filling the rolls of the enlisted ranks was much more difficult then that experienced by the North because most of the "better" men had already joined the army. Even when the Navy Department offered 50 dollars as an incentive, there were few takers. To compensate for the shortage of seamen, or "Jack Tars" as they were called, the Confederate Navy was forced to detail men from the army to help man their riverboats. There was an immediate uproar with this arrangement, however, since the army was highly reluctant to release their troops to serve on board navy vessels, troops they needed on the frontlines. Even the soldiers themselves disdained the thought of serving on a boat. Nevertheless, the army relented and would grudgingly detail small contingents of soldiers to serve on the riverboats for only short periods of time. The manpower shortage lightened a bit in March of 1864 when the Confederate Congress passed a general conscription law, and at the same time the navy picked up nearly one thousand men from the army. Consequently, by the end of that year the enlisted ranks peaked at slightly over 3,600 sailors.

Another source for obtaining seamen was the use of foreign crews. This was especially true for the commanders of Confederate commerce raiders, like the CSS *Alabama*, *Shenandoah*, and *Rappahannock*, who depended on foreigners, sometimes exclusively, to staff their ships. These crewmembers were regularly sought after and were handsomely paid volunteers. The job benefits that attracted many of them were double pay in gold, generous rations, tobacco, grog twice each day, and the enticing prospect of prize money. In essence, therefore, the Confederate Navy was largely made up of army soldiers, conscripts, and foreign sailors. Black sailors served aboard only one Southern vessel, the gunboat CSS *Chicora,* where three such sailors enjoyed life in the Confederate Navy.

Life aboard a Confederate ship wasn't unlike that in the Union, owing to the fact that the commanders were previously officers in the Union Navy. Slight variations did occur, however, depending on the whims of the captain. Otherwise, the discipline was the same, as was the daily routine of drills, drills, and more drills.

Dining room fare was far superior in the navy than it was in the Confederate army, where food was always bad or in short supply. This was well expressed by one Southerner who experienced both: "Got dinner, pork, peas and hard bread, good living to what we've been use to in the army." Navy food in the Confederacy consisted mostly of hard bread, pork or beef, and green beans. Unlike the Union Navy, the Southerners maintained their ration of grog, usually a half-pint of wine per day. But, similar to the Jack Tars of today, greater quantities of grog were consumed on shore leave than could be handled.

Seamen were paid between $14 and $18 a month. Landsmen received $12, and "boys" got $8, although crewmen on commerce raiders were usually paid slightly more, and usually in gold.

Aside from manpower constraints, the enormous problems and insurmountable obstacles the Confederacy had to overcome in building a new navy was placed in the capable hands of 54-year-old Stephen R. Mallory. Born in Trinidad and raised in Key West, Florida, Mallory was President Davis' personal choice to be secretary of the navy. Before being elected to the U.S. Senate in 1851, he held various occupations, such as a county judge and customs collector, and also spent time in the Seminole War when he was 24 years old.

During his tenure in the U.S. Senate he became chairman of the all-important Naval Affairs Committee in 1857 and, as a result, gained considerable notoriety and respect as an authority on naval development and naval affairs. Meanwhile, Mallory's highly regarded reputation was also making a decided impact on a Southern senator from Mississippi, Jefferson Davis. Mallory's extensive background on naval matters undoubtedly landed him the appointment to head the Navy Department, and with it the seemingly impossible task of building a navy from nothing.

Not everyone, of course, shared Davis' high opinion of Mallory's competence as Secretary of the Navy. The editor of the *Richmond Examiner* had a few choice words to describe Mallory when he wrote that the secretary was "... a notoriously weak man, who was slow and blundering in his office, and a butt in Congress for his ignorance of the river geography of the country." Disregarding what others thought, Mallory's confidence in his own abilities was manifestly illustrated in his acceptance of this huge burden and his determination to succeed.

Under his leadership, ironclad warships were reintroduced, as was the use of heavy metal rams, both effective weapons against wooden ships. He also instituted the concept of underwater mines, or torpedoes; and under his tenure was launched the first prototype submarine, the CSS *Hunley*, to sink an enemy ship. Mallory proved his capacity to innovate under extreme pressure and was the only Cabinet member to remain in office to the very end.

The goals Mallory established reflected President Davis' desire to develop a naval strategy for "... the protection of our harbors and commerce on the high seas...." Considering the limited resources at his disposal, Mallory's initiatives were quite ambitious. His vision was to acquire an effective fleet of cruisers to destroy Northern commercial shipping, and to defend the major rivers, ports, and cities of the Confederacy against Northern incursion with ironclad gunboats.

To accomplish this, Mallory organized the Confederate Navy to resemble in most respects its Union counterpart. He divided the Navy Department into five bureaus — the Bureau of Orders and Detail, the Bureau of Ordnance and Hydrography, the Bureau of Provisions and Clothing, the Bureau of Medicine and Surgery, and the Bureau of Naval Construction. Unlike the Union organization, however, each bureau chief reported to Mallory directly. Bureau chiefs held the rank of captain but were later promoted to commodore.

One of the very first initiatives taken by Mallory was to start the process of procuring ships and machinery he felt the C.S.A. would need to establish a respectable naval force. In addition, he had to attract a skilled labor force to operate the machinery once it was set up in the factories. To carry out this assignment, in February 1861 he sent Raphael Semmes, a 52-year-old former Union Navy commander on a shopping expedition to New York City. In reference to finding equipment and workers, Semmes summed up the dire straits his new country found itself in when he stated, "The persons alluded to were to be mechanics skilled in the manufacture and use of ordnance and rifle machinery, the preparation of fixed ammunition, percussion caps, etc. So exclusively had the manufacture of all these articles for the use of the United States been confined to the North ... that we had not even percussion caps enough to enable us to fight a battle or the machines with which to make them."

Semmes conducted his business quite openly in New York City, as he would later write. "I found the people everywhere not only willing but anxious to contract with me. I purchased large quantities of percussion caps in the city of New York and sent them by express without any disguise to Montgomery. I made contracts for batteries of light artillery, powder, and other munitions, and succeeded in getting large quantities of the powder shipped. I made a contract, conditioned upon the approval of my Government, for the removal to the Southern states of a complete set of machinery for rifling cannon with the requisite skilled workmen to put it in operation." But the one problem he did have was finding what he considered suitable ships, and without the ships the expedition was considered a failed venture. Bringing back guns and ammunition was relatively easy, but most of all Mallory wanted — and expected — to acquire ships as well.

In addition to Semmes, the Confederacy had many other agents in the field. They were dispatched to Philadelphia, New Orleans, and Baltimore, as well as to other countries (such as England, France, and Canada), all in the quest for more ships, parts, equipment, materiel, and skilled craftsmen and laborers.

During the course of the war, one significant difference between the two sides was in terms of innovative ideas. The North was somewhat behind the curve in this regard. Northern naval officers and administrators relied almost exclusively on the tried and true methods of traditional history and conventional weapons, whereas the South, having no tradition to fall back on, was a master of improvisation.

For his part, Mallory understood that buying a few small ships here and capturing a few more there would not satisfy his long-range needs. And without adequate quantities of shipyards, raw materials, and skilled labor, he also knew the Confederate government would not be able to compete with the North in building new ships. So, considering all the obstacles, it became self-evident that if Mallory wanted new ships, and built to the highest quality, he would have to go to Europe, and that's exactly what the Confederate Navy did.

In May 1861 James Dunwoody Bulloch, a Georgian and 14-year veteran with the Union Navy, was sent to England to negotiate with British shipbuilders for the construction of commerce-raiders. It was hoped that with Bulloch's expertise on ships, and his experience with naval affairs, he would be able to acquire swift, sleek, and powerful cruisers for the Confederate Navy. Bulloch surpassed Mallory's expectations, being solely responsible for equipping the Southern navy with several state-of-the-art warships, such as the *Alabama*, *Florida*, and the *Shenandoah*, ships that were instrumental in destroying the Northern commercial fleet.

The Navy Secretary was well aware that in 1860 France had converted wooden vessels into armored warships and had conducted successful trials on their performance. Based on these European experiments, Mallory envisioned Confederate ironclads equipped with iron rams as a feasible way to destroy the wooden blockade ships. Taking full advantage of the merits of ironclad technology, in June of 1861 Mallory initiated an engineering study on the design and construction of an ironclad ram. As a result of that study, the following month approval was given to raise the sunken frigate *Merrimack* at the Norfolk Navy Yard and, based on accepted designs, convert her into an ironclad gunboat. Several weeks later, with his war chest brimming over with new cash, Secretary Mallory also ordered the construction of four additional ironclads, for all intents and purposes the beginning of his armored gunboat river fleet. Two of these vessels, the *Arkansas* and the *Tennessee*, would be built in Memphis, while New Orleans was the site for the construction of the *Mississippi* and the *Louisiana*. Because of their superior maneuverability, these ironclad gunboats would be the first to challenge the Union fleet on the Mississippi River.

Mallory also vigorously pursued other avenues to build up his navy into a competitive fighting force. He knew the South wouldn't have a navy that in any way, shape, or form could challenge the Union fleet now preparing to launch a blockade of Southern ports. But although he was lacking the ships and the manpower to counter this threat, he would fight his enemy with new ideas and with bold defensive weapons. Utilizing the old maxim that necessity is the mother of invention, Mallory brought his innovative skills to the fore by implementing a defensive strategy novel for its brashness and revolutionary in its defensive capabilities. Called torpedoes, Mallory instituted the concept of underwater mines to guard access to Southern harbors and rivers. Placed in command of harbor defenses, Cmdr. Matthew F. Maury soon had a network of explosives that inflicted considerable damage on Union shipping, and in time would become a source of major concern for Union naval officers attempting to patrol Southern waters. Mallory would also initiate the use of "torpedo boats." Small and cigar-shaped, these half-submerged vessels were the forerunner of submarines. They were constructed with a long spar protruding from the bow, and by fixing a contact mine to the end of the spar, these weapons would be used to attack wooden blockaders.

Despite all the adversity, by the end of 1861 the Southern fleet consisted of about 35 ships, 21 of which were steam driven, and the Navy Department had issued contracts for about 40 more. Furthermore, efforts were begun to construct cordage plants and manufacturing facilities to turn out steam engines and boilers, while blockade-runners were furnishing the military with guns and ammunition. The production of gunpowder was substantially increased through the creation of a Niter and Mining Bureau, which oversaw the mining of potassium nitrate, a vital ingredient of gunpowder. In addition, plans were drawn up to build a new powder mill in South Carolina for the production of cannon powder, and additional foundries and rolling mills at Charlotte, North Carolina, Atlanta, Georgia, and Selma, Alabama.

Consequently, for Secretary Mallory the formation of his budding navy appeared to be gaining momentum. He had the beginnings of a navy in the Mississippi, and with the anticipated launching of their four ironclad river gunboats, as well as the ironclad *Virginia* in Norfolk, along with the promise of new English-built commerce-raiders, the Confederate Navy had come a long way and was nearly primed for battle.

7

Naval Blockade and Blockade-Runners: April 1861–December 1862

Two days after President Davis issued his appeal for privateers, on April 19, 1861, President Lincoln issued a proclamation of his own which said, in part, "Now, therefore, I, Abraham Lincoln, President of the United States, with a view to the ... protection of public peace and the lives and property of quiet and orderly citizens pursuing their lawful occupations ... deemed it advisable to set on foot a blockade of the ports with the States aforesaid...."

Before Lincoln announced this new initiative, however, there was one technical and rather sensitive point of international protocol that had to be considered and handled diplomatically. There was a question as to what impact the blockade of Southern ports would have on the legitimate rights of foreign trade and foreign recognition, especially from England and France. This extremely sensitive matter was resolved when the Lincoln administration, through its Minister to England, Charles F. Adams, obtained the assurances of the British government that the blockade would be respected, and that formal recognition of the Confederacy as an independent country was not forthcoming. In New Orleans at the time were about 30 fully loaded British transports, and, understandably, a declaration of neutrality was the only course of action for England to take in order to protect their property from seizure. Accordingly, on May 13 the British government announced its neutrality in what they recognized as a state of belligerency between the North and the South. Soon afterwards, other European countries would follow England's lead.

The use of a naval blockade wasn't exactly a new concept. Blockades were used by other nations, such as England, France, and Spain, during the Napoleonic Wars. Not considered a novel military tactic, the blockade was first proposed by General-in-Chief Winfield Scott, Lincoln's military advisor. In his opinion, minimally trained civilians and inexperienced militia troops could not possibly sustain an armed invasion of the South, especially within the limits of a three-month tour of duty. In lieu of an invasion of Southern territory, therefore, his plan called for encircling the Confederacy with blockading ships along the seacoasts and a fleet of gunboats patrolling the length of the Mississippi River. The ensuing strangulation of the Confederacy would ensure that all food and materials imported by the South from Europe and the Western States, as well as all farm product exports for cash, would be promptly choked off. For this reason it was known as the "Anaconda Plan."

At first Scott's idea was soundly ridiculed as being much too defensive. Also, to carry out this plan effectively would take time. Naval manpower resources would have to be recruited and trained, and a considerable number of ships constructed to insure its ultimate success. If public opinion polls were taken at the time, as they are today, they would show that public sentiment was overwhelmingly in favor of immediate, decisive action against Richmond — now, rather than later. The public outcry for a march on Richmond won the day and set in motion plans leading to the first battle of Bull Run in July. In spite of all the criticism, however, in the final analysis the Union's overall naval strategy was in essence Scott's "Anaconda Plan."

In Washington, Secretary Welles began to contemplate the scope of the navy's expanding role in the coming conflict and to assess his materiel capabilities towards implementing an effective blockade of the Confederate coastline.

For the first time, large scale naval planning was imperative to meet the demands of comprehensive mission objectives. In addition to its prime task of establishing and maintaining the blockade, the navy was also responsible for moving troops and supplies in support of joint army/navy operations against coastal ports and fortifications. Furthermore, it was also charged with carrying out unilateral strikes on battery emplacements and other enemy coastal targets, to pursue and destroy Confederate privateers and commerce-raiders, and to maintain a strong presence on the Mississippi, Ohio, and Potomac rivers, and their tributaries.

To satisfy the wartime demands imposed upon the navy, Secretary Welles required a large inventory of ships and guns, and a corresponding pool of officers and able-bodied seamen to serve on them. As Welles continued the assessment of his department, it became quite apparent that at present the navy was far too inferior for such an enormous task. The navy inventory at the time consisted of approximately 90 ships, only 42 of which were commissioned. Of the commissioned ships, 25 were assigned to foreign stations and 12 were in the Home Squadron scattered along the eastern U.S. seaboard. The others were either moored in a reserve status in some port or merely languishing in disrepair at any one of the Union shipyards.

At the time, Union warships were primarily assigned for duty in six squadrons, five of which were scattered around the world. Four ships were in the East Indies, eight off the coast of Africa, seven in the Pacific, three in the Mediterranean, and three in the waters off Brazil. Currently, twelve ships were assigned to the Home Squadron, a fleet based in Hampton Roads, off the coast of Virginia, and used to protect U.S. interest at or near home.

The ships of the Home Squadron consisted of seven steamers — the *Pawnee, Brooklyn, Pocahontas, Wyandotte, Mohawk, Crusader,* and *Powhatan.* Also included in the squadron were five sailing ships, the *Cumberland, St. Louis, Sabine, Supply,* and *Macedonian.* The most powerful in terms of firepower was the *Sabine,* with 50 guns, followed by the 25-gun *Brooklyn,* and the *Cumberland,* with 30 guns. In desperate need of his warships, Welles did not hesitate to recall the squadrons from the Mediterranean, East Indies, Africa, and Brazil.

Secretary Welles soon learned, however, that having the ships of the Home Squadron on hand would not entirely satisfy his immediate objective. He was informed that most of the ships were extremely limited for the blockading action because they drew too much water to enter Southern ports, which were too shallow, and none of them were designed to pursue privateers and blockade-runners. One of his first priorities, therefore, was to order the construction of improved, state-of-the-art warships for a new and more aggressive navy.

This rebuilding effort, an enormous undertaking, would mobilize all the resources of the Union and would cost the government millions of dollars. To accomplish his objectives, Welles had to consider three different and distinct types of vessels. First, he had to contract for swift and shallow-drafted ships to enforce the blockade and to pursue blockade-runners. He also needed sturdy and well-armed cruisers for tracking and engaging commerce-raiders on the high seas, and small, highly maneuverable gunboats for patrolling the inner network of rivers to safeguard army bases and supply depots.

Building new ships would take time, so to satisfy the emergency of the moment Welles began a stopgap program of refitting existing merchant marine vessels and to purchase or charter as many commercial ships as were available. This initial effort translated into contracts being issued for over 150 vessels, of which 50 were new warships, including screw-propelled frigates, sloops, side-wheel steamers, and over 20 new screw-gunboats. Until the new vessels were completed, however, the Home Squadron and several refitted ships from the merchant fleet would have to do what they could to spearhead the blockade.

The blockade would cover slightly over 3,500 miles and extend from the Chesapeake Capes to the mouth of the Rio Grande. With nearly 200 inlets, harbors, and river mouths to cover, the task appeared insurmountable.

The imposition of the blockade was swift, occurring within a few weeks of Lincoln's order. On May 9, for instance, the USS *Niagara*, a 12-gun screw frigate just back from Japan, began intercepting ships outside Charleston Harbor. Three days later, 60-year-old Capt. William W. McKean, her commander with 46 years in the navy, captured his first prize. And when McKean was selected to replace Capt. Henry A. Adams at Pensacola on May 25, he dispatched the USS *Powhatan*, Lt. David D. Porter commanding, and the USS *Brooklyn*, under Cmdr. Charles H. Poor, to blockading duty outside the mouth of the Mississippi River.

Likewise, Cmdr. Garrett J. Pendergrast, of the USS *Cumberland*, also began patrolling the waters of the Chesapeake Capes in May. Within days of giving his notice, he seized the first ship challenging the blockade, stopping fifteen more transports over the next two weeks.

By June, several dozen Union ships were taking part in the blockade, with more being added over the weeks and months ahead. However, as the number of ships increased, the naval blockade became more widely dispersed. To improve the management and the efficiency of the growing fleet, the navy wisely organized its forces into two Blockading Squadrons. They included the Atlantic Blockading Squadron and the Gulf Blockading Squadron. Flag Officer Silas Stringham commanded the Atlantic Blockading Squadron; but, following his win at Hatteras Inlet, he was severely chastised in the press for failing to continue his campaign into Pamlico Sound. Unable to cope with the harsh criticism, he tendered his resignation in September of 1861. Shortly after Stringham resigned, the squadron was reorganized further into two smaller squadrons. The first was the North Atlantic Blockading Squadron, which patrolled the coastline of Virginia and North Carolina, and used Hampton Roads as its base of operations. The second was the South Atlantic Blockading Squadron, whose ships cruised the waters off the coast of South Carolina to the tip of Florida. Port Royal, on the southern coast of South Carolina, was used as its supply base after it fell to Union forces in November.

Similarly, the Gulf Blockading Squadron, under the command of Flag Officer William Mervine, was also divided into two smaller blockading squadrons. The East Gulf Blockading Squadron patrolled the Gulf side of Florida, from Key West to Pensacola, and was based at Key West. The West Gulf Blockading Squadron established its cordon along the shores from Pensacola, Florida, to the Rio Grande. Its home port was initially Ship Island,

Mississippi, until the Union regained the Pensacola Navy Yard on May 10, 1862. A third division was also formed in September. Called the Mississippi River Flotilla, it was responsible for action in the upper waters of the Mississippi River.

The number of vessels in any one squadron depended to a large degree on the scope of its mission. To successfully support General Grant's Vicksburg campaign in 1863, for instance, the Mississippi River Squadron employed 12 ironclad steamers, two gunboats, 10 steam transports, several mortar boats, and six other smaller crafts, such as a hospital ship, mail boat, and tugs.

Although the Confederate coastline extended for over 3,000 miles, the Union blockade focused primarily on ten major ports, some to a greater extent than others. These ten were determined to be the most vital to the Confederacy because they were the only ones with rail connections, including six that connected to the interior and were the prime targets. The six ports were Wilmington, Charleston, Savannah, Pensacola, Mobile, and New Orleans. The other four were Norfolk, Virginia; Beaufort and New Bern, North Carolina; and Fernandina, Florida.

As mentioned earlier, in May 1861 the USS *Cumberland* seized the first Confederate ship attempting to run the blockade in the waters of the Chesapeake Capes. The Confederate ship was a much slower merchant vessel; although it failed to get by the blockade, through the summer of 1861 many more tried and most succeeded. During the early months of the blockade, the Union cordon, if it can be described as such at that time, was quite thin and, as a consequence, easily penetrated. One Richmond observer remarked, "At first Mr. Lincoln's proclamation was laughed at to scorn in the South. The vast extent of South Atlanta and Gulf coast, pierced with innumerable safe harbors, seemed to defy any scheme for hermetic sealing. The limited Federal navy was powerless to do more than keep loose watch over ports of a few large cities, and, if these were effectually closed, it was felt that new ones would open."

According to international agreements, a blockade could not be declared by a warring country or respected by other nations unless it was proven to be "effective" and enforced around the clock. In fact, there were provisions included in the 1856 Declaration of Paris that governed the implementation of blockades, which read, "Blockades, in order to be binding, must be effective; that is to say, maintained by forces strong enough to prevent access." Although the U.S. was not a signatory to this agreement, the European nations did honor the U.S. blockade anyway; and after the first year there were many who praised the blockade for its effectiveness and its efficiency.

The growing effectiveness of the blockade was aptly described by one Confederate officer who recalled after the war that the blockade had "shut the

Confederacy out from the world, deprived it of supplies, [and] weakened its military and naval strength."

Not only did the blockade deny huge amounts of supplies to the military, it also vastly reduced the quantities of imported and domestic goods and food to the citizens of the South. The blockade was indeed an economic embargo designed to prevent imports and exports from arriving or leaving Southern shores. The strategy being, without these imported goods the Southern war effort would eventually wither and die. In addition, by regaining control of the Mississippi River in 1863, the Union cut the Confederacy in two, significantly reducing the internal shipments of food and other essentials from the western farmlands to the Southern military forces.

This created a period of terrible suffering for the Southern people, both the once rich and the poor alike. There were times when the aristocracy, as well as the working class, had to grovel over meager stores of practically everything, and face exorbitant prices for the simple necessities of life. Even in the early phases of the blockade, in the fall of 1861, the effects from shortages were already being experienced by a Charleston merchant who complained, "Business perfectly prostrated everything enormously high salt selling at 15 and 20 cents a quart hardly any shoes to be had dry goods of every kind running out." In many major Southern cities the discontent over widespread shortages, high inflation, and exorbitant prices provoked unbridled riots and raging crime as its starved citizens looted and plundered to preserve their very existence.

As the number of Union ships increased, and the navy's operating procedures improved, the blockade gradually grew tighter and more effective; as a result, the much slower merchant vessels found it increasingly difficult to evade the persevering patrols.

British entrepreneurs did their best to correct this inequity by contracting with Confederate agents for a special type of vessel especially designed to challenge the blockading fleet. Constructed principally in Liverpool, the new ships were called blockade-runners. They were small, unarmed side-wheel steamers built for speed. Blockade-runners were also shallow drafted and cleverly designed, with a unique low profile that made them difficult to spot at a distance.

England and France would not interfere with the Union blockade and carefully avoided it at all cost. Therefore, all of their exported goods to the South, as well as Southern cotton going to Europe, were delivered to Nassau, Bermuda, and Havana, ports of call now transformed into bustling centers of commercial activity, and havens for gamblers, adventurers, shysters, and other unseemly characters. Under international law, of course, ports of foreign neutrals could not be blockaded.

Blockade-runners picked up the cargoes from any one of these bustling ports, dashed quickly towards the U.S. mainland, and then attempted to slip through the blockade into a Southern port. The principal Confederate bases for the blockade-runners on the east coast were Wilmington and Charleston. Wilmington was a prime port because it enjoyed the protection of the favorable geographical features of the surrounding area; from Fort Fisher, the strongest fortification in the Confederacy; and from two ironclads, the *North Carolina* and the *Raleigh*, both guarding the approaches to the city. Charleston was also a favorite. Considered the most defended city in the South, Charleston was situated deep within a harbor surrounded by numerous batteries, underwater mines, and the heavy guns of Fort Sumter. Goods picked up at Havana were usually destined for New Orleans or Mobile, ports also protected by highly armed forts.

By the end of 1862 the Union blockade fleet was much larger and much more organized; and, with the exception of Charleston and Wilmington, most of the ports on the East Coast had been retaken and were now occupied by U.S. army troops. This afforded the Union Navy the ability to concentrate more ships outside Wilmington, where the blockading cordon was organized into three arching tiers. The new procedures that governed the operation of the blockading fleet directed that small picket boats would constitute the first tier and patrol the vicinity of the immediate shoreline. When a blockade-runner was spotted heading out to sea, the picket ship would fire a signal rocket, which in turn brought all the Union warships in the area converging on that sector. In the event the runner evaded the second tier, a third force was stationed farther out that not only watched for incoming ships but also for those runners who eluded the second tier vessels.

The owners financing the bloackade-runners, however, would not be denied. The enormous profits realized from their investments compelled them to institute more cunning and evasive techniques. They soon acquired faster and sleeker ships to outrun their pursuers, some capable of reaching incredible speeds of 18 knots. One bloackade-runner, the *Ella and Annie*, was so fast that after she was captured the Union Navy renamed her the USS *Malvern,* which then became the flagship of Rear Admiral David D. Porter. In addition to designing the vessels with very low profiles, the crafty British shipbuilders devised other tricks to elude the Union Navy. Telescoping smokestacks were devised to shrink the blockade-runners' silhouette even more, and the type of coal burned in the furnaces was of critical importance. Using anthracite coal for fuel was calculated to produce as little smoke as possible, and painting the ships gray — to blend in with the surrounding sea and fog — was also successful. One of the favorite diversionary tactics was for an accomplice to shoot off signal rockets, like the Northern picket boats would do as a signal of an approaching runner. In this case, the signal sent the Union Navy steaming off towards the suspected sector while opening up the sea-lanes for the actual blockade-runners to make their mad dash to port. Also, to increase their success at eluding the blockade, attempts were mostly made on moonless nights, in bad weather, or in the fog. The blockade-runners were all unarmed because, under international law, if a non-belligerent vessel used armed force in her own defense, the captain and crew could be arrested and tried in court as pirates.

Crewmembers of most blockade-runners were usually foreign sailors, mostly British subjects attracted by the tales of instant fortunes. This was something of a problem for the Union because, not wanting to create an international incident, the Northern authorities were forced to release all foreigners captured on blockade-runners. On the other hand, any Southerners on board were locked up as prisoners of war. Since it was illegal under British law for an Englishman to render service to a warring nation, it was standard practice for British captains to sail under an alias.

For these sailors, life on board a blockade-runner was quite exciting. One such officer wrote, "Nothing I have ever experienced can compare with it. Hunting, pig-sticking, steeple-chasing, big-game hunting, polo — I have done a little of each — all have their thrilling moments, but none can approach running a blockade." This adrenaline rush was also expressed by another sailor who described his first sight of a pursuing blockader as "a thrill of intense pleasure and excitement almost delirious [that] animated me; all [were] moved with the strange emotion wavering between success and capture as soon as the steamer was seen from the quarterdeck."

Those sentiments were in stark contrast to that of a Federal blockade crewmember who lamented, "Day after day, day after day, we lay inactive, roll, roll." There was also the Union sailor aboard the USS *Brooklyn* blockading the mouth of the Mississippi for two months in 1862 who wrote: "It is impossible to describe the monotony of the life on board ship during this period. Most of the time there was a dense fog, so thick that we could not see the length of the ship. The fog collected in the rigging, and there was a constant dripping from aloft like rain, which kept the decks wet and made things generally uncomfortable. No news was receive from the North, and our waiting and watching seemed endless."

Running the blockade was enormously profitable and, to the Liverpool entrepreneurs sponsoring that venture, certainly well worth the risk. The expenses of constructing and operating the ships prohibited anyone but wealthy private firms from making the capital investment. After two or three successful expeditions, the ship was usually paid for, and from then on everything was clear profit. In some instances, investors made fortunes as high as an estimated $20 million dollars over the four years of the Civil War.

On such small ships cargo space was always a problem. Crates, barrels, and bales were stowed everywhere, even in the staterooms and the captain's cabin. Once unloaded the cargoes were then sold at auction at exorbitant prices. It was a very lucrative business in which the daring blockade-runner could reap great rewards. Cargoes included such items as guns, gunpowder, cannon, rifles, ammunition, shoes, blankets, medicines, salt, tea, liquor, lace, perfumes, clothing, and machinery. Some articles, particularly luxury items like cigars, wines, perfumes, and silks, could bring profits of 500 to 600 percent. In fact, luxury goods were such moneymakers that, initially, runners preferred shipping them into port instead of military hardware. Eventually, to correct this problem the Confederate government was forced to impose restrictions on luxury items entering its ports. It mandated that half of the cargoes would be reserved for government materials, and, in addition, applied fixed purchasing rates on government goods. Another solution for the Confederacy found them operating their own blockade-runners, four of them, in fact — the *Owl, Bat, Deer,* and *Stag.* In many cases, the owners of blockade-runners made huge amounts of money on goods brought into Confederate ports and then made even more money selling the cotton taken out on the return trip for ten times the original price. This was particularly true when cotton prices soared up to ten times the pre-war levels. The payoff for the crews would typically average about $5,000 for the captain and $3,000 to the officers, while a seaman received around $250 for each round trip, always paid in gold.

Even the sailors aboard Union blockade ships could earn extra money under certain circumstances, although not as much as their adversaries. Union vessels were required to split the proceeds of every prize captured with the government. After the prize money was split, the captain always received the lion's share of the balance, and the rest was distributed to the officers and crew. Even though large rewards were rare, a lucky capture could bring tens of thousands of dollars to the captain, down to several thousand for each crewmember. Wilmington, with its heavy traffic of blockade-runners, was therefore choice duty for the blockaders.

The CSS *Robert E. Lee* ran the blockade some 21 times before being captured in November 1863 and then re-christened the USS *Donelson.* But her success story was far from being the benchmark. The overall odds for getting through the Union fleet was estimated to be about 90 percent at the beginning of the blockade, while near the end of the conflict it was thought to be around 50 percent. Success for any blockade-runner, however, varied to a large degree on many factors, ranging from the type of propulsion used and the weather conditions, to the port in question and the porosity of the Union fleet at that point on that particular day. The success rates varied from year to year and even for the time of the year. In all likelihood, any analysis that arrived at some efficiency measurement for the overall effectiveness of the blockade would certainly still be a highly questionable estimate.

Even if it was true that at least half of the blockade-runners were getting into port in the later years of the war, in terms of delivering sufficient quantities of consumables to the people, and ample amounts of munitions of war to the military, the blockade-runners failed. As mentioned earlier, blockade-runners were small ships, and as a result could not carry large quantities of cargo. Compounded by the grossly inadequate network of rail lines in the South, and their underdeveloped transportation system, the needs of the Southern people and of the military were far from being met. Without question, therefore, the Union blockade proved to be a significant strategic tactic against the Confederate war effort. Its very presence heavily contributed to the diminished capacity of the Confederate army to wage war, and was also the impetus that sparked the loss of fighting spirit within the Southern people.

The initial inefficiency of the blockade had lulled the South into a false sense of security. So gradual was the growth of the Union naval forces, and so slow and consistent was the occupation of Confederate ports, that before the South realized it, the "Anaconda" had tightened its unrelenting grip. Blockade running continued for sure, but it gradually diminished as Federal forces slowly and methodically occupied each Confederate port one by one.

At the end of 1862 only two Confederate ports on the east coast, Charleston and Wilmington, still remained under Southern control and open to the most daring of the blockade-runners. Be that as it may, those blockade-runners and the new and improved wartime industrial output of the South managed to barely keep the Southern military functioning, albeit at a very low level.

8

Confederate Privateers and Commerce-Raiders: April 1861–November 1865

Privateers are privately owned vessels armed and sanctioned by a warring government to attack and capture enemy merchant ships on the high seas. This was exactly the type of enterprise President Davis was calling for in his proclamation on April 17, 1861.

Responding to the president's appeal were ship owners from Liverpool, England, several Southern cities, and, reportedly, even from the North as well. Selected applicants were then issued letters of marque, certificates that granted them the authority to prey on Northern shipping. The motivation, of course, was the huge financial rewards the ship owners could pocket from the sale of their prizes. Forty-eight ships received these certificates, although less than half actually took part in the action.

The Confederate Congress authorized privateering on May 6, and within a week nearly two-dozen ship owners were embarking on a practice last used by the United States in the American Revolution and the War of 1812, a practice the United States exercised with much success. Although it was later outlawed by the Declaration of Paris in 1856, the United States was unwilling to abandon privateering and consequently did not participate in the signing. At any rate, since the Confederacy didn't exist at the time, the South was certainly free to impose privateering as it saw fit.

The intent of the Confederacy for applying this tactic was twofold. First, it would disrupt Northern commercial shipping to Europe. In so doing, it was hoped that England and France would be forced to intervene on behalf of the Southern side and perhaps compel them to insist that Lincoln lift the blockade. Second, Davis wanted to create a diversion sufficient enough to distract the blockading ships away from their patrols, which in most sectors along the Atlantic seaboard at that time were extremely thin, making many merchant ships easy pickings. In fact, in the first five months the privateers, mostly out of Charleston, New Orleans, and Hatteras Inlet, captured over 50 Union merchant ships.

The role of the privateer was short-lived, however. Its demise, in fact, began only two months after it started, when, on June 1, England announced that all privateers would be prohibited from bringing their prizes into British ports. Soon afterwards other foreign neutrals would follow England's lead. The only option now remaining to the privateers was to penetrate the blockade of the Southern coastline. But as the Union blockade expanded its surveillance and tightened its cordon, the slower moving privateers found it exceedingly difficult, if not impossible, to bring their prizes into Southern ports. As a consequence, by the end of 1861 privateering had just about run its course. Nevertheless, the ship owners had little reason to celebrate, because to continue their destructive pursuit of the U.S. commercial fleet the Confederates now turned to their growing fleet of armed steamers, a new and much more serious threat to the shipping industry.

They were called commerce-raiders, and the biggest difference between them and privateers was that, besides capturing the merchant ships, the raiders were also authorized to destroy and sink them.

The use of commerce-raiders against Union merchant ships began shortly after Confederate envoy Raphael Semmes returned from New York in April of 1861. A native of Maryland, and a U.S. naval officer since 1826, Semmes resigned his commission in February while serving as a commander in the Lighthouse Service. His decision was influenced by the secession of Alabama, his adopted state; and as a consequence of his "desertion," Semmes was reviled in the North for turning his back on the Stars and Stripes, a banner he served under for 35 years. Shortly after joining the Confederacy, he was sent to New York by President Davis to procure much needed machinery, munitions, and ships in order to jump-start the formation of a naval force for his new government. The effort proved to be a disappointment, however, failing to accomplish the lofty goals envisioned by President Davis.

Upon his return from New York, and eager to return to sea, Semmes was one of the first to propose using armed Confederate ships against unarmed U.S. merchant vessels. Secretary Mallory was in full agreement with this scheme, and to consummate the new strategy, in April Semmes was given command of a small steamer tied up in New Orleans. The decrepit vessel, called the *Habana*, was once a passenger steamer on the New Orleans to Havana line, but in a matter of weeks she was converted into the Confederacy's first armed cruiser. Equipped with one 8-inch rifle in pivot and four 32-pdrs. broadside, she was commissioned the CSS *Sumter*, after the battered fortification in Charleston Harbor — now a symbol of Confederate sovereignty.

With a staff of Confederate naval officers to direct the predominately foreign crew, Semmes was under orders to create as much havoc as he could on U.S. shipping interests. But first, to leave New Orleans he had to penetrate the Union blockade patrolling the waters outside the Mississippi Passes, the four channels that branched out from the Mississippi delta. The four principal channels were called the Southwest Pass, the Pass a l'Outre, the Northeast Pass, and the South Pass. Patrolling the waters of the Gulf just outside the Passes were two Union ships, the USS *Brooklyn*, under Comdr. Charles H. Poor, and the USS *Powhatan*, commanded by Lt. David D. Porter, both recently assigned to blockading duty following the Fort Pickens incident. For the crews of the two Union ships, blockade duty was far from ideal. With the crews unaccustomed to prolonged idleness, the days dragged by from the sheer monotony of a 24-hour watch, and in time this growing boredom and restlessness became a great concern to the commanders. The sweltering heat and swarming mosquitoes only added to the misery experienced by the seamen.

Lt. Porter suspected that the *Sumter* was preparing to make a break through the blockade. He had witnessed the frequent visits downriver of the *Ivy*, a Confederate side-wheeler used by Semmes as a scout to bring back information on the location of the two Union blockaders. Both Union commanders were at a disadvantage, however, because they could not leave their stations for long without opening an escape route for Semmes.

Just such an opportunity came on June 30 when the *Brooklyn* was called away from her position outside the Pass a l'Outre to investigate an unknown ship eight miles away. Demanding all the engine power the *Sumter* could muster, Semmes steamed from the Pass and made a break for the open waters of the Gulf. Quickly spotted by the *Brooklyn*, however, the *Sumter* was under immediate pursuit and would have been captured if not for a sudden squall that created high winds and swift currents favorable to the Confederate ship and enabled the *Sumter* to escape. Once clear of the Union warship, the first Confederate commerce-raider was loose in the Gulf, free to carry out its destructive mission. Amid cheers of the crew entwined in the rigging, Semmes headed for Cuba.

The *Brooklyn* and the *Powhatan* were the only blockading ships in the Gulf to guard the mouth of the Mississippi River. It was quite obvious to some people, especially after the escape of the *Sumter*, that more Union ships were necessary in that section of the Gulf. This shortcoming provoked much criticism, particularly from Lieutenant Porter, who was not one to mince words. Angrily berating the Assistant Secretary of the Navy, Gustavus V. Fox, Porter wrote, "This blockade is the greatest farce on earth." In Washington, Welles readily agreed that more surveillance was needed there and assigned a small squadron of four vessels, under Capt. John Pope, to patrol the lower segment of the Mississippi River.

Now free to cruise the open waters around Cuba, within two weeks the *Sumter* left her first prize in flames and managed to capture six others, bringing the prizes into the port of Cienfuegos, Cuba. In response to an inquiry from the local officials, however, the Spanish government in Madrid advised the Cubans that Spain was following the policy already established by England, specifically that prizes are to be refused admittance into their ports, and directed they do the same. Losing his battle to gain entry into port, Semmes left his prizes in the hands of a caretaker and steamed back out to sea. Cuban authorities ultimately released the six prizes back to their crews.

Following a short stay for fuel and repairs at the Dutch Island of Curacao in the last week of July, Semmes took the *Sumter* along the coast of Venezuela, where he captured and burned two more merchant ships. In August he stopped for coal and provisions at the neutral ports of Surinam and Trinidad, which also afforded him the opportunity to release the prisoners from the two prizes encountered earlier. Never staying long in any one place, the *Sumter* departed Trinidad on August 25 for the waters off Brazil, where three more ships were overtaken and destroyed in September and October, before visiting the island of Martinique in November. All the while, Semmes managed to elude a dozen Union warships, including the *Powhatan, Iroquois, Keystone State, Niagara, Richmond,* and *San Jacinto,* sent out by Secretary Welles to stop him.

By this time, Porter had taken a keen interest in capturing the *Sumter* and was in hot pursuit aboard the slower and older side-wheeler *Powhatan.* "I will follow her as long as my engine holds together," he wrote Fox. And Porter did just that. He tracked the *Sumter* from August 14 to October 10, 1861, at times within a day of catching her, until his engines and boilers gave out and forced the *Powhatan* into New York for repairs.

In December, concerned that Federal warships were on his trail and closing in, the Confederate commander set his course for Cadiz, Spain, again escaping the Union's relentless pursuit, somehow always managing to stay one step ahead.

At Cadiz, Semmes released his prisoners and was finally able to get needed and long overdue repairs to his ship before moving on to Gibraltar. It was now January 1862, and by this time the *Sumter,* a rather fragile and unlikely looking menace, had captured some 18 ships, seven of which were burned. If the Union navy had a most-wanted list, Semmes would undoubtedly have been at the top.

The presence of the *Sumter* in Gibraltar, however, spelled doom for the first Southern commerce-raider. Unable to get badly needed coal because of his growing reputation as a "pirate," a distinction he loathed, and under constant surveillance by a flotilla of Union ships across the harbor, the Confederate authorities in Richmond saw the futility of continuing his exploits. Unable to secure provisions or major repairs, he was ordered to sell his ship and return to England.

On the night of February 6, 1862, the new owner of the *Sumter*, an Englishman, quietly sneaked her pass the Union flotilla, which was still across the harbor, and sailed her out to sea. Renamed the *Gibraltar*, she became a blockade-runner in the summer of 1863. Although she managed to survive the war, the *Gibraltar* was lost off the coast of France some years later.

On April 15, with his officers in tow, Semmes boarded a blockade-runner in Liverpool, England. Their destination was Nassau, a brief stopover on his return to the C.S.A.

Although the number of merchant ships Semmes had intercepted was relatively small, the mere presence of the *Sumter* on the seas was interpreted as a real threat to the shipping industry. This anxiety over the increased risks of losing ships, cargoes, and crews quickly escalated into skyrocketing cost of maritime insurance. In some cases insurance costs increased 900 percent, adding another burden to an already financially desperate industry. Consequently, during the early months of privateers, and with losses mounting from the *Sumter* raids as well, the U.S. commercial shipping industry became extremely concerned over the possibility of losing their huge investments, either outright to the enemy or from the financial strains suffered from merely staying in business. When their appeals to Washington for help went largely unheeded, scores of ship owners panicked. Afraid of impending financial disaster, they were compelled to sell off their vessels and/or businesses to foreign neutrals (ironically, with England being the predominate beneficiary).

Around the same time that the Confederacy launched the *Sumter*, in April of 1861 the Confederate government received a telegram from a civilian captain of a mail steamer. In the wire a 35-year-old Georgia man was offering his services and expertise to the new and uninitiated Navy Department. His name was James Dunwoody Bulloch, one of the few acknowledged experts on naval matters and its ships, and he was willing to relinquish his command to assist the fledgling Confederacy.

Impressed by this offer, Secretary Mallory immediately accepted, and Bulloch found himself in Liverpool, England, on June 4, working as a Confederate purchasing agent in search of warships, munitions, and any other navy equipment he could get his hands on. Mallory's unrestrained enthusiasm was based on the extensive background Bulloch had acquired over 14 years in the

U.S. Navy, and his eight years of experience in commercial shipping. The experience and knowledge Bulloch possessed on ships, the navy, naval customs, and international shipping laws gave him skills not otherwise available to most Confederate agents. In addition to his technical know-how, he also possessed a diplomatic savvy that allowed him to move easily within English circles, a very desirable attribute for a Confederate deal-maker.

Discussing his enthusiasm to join the Southern cause, Bulloch once wrote, "My heart and head were with the South. My sympathies and convictions were both on that side, although my personal interests were wholly, and my personal friendships were chiefly, in the North."

Within a short time of his arrival in England, Bulloch completed negotiations with a Liverpool shipyard for a contract that ultimately constructed the commerce-raider *Florida*. And a few months later he scored again, contracting with the John Laird & Sons shipbuilders for the most famous Confederate raider of them all, the *Alabama*.

Regarded as an unsung hero of the Confederacy, Bulloch was the most successful of the many purchasing agents sent to Europe. Indeed, his successes were directly responsible for the very existence of the Confederacy's most dreaded commerce-raiders, and, in turn, for the resulting success and fame of their captains. He was also one of the principal procurers of war supplies from England, purchasing enormous quantities of material, such as ammunitions, rifles, artillery, side arms, sabers, and medical supplies. In fact, at one point early in his career Bulloch bought a steamer in England, the *Fingal*, and took her to Scotland where he secretly crammed it full of military supplies. As he would later comment, "no single ship ever took into the Confederacy a cargo so entirely composed of military and naval supplies." Taking charge of the new ship himself, he crossed the Atlantic in November of 1861 and, with a British crew, easily eluded the Union blockade in heavy fog, bringing the *Fingal* into the port of Savannah. Shortly afterwards, however, ships of the South Atlantic Blockading Squadron were anchored outside the Savannah River preparing to take over Tybee Island, located at the mouth of the river. Finding he was unable to leave Savannah with his cotton-laden ship because of the heavy concentration of Union vessels offshore, the *Fingal* was promptly accepted by the Confederacy to enhance their tiny navy. She was cut down, ironclad armored, rearmed, and christened the ram CSS *Atlanta*. Bulloch, meanwhile, returned to England on a blockade-runner by way of Wilmington in March of 1862.

It is interesting to note that to avoid breaking international neutrality laws, specifically the Neutrality Proclamation and the Foreign Enlistment Act, the British shipbuilders, of course with the acquiescence of Bulloch, would refer to the ships in their contracts by the builder's name, an alias that at times was only a number. On paper, for instance, the CSS *Florida* was first called the *Oreto,* and later the *Manassas,* while the future CSS *Alabama* was merely identified as #290 and, prior to her christening, as the *Enrica.* This was done to conceal the real owner of the ship and therefore the obvious nature of the contract. Another way to circumvent the law was accomplished by eliminating any requirements for ordnance, shot and shell, or any other weaponry, from the contract. When Bulloch solicited legal interpretations of the British neutrality laws, he was advised, "The mere building of a ship within Her Majesty's dominions ... is no offense, whatever may be the intent of the parties, because the offense is not the building but the equipping." Consequently, after any of his ships were launched from the British yards, they were taken to the Azores or to an island in the Bahamas, where the ship would then be equipped with her firepower and commissioned under her real name.

Although it became fairly obvious that the ships were being built for the Confederacy, for the most part British authorities looked the other way — not only because there was always the lack of solid evidence to prove it in court, but also because they were reluctant to interfere with the benefits it brought to the English economy, and to protect the lucrative business and financial opportunities enjoyed by the British shipbuilders. Their silent acquiescence also extended to the illegal use of British subjects on Confederate warships, and the Confederate use of foreign ports flying the British flag. England, however, would pay dearly for its cavalier attitude in a lawsuit brought by the U.S. after the war called the "Alabama Claims."

In March 1862 Bulloch was ordered by Secretary Mallory to negotiate a deal for even more formidable warships that could challenge the ever-growing fleet of Union blockaders. Consequently, in July a contract was signed with the Laird shipbuilders for two state-of-the-art steam driven rams to be delivered in April and May of 1863. The specifications called for the ships to be iron-plated and to come equipped with a seven-foot underwater lance, or ram, protruding from the bow. Each ship would also carry two 9-inch rifled guns enclosed in twin-armored turrets. These were just the ships Mallory needed to wage warfare against the wooden Union fleet patrolling the Confederate coastline.

However, by the spring of 1863 it became quite evident that the Confederate flag would not flutter from either ship.

The British Government had stepped up its surveillance of Confederate shipbuilding activity, and, as a result, Bulloch found it increasingly difficult to conceal the real intent for the rams — or their ultimate owner.

Bulloch's problems with the English began when vessel #290, now called the *Enrica,* was launched on May 15, 1862. Around that time, British authorities were presented with enough reliable evidence from the U.S. Consul in

Liverpool to prove unequivocally that the owner of *Enrica* was, in fact, the Confederate Government. Therefore, armed with the proper legal documentation, British authorities were preparing to seize the *Enrica* in the name of the crown. In July, however, Bulloch was tipped off ahead of time on the imminent confiscation of the ship. Only hours before the British officials arrived, however, Bulloch ordered his British captain and a makeshift crew to sail from the harbor on the pretense of conducting additional sea trials. The next morning *Enrica* was on her way to the Azores.

The British authorities were highly incensed and extremely embarrassed over this episode and vowed to tighten their enforcement of the neutrality laws even more. It appeared as if the shipbuilders, as well as Bulloch, could no longer avoid running afoul of the British statutes.

Nevertheless, the Confederates would not be deterred. In yet another effort to bypass the neutrality laws, Bulloch was ordered to sell the two Laird rams to French agents representing the Viceroy of Egypt. It was all part of a grand scheme that would eventually bring the ships back into Confederate hands in the waters outside Mexico. But the United States Government, in the person of Ambassador Charles Francis Adams, exerted a considerable amount of pressure on the English to prevent the ships from leaving port. Remembering the embarrassing incident with ship #290, alias the *Alabama*, the two rams were seized on September 3, 1863; and, following many months of haggling, the British government ended up buying the two ships from the agents, and Her Majesty added the rams to her own fleet.

All was not lost, however, for between 1863 and 1864 Bulloch continued to use his finely honed and manipulative skills, both technical and social, to negotiate contracts for five blockade runners, the *Coquette, Owl, Bat, Stag,* and *Deer*. He also purchased one additional vessel that went on to be the successful commerce-raider *Shenandoah*.

Up to this point, Secretary Mallory's foreign shipbuilding effort dealt mostly with English yards. But to the consternation of Mallory, as well as his purchasing agents in England, British law was proving to be extremely frustrating. The Crown's intensified enforcement of the laws, albeit only at the aggressive insistence of the U.S. Government, was making it very difficult for the Confederacy to get the ships out of the country.

It was widely accepted at the time that the French shipbuilders were also master builders of ironclads, having experimented with this new technology for a number of years. Taking advantage of the seemingly cordial relations between the Confederacy and the French Government, and at the same time the reputation of the French craftsmen, on July 13, 1863, Bulloch contracted for six ships. They were four small wooden corvettes and two ironclad rams, each ram being equipped with twin turrets. Within two months, news of the deal had leaked to the U.S. Minister in France, who wasted little time in filing a formal protest. The following February the French Government placed a hold on their departure and also ordered all six ships sold abroad. Through legal maneuvering, however, Bulloch did manage to have one ironclad transferred to the Confederacy from Denmark, her new owner. Arriving in Havana, Cuba, a month after Lee's surrender in 1865, the CSS *Stonewall* was later turned over to the U.S. Government.

In Nassau, Confederate authorities intercepted Commander Semmes in June 1862; instead of continuing on to Richmond, he was told to report to England to take over a new command. His ship, he was told, was the newly built *Enrica*, anchored outside the Laird Shipyard, having been launched in May and now waiting for her crew.

But, as mentioned earlier, quickly evolving events with the British Government and their neutrality laws had forced the speedy departure of #290 and, in turn, had also altered the Confederate program. Accordingly, following his arrival in Liverpool, Semmes, who was now in the company of agent Bulloch, departed on August 13 for the Azores, where #290 was christened and turned over to her new commander.

Describing the clean and pristine condition of his ship at her christening, Semmes remarked with pride, she was "like a bride, with the orange wreath about her brow, ready to be led to the altar." Over the next few days she was fueled, provisioned, armed, and, with a new Confederate flag proudly waving from her mast, renamed the CSS *Alabama*.

For Bulloch, this was indeed a difficult time. He had paid special attention to the *Alabama* as she was being built and grew to admire the grandeur of the new ship. He thought, "She was as fine a vessel, and as well-found, as could have been turned out of any dockyard in the kingdom, equal to any of Her Majesty's ships of corresponding class in structure and finish, and superior to any vessel of her date in fitness...." In fact, he was hoping to command her himself and was quite disappointed when Semmes was selected instead. The authorities in Richmond preferred to offer Semmes the command of the *Alabama*. He had gained some degree of notoriety from his exploits aboard the *Sumter*, and it was only fitting that he should continue with his destruction of Northern shipping, while Bulloch's successes made him more valuable negotiating ship contracts.

Staffed with Confederate officers and a British crew, on August 24, 1862, the *Alabama*, representing a massive $250,000 investment, steamed out of the Azores on her maiden voyage as a commerce-raider. For the next 22 months, from August 1862 until June 1864, the *Alabama* would make history with her piratical tactics against the U.S. shipping industry.

For a wooden ship, the 8-gun *Alabama* represented the latest state-of-the-art engineering and was a marvel of naval architecture. She was described as a model of "perfect symmetry," and "she sat upon the water with the lightness and grace of a swan." Under sail she was able to cut through the sea at up to 12 knots, even more when assisted by her engines. She was equipped with an innovative new device, a condenser, which supplied more than enough fresh water for her crew, and a screw propeller that in 15 minutes could be lifted out of the water to reduce drag when under sail. Painted black, she looked as menacing as she would later prove to be.

A week and a half later, the *Alabama* claimed her first victim, followed in quick succession by nine others, all whaling ships and all of them burned in the waters around the Azores.

Sailing west from the Azores to the U.S. coastline, Semmes set his course along the commercial sea-lanes, the superhighway used by the shippers that connected New York with Europe. In these waters pickings would be plentiful.

As predicted, with no one to challenge his escapades, Semmes captured ten more defenseless merchant vessels on his crossing from the Azores. After appropriating needed provisions from his captured ships and locking up their crews, ten more burning hulks were sent to the deep before the *Alabama* headed south for the waters of the Caribbean. At Martinique, Semmes sailed into port for supplies and fuel from his waiting tender and to release his prisoners.

It was now November 1862 as the *Alabama* steamed towards the Gulf of Mexico. Arriving the following month, Semmes was utterly amazed that federal warships were never in sight to challenge him.

By this time, some 24 U.S. merchant ships had fallen victim to the *Alabama* and her notorious captain, whose exploits at sea were widely publicized, and who was still being characterized as a "pirate" by Northern newspapers.

In the late afternoon of January 11, 1863, the *Alabama* was off the coast of Galveston, Texas. Suddenly, a federal gunboat was spotted racing directly towards the Confederate intruder. It was the side-wheeler USS *Hatteras*. Although armed with five guns and covered in iron plate, she was definitely no match for the wooden Southern cruiser. Semmes immediately steamed away, forcing the pursuing challenger to distance herself from the rest of the fleet. At nightfall, the *Alabama* turned back on the *Hatteras*, sending shells screaming from her broadsides into the Union ship. As the two ships traded gunfire at a range of only 100 feet or so, the *Hatteras* was severely damaged by direct hits to her engine room, which disabled the craft, and by subsequent impacts that ruptured her iron plates. With their vessel now ablaze, within 15 minutes the crew of the *Hatteras* was forced to abandon ship and now claimed the dubious distinction of having served on the only Federal warship sunk by the Confederate Navy in an engagement at sea.

Running low on fuel, the *Alabama* sailed off for Jamaica where Commander Semmes released his prisoners, a practice he would follow with all his captured crews. With the ship replenished and the crew rested, on January 25 the *Alabama* headed out to sea to continue her relentless search for more victims.

Leaving a long trail of burning ships in her wake, their cargoes confiscated and stowed in her belly, the rebel raider arrived in the waters off Brazil on the 10th of April. Here, at a penal island, he took on coal and captured some 15 more ships, 13 of which were destroyed, their crews dutifully transported to the coast, although always after surviving under appalling and inhumane conditions. Now with 53 captures to her credit, in July Semmes sailed across the South Atlantic, stopping just north of Cape Town on the 26th.

Ten days later, the *Alabama* encountered another merchant ship, the *Sea Bride*. To the delight of the local inhabitance, the pursuit and capture of the American vessel was an exciting and thrilling spectacle to watch. Drawn to the seacoast, hundreds of onlookers cheered at the sight of a Confederate commerce-raider in action. The *Sea Bride*, like many of others before her, lit up the nighttime sky.

After looting and torching three more merchant ships navigating through the Indian Ocean, the *Alabama* stopped at Singapore for a couple of days in December before returning to Cape Town on March 20, 1864, capturing three more prizes along the way. Departing five days later, Semmes took his tired and worn out ship north, seizing his last four prizes in the process.

Passing the Azores where she began her journey several years earlier, and badly in need of repairs, the *Alabama* finally anchored off Cherbourg, France, on June 11.

Reminiscing aboard the *Alabama* of his exhausting expedition, Semmes wrote, "The poor old *Alabama* was not now what she had been then. She was like the wearied foxhound limping back after a long chase, footsore, and longing for quiet and repose. Her commander, like herself, was well-nigh worn down. Vigils by day and night, the storms and the drenching rain, the frequent and rapid change of climate — now freezing, now melting or broiling, and the constant excitement of the chase and capture — had laid, in the three years of war he had been afloat, a load of a dozen years upon his shoulders."

Meanwhile, the federal warship USS *Kearsarge* was anchored off the coast of Holland on June 12 when an urgent telegram arrived from the U.S. Minister to France alerting her commander that the *Alabama* was in Cherbourg. Cmdr. John A. Winslow frantically gathered up his crew and, under full steam, raced directly towards the French coast. Having spent the past year chasing down

Confederate commerce-raiders, the Union commander could not resist this opportunity to bag the best and the vilest of them all.

Several days later, Semmes received word that the *Kearsarge* had arrived in Cherbourg and was positioned outside the breakwater. The Confederate commander, however, under the impression that the *Kearsarge* was in Cherbourg merely to pick up the *Alabama*'s prisoners, relayed his desire to engage the Union warship in battle. In his reply Winslow strongly chided Commander Semmes by telling him that his sole purpose for coming to Cherbourg was only to fight.

At this time Semmes was feeling quite ill. Suffering with a fever, he lost the strength to continue, writing earlier that his health had "suffered so much from a constant and harassing service of three years, almost continuously at sea, that I shall have to ask for relief." Nevertheless, knowing his ship and his crew were also showing the wear and tear of thousands of miles and twenty-two months at sea, Semmes chose to give battle to the federal warship. This was his chance to prove that the *Alabama* wasn't a privateer but was, in fact, a true ship-of-war, and that he was not a pirate but a naval commander carrying out his duty. It would be a duel between two old shipmates that as lieutenants had shared the same cabin 17 years ago in the war with Mexico.

Word of the impending battle had spread very quickly throughout the region. Like the epic clash of the ironclads in March of 1862, the duel captured the imagination of the people living in the surrounding villages and in cities miles away. An estimated 15,000 people came to Cherbourg to witness the fight. They lined the coastline and the heights and watched from the many private boats that crowded the channel on that historic day.

At last the anticipation was over. At 10 a.m. on June 19, a Sunday, the two ships approached each other in the English Channel and, amid the cheering throng, were joined in battle.

The two ships appeared to be evenly matched. Both ships were screw steamers around the same size, and both were powered by dual engines. Firepower aboard the *Alabama* consisted of eight guns — six 32-pdr. smoothbore broadsides, one 68-pdr. pivot smoothbore, and a rifled British 110-pdr. Blakely pivot gun. The *Kearsarge* was armed with seven guns — four 32-pdr. broadsides, one 30-pdr. rifle, and two formidable 11-inch smoothbore Dahlgrens on pivot fore and aft. One additional piece of defensive equipment employed by the *Kearsarge* were iron chains, which hung down the sides of the ship to protect the engines and boilers from a direct hit.

Aboard the *Alabama* the crew was supremely confident of their ultimate victory. After all, they had the experience of capturing over sixty merchant ships behind them, experience that would serve them well against the *Kearsarge*. Steaming out well beyond the three-mile limit, each ship defiantly approached the other, gun crews impatiently waiting to release their first salvo. Finally, firing from a range of 1800 yards, a few minutes before 11 a.m. the *Alabama*'s first broadside echoed through the channel, missing wildly and passing harmlessly through the Union rigging. Then came a second shot, and a third, each one well off the mark. The maneuvering of the two ships eventually forced them into a circular track, each ship circling the other in a counter-clockwise direction, both bobbing and weaving like prizefighters as they plowed through the churning wake. As the two ships tightened their circle to a range of 500 yards they continued to trade broadsides with little effect.

The *Alabama* was the first to score a direct hit, severely damaging the *Kearsarge* and injuring three crewmembers from the impact of a 110-pound shot from her Blakely. Although the *Alabama* had drawn the first blood and appeared to be gaining the initiative, the *Kearsarge* quickly returned fire, her Dahlgrens disabling the *Alabama*'s steering. The momentum began to shift as the well trained and highly disciplined gunners of the *Kearsarge* continued to lob shells into their crippled adversary. The crew of the *Alabama* soon learned that the experience gained from capturing unarmed vessels was no match for actual combat. Finally, a mighty blast from the *Kearsarge*'s 11-inch pivot Dahlgren scored the fatal blow, opening the hull at the waterline of the Confederate cruiser. The *Alabama* was badly damaged and in serious trouble. Taking on water rapidly, Semmes had little choice but to lower the colors and order all hands to abandon ship. It was now noon. At 12:24 the infamous Confederate cruiser disappeared beneath the waves, coming to rest in 45 fathoms of water.

Of the *Alabama*'s 144 men, 21 died. The only casualties suffered by the *Kearsarge* were the three men wounded at the outset of the battle.

The *Kearsarge* and several other boats in the area managed to rescue the crew of the *Alabama*. Semmes and several staff officers, meanwhile, were picked up by one of the private boats witnessing the battle and taken to England, where Semmes was enthusiastically wined and dined by the British elite. When he returned to the Confederacy he was praised by the Confederate congress, promoted to rear admiral, and given command of the James River Squadron.

In an attempt to save face, however, Semmes would later complain that Winslow's use of heavy iron chains to protect the hull of the *Kearsarge* was a form of armor and represented an unfair advantage, which contributed to his defeat — as did the stale powder he was forced to use, which caused the failure of many of his shells to explode.

Winslow, on the other hand, was also received as a national hero and, by direction of President Lincoln, promoted to commodore.

In her 22 months at sea, the *Alabama* always managed to elude capture. And during this period she seized no less than 64 Union ships, 52 of them just in the first ten months. With the exception of the USS *Hatteras*, all were federal merchant vessels. Fifty-four were destroyed, eight were released under ransom-bond, one was sold to an Englishman, and one was converted to a Confederate warship, the CSS *Tuscaloosa*.

With the *Alabama* gone, the ships of the U.S. Navy could now focus on the CSS *Florida*, still actively engaged in hunting down merchant ships off the East Coast.

The first commerce-raider contracted for by Bulloch, the *Florida* was built in England and was fraudulently represented as a ship destined for the Italian Government. Although suspected by the U.S. Government to be a warship in disguise, the charges could not be proven. When an "agent" for the Italian Government, who swore to be the owner, appeared with her English commander, the ship was released in March of 1862. In August, shortly after receiving her commission and ordnance at Nassau, the *Florida*, under the command of Lt. John N. Maffitt, set her sails for the waters of Cuba.

Problems, however, plagued the ship from the very start. The *Florida* had sailed without a full complement of crewmen, having lost around 20 men in Nassau that were bribed by the U.S. to jump ship. Even worse, her two 7-inch and six 6-inch rifled Blakelys were useless without several vital parts that had not arrived with the rest of the ordnance. If that wasn't enough, a few days out of Nassau a fierce epidemic of yellow fever broke out and raged throughout the ship. As a result, the entire crew required immediate medical attention in Cuba, including her commander.

Unable to obtain the parts or able-bodied seamen in Cuba, the following month Maffitt returned to the U.S. mainland by successfully running his defenseless ship through the Union blockade to the Confederate port of Mobile.

Four months later, on January 15, 1863, the fully staffed and fully equipped *Florida* headed back to sea, again eluding the federal blockade, despite the increase in Union blockaders patrolling the area. From January through the middle of July her course ranged to the south along the coast of Brazil and then north as far as New England. During this time, on February 12, she captured the largest prize of any cruiser, burning the *Jacob Bell*, a ship engaged in the U.S.–China trade worth some two million dollars. After she evaded a Union warship off the coast of Nantucket, Maffitt reset his course southward again, arriving in Bermuda on the 15th of July. At this point the *Florida* was in desperate need of major repairs, which couldn't be obtained in Bermuda. Crossing the Atlantic at the end of July, the *Florida* sailed to France, anchoring in the harbor at Brest.

Too ill to continue, on September 17 Maffitt was removed from command and replaced by Lt. Charles M. Morris. In February of 1864 Morris sailed the *Florida* back across the Atlantic to Martinique, returning to Bermuda in May.

Although not as formidable as the *Alabama*, the *Florida* by this time had captured 28 prizes. After sailing from Bermuda she managed to capture eight more in the northern sea-lanes until she was forced to flee from pursuing Federal cruisers for a second time. Traveling south again, she finally entered the port at Bahia, Brazil, on October 5, with two more captures along the way.

Also anchored at Bahia, however, was the Federal warship USS *Wachusett*, under Cmdr. Napoleon Collins. The Union commander could not believe his eyes, and despite the neutrality of Bahia he could not resist the temptation of sinking the Confederate raider responsible for destroying 38 U.S. merchant ships. In the wee morning hours of October 7 the *Wachusett* attacked. The intent was to destroy the *Florida* by simply broadsiding her where she anchored. Once the Confederate ship was wounded and sinking, the Union cruiser would then quickly steam out of the harbor. But the *Wachusett* failed to impact the *Florida* solidly with a direct and head-on attack, instead only striking a glancing blow. Following the failed ramming, a small gunfight ensued between the few Confederate crewmembers on board and a *Wachusett* boarding party. The *Florida* was quickly captured, immediately taken out of the harbor, and taken directly to Hampton Roads, Virginia.

The Brazilian authorities were highly incensed over this blatant disregard of their neutrality and demanded the return of the *Florida*. The U.S. authorities agreed, but shortly before the *Florida* was to sail, she was rammed by an army transport negotiating through the heavy traffic of Hampton Roads. Although damage was reported to be minimal, she was moved to Newport News where she mysteriously sank to the bottom of the channel that same night. Despite the obvious repercussions and questions surrounding this incident, the Navy Department was quite pleased that the Confederate commerce-raider was no longer a threat, and, as a result, culpability for this "accident" was never determined.

At last, two of the most productive Confederate raiders were no longer a threat to the U.S. commercial shipping fleet, but it was too late. In spite of their demise, the efforts of these two ships had already caused a catastrophe to the U.S. shipping industry. Not only from the number of ships destroyed, but also from the psychological effect they had on the owners and their investors.

Before the war the U.S. took great pride in the success of its commercial fleet. Its capacity to reach the most distant ports of the world was an inspiration to everyone. By the end of the Civil War, however, the Confederate strategy of commerce-raiders had decimated the American shipping industry. Through the latter half of 1861, when the threats of privateering and the menacing exploits of the CSS *Sumter* first appeared to endanger the very survival of their fleet, a few commercial ship owners panicked and, to protect their investments, sold out their business interests to English buyers. With the increased threat from commerce-raiders such as the *Alabama* and the *Florida,* among others, however, this paranoia grew to such proportions that eventually half of the U.S. commercial shipping industry sold out, graciously taken over by Great Britain, who now boasted of having the number one merchant marine fleet in the world.

The Southern goal was to bring the Union to its knees by destroying the commerce of the Northern States. But materially, the North suffered very little by the efforts of the Confederate raiders. Imported supplies and foodstuffs for both the military and the civilian populace were still quite plentiful. In the end, commercial shipping in and out of the North had not changed at all, except that now most of the goods were transported on ships flying the British flag.

The *Alabama* and the *Florida* were the most famous of the commerce-raiders, but the Confederacy did have several other cruisers that deserve mention.

The CSS *Georgia,* a new screw-steamer, was bought in England by Matthew F. Maury, a former Union naval officer and, like Bulloch, a Confederate purchasing agent in Liverpool. The *Japan,* as she was called, was bought in March 1863 through an intermediary to conceal the true nature of the purchase. With a British crew and British armament, she was commissioned at sea the following month under the command of Lt. William L. Maury, and traveled a course through the Caribbean and along the coast of Brazil, eventually sailing to Africa, France, and on to England.

The *Georgia* was credited with only nine captures because of two glaring defects: her lack of auxiliary sail power and her limited coal capacity. These two design flaws made the ship much too slow to compete in an enterprise where speed was critical. Having no other choice, Commodore Samuel Barron, of Hatteras Inlet fame, and who now controlled the operations of all Confederate raiders in Europe, decided to retire her as unfit for commerce-destroying duty. The *Georgia* was disarmed and sold on June 1, 1864, to an English merchant who, in turn, chartered her to Portugal. But when information was received disclosing her destination, the U.S. Government immediately ordered her seized at sea. Following her capture by the USS *Niagara,* she was brought to the U.S. and condemned by a prize court, an action subsequently upheld by the U.S. Supreme Court.

The CSS *Tallahassee* was originally a blockade-runner. She was refitted, armed, and later commissioned at Wilmington, North Carolina, on July 20, 1864. Skippered by Cmdr. John T. Wood, the *Tallahassee* sailed the following month up the East Coast by New York and New England to the waters off the coast of Halifax, capturing a total of 33 prizes. Incredibly, her first fourteen captures occurred in just two days, August 11 and 12. Her success, however, had attracted a number of Union cruisers bent on ending her mischief, and forced her to sail back to the safety of Wilmington, successfully running the blockade on August 26.

Renamed the *Olustee*, in October she sailed northward as far as the entrance to the Chesapeake Bay, capturing six more prizes before returning to Wilmington. The *Olustee* was then converted back to a blockade-runner, the *Chameleon*, transporting cotton to Bermuda. In December of 1864, on her return trip with supplies for the Confederate army, she was unable to avoid the Union blockade. With no other option, the *Chameleon* dropped her supplies in Nassau and steamed for Liverpool. She was eventually seized by British authorities and handed over to the U.S. in 1866. The U.S. eventually sold her to the Japanese Navy.

The CSS *Chickamauga* was also converted from a blockade-runner at Wilmington and began her first cruise on October 28, 1864. After capturing only five prizes she escaped from a growing number of pursuing Union warships and sailed to Bermuda. However, with the British now stringently enforcing their neutralization laws, her captain, Lt. John Wilkinson, was allowed only enough coal to return to the closest Confederate port. After only three weeks at sea her raiding days were over. In February of 1865 she was burned to prevent capture.

The CSS *Shenandoah*, the only Confederate raider to circumnavigate the globe, was a commercial vessel purchased by Bulloch in England and, like the others, secretly armed, commissioned, and renamed at sea in October 1864. At this late date, most of the commercial ships flying the U.S. flag had disappeared from the seas. In that light, the *Shenandoah*'s commander, Lt. James I. Waddell, was ordered to pursue "the great American whaling fleet, a source of abundant wealth to our enemies and a nursery for their seamen." The *Shenandoah* stopped at Melbourne on January 25, 1865, then sailed past New Guinea to Ascension Island, through the Amphitrite Straits, and into the thick ice of the Sea of Okhotsk off the coast of Russia. On June 16 she entered the Bering Sea and by early July had passed into the North Pacific. By that time the *Shenandoah* had made 38 captures, 25 of them from the fishing fleet in the Bering Sea. To many in the North, however, her success was somewhat qualified, owing to the fact that her prey was largely small vessels from the commercial whaling fleet. Mostly out of New Bedford, Massachusetts, the whalers were thought to be unnecessarily victimized by the incursion of the powerful Confederate cruiser.

In the Pacific, in August, Lt. Weddell learned that the war was over and that Jefferson Davis had been imprisoned. Accordingly, he steamed south around Cape Horn and back across the Atlantic to Liverpool where the *Shenandoah* finally surrendered on November 6, 1865, after a 17,000-mile voyage. She was later transferred to the U.S. and sold to the Sultan of Zanzibar.

At the end of the war the U.S. Government determined that the British owed compensation for their role in the damage to its commercial shipping and whaling industry. The claim was for monetary damages, in order of their severity, caused by the *Alabama, Shenandoah, Florida, Tallahassee, Georgia, Chickamauga, Sumter, Nashville, Retribution, Jefferson Davis, Sallie,* and *Boston.*

It should be noted that most of the crews aboard the commerce raiders were British subjects, their ordnance was British made, British ports were often used for activities that were in direct violation of their Neutrality Act, and six of the ships were actually built in British yards.

Collectively referred to as the "Alabama Claims," the proceedings were held in Geneva and negotiated by representatives from the U.S., Great Britain, Brazil, Italy, and Switzerland. The $16 million finally agreed upon in 1872 represented only the damages inflicted by the *Alabama*, the *Shenandoah*, and the *Florida*. The arbitrators concluded that England was not liable for damages from the other nine vessels. Of the $16 million, the compensation for the damages caused by the CSS *Alabama* alone accounted for nearly half the total.

The loss of the *Alabama* and the *Florida* had for all practical purposes closed the chapter on the Confederate commerce-raiders. By the end of 1864 nearly all of the major raiders were gone and the Confederacy itself was in dire straits, experiencing the final stages of its own existence.

In 1984 a French Navy mine-hunter detected the remains of the *Alabama* off the coast of Cherbourg. A joint French-American Scientific Committee was formed in October 1989, which established the basis for international cooperation in archaeological research and for the protection of the historic shipwreck. The *Alabama*'s Blakely gun was recovered in 1994. In France, while undergoing conservation treatment, the gun was found to be fully loaded. Incredibly, when the shell was defused in March 1995 the powder was found to be intact and just as dry as it was 131 years earlier. As of July 1995, 18 objects were recovered and the pivot gun was now visible. However, as of this writing, the search continues for the 32-pounders.

9

North Atlantic Naval Campaigns: August 1861–October 1864

During the course of implementing the cordon along the Atlantic seaboard, it became quite evident to the navy that the lack of supply bases was having a major impact on the effectiveness of the blockade. With the loss of the Norfolk Navy Yard, the Atlantic Blockading Squadron was using Hampton Roads, at the entrance to the James River, as its base of operations. Consequently, an enormous logistics problem soon became apparent whenever any of the blockading ships in the squadron required repairs, ran out of coal, fresh water, or any other necessity. They were forced to steam all the way to Hampton Roads to replenish their supplies, or to either the Brooklyn or Philadelphia Navy Yard for repairs. Depending on where the ships started from, the round trip could take months. In the meantime, their positions at sea remained vacant for considerable periods of time, creating huge voids in the blockading line. At the recommendation of Secretary Welles, a four-member Board of Strategy was formed, chaired by Capt. Samuel F. DuPont, commander of the Philadelphia Navy Yard, to investigate the problems of implementing the blockade and to recommend corrective action. Other members of the board were: Major John C. Barnard, of the U.S. Corps of Army Engineers; Capt. Charles H. Davis, U.S. Navy; and Prof. Alexander D. Bache, Superintendent of the Coast Survey.

Following its deliberations in August 1861, the board proposed seizing a Southern port and converting it into a naval supply base. Once achieved, the additional base would guarantee an efficient means for quickly serving the needs of the blockading ships. Since it had to be conveniently located, they selected

Port Royal, South Carolina, and Captain DuPont would be the commander in charge of the expedition. In addition to Port Royal, the board also recommended the seizure of Hatteras Inlet by an expedition to be led by Flag Officer Silas H. Stringham, commander of the Atlantic Blockading Squadron.

Hatteras Inlet was one of several land gaps in a 200-mile long series of barrier islands. The gaps, or inlets, allowed ships in the Atlantic to gain entrance to the coast of North Carolina. Hatteras Inlet led into Pamlico Sound and was significant because, for the Union, it was the most troublesome of them all. Pamlico Sound had become a magnet for blockade-runners and privateers in view of the fact that the railroad at that point, the Atlantic & N.C.R.R, was one of the conduits for supplies reaching Richmond. Another factor was that privateers out of Pamlico Sound were continually ambushing unsuspecting Northern commercial vessels sailing in the area, which in turn provoked an immediate outcry for action from the shipping industry.

On August 26, in the very first joint military action of the war, Flag Officer Stringham, commanding seven warships, was joined at Fort Monroe by Gen. Benjamin F. Butler and approximately 900 troops aboard three transports. The Union fleet under Stringham consisted of the *Minnesota*, his flagship, the *Wabash, Harriet Lane, Monticello, Pawnee, Susquehanna*, and the lone sailing ship, the *Cumberland*. Their mission was to put a stop to the infiltration of Confederate runners and privateers into the Sound by gaining control of Hatteras Inlet.

Stringham and Butler planned to accomplish this feat by capturing the two log and sand forts under the command of Major W. S. G. Andrews that were guarding the entrance to Pamlico Sound on the southern tip of Hatteras Island. Fort Clark, the smaller and less fortified of the two, stood on the ocean side of the Island, at the entrance to Hatteras Inlet, while Fort Hatteras was located on the far side of the Island, only a half-mile away.

The Union plan was simple. It called for the *Minnesota, Susquehanna*, and *Wabash*, towing the *Cumberland*, to bombard the forts into submission from the front while Butler's troops landed on the beach and stormed the forts from the rear.

Approximately three hours into the battle, however, around midday of August 27, the ammunition for the five guns at Fort Clark had run out. Considering the limited number of options to survive his present dilemma, the troop commander, Col. William F. Martin of the 7th North Carolina Infantry Regiment, had little choice but to abandon the fort. After conferring with the other commanders, he ordered his troops to Fort Hatteras, the larger and, with 25 guns, more heavily armed. Meanwhile, about 320 of Butler's men, who had landed earlier three miles up the coastline, proceeded to file into the now deserted Fort Clark.

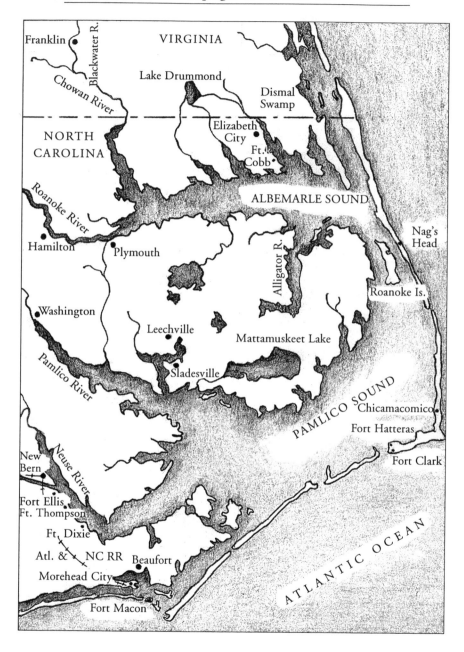

Franklin

Blackwater R.

VIRGINIA

Lake Drummond

Chowan River

Dismal
Swamp

Elizabeth
City

NORTH
CAROLINA

Ft.
Cobb

Roanoke River

ALBEMARLE SOUND

Nag's
Head

Hamilton

Plymouth

Alligator R.

Roanoke Is.

Washington

Leechville

Mattamuskeet Lake

Pamlico River

Sladesville

PAMLICO SOUND

Chicamacomico

Fort Hatteras

New
Bern

Neuse River

Fort Clark

Fort Ellis
Ft. Thompson

Ft. Dixie

Atl. & NC RR   Beaufort

ATLANTIC OCEAN

Morehead City

Fort Macon

North Carolina Sounds

The next morning the fleet resumed its bombardment of Fort Hatteras, blasting the Confederate occupants with shells from their 10-inch and 11-inch guns. In the meantime, Flag Officer Samuel Barron C.S.N., representing the Confederate Navy and in charge of defending the Virginia and North Carolina coastlines, had arrived with several hundred reinforcements to take over the command. By this time Colonel Martin understood the futility of further resistance and, with Barron's acquiescence, surrendered the fort along with the garrison of Confederate soldiers.

Shortly after noontime, the three Confederate officers, Barron, Martin, and Andrews, joined Stringham and Butler aboard the *Minnesota* for the formal signing of the surrender terms, which were fully unconditional. Later, as a prisoner aboard the *Minnesota,* Barron explained the reason for his capitulation. "During the first hour the shells of the ships fell short, we only firing occasionally to ascertain whether our shots would reach them, and wishing to reserve our very limited supply of ammunition until the vessels might find it necessary to come nearer in; but they, after some practice, got the exact range of the 9, 10, and 11 inch guns, and did not find it necessary to alter their positions, while not a shot from our battery reached them with the greatest elevation we could get."

Although the battle was ultimately successful for the Union side, for General Butler the mission began rather badly. Three miles up the beach from Fort Clark, the Union troops making the amphibious landing, about 320 infantrymen from the 9th and 20th New York Volunteer Regiments, had to deal with extremely severe weather conditions. Strong, gusty winds and heavy surf capsized many of the small boats used in the landing, rendering their weapons and gunpowder useless and their food unfit to eat. As a result, the troops were without food for several days and were unable to fire a single shot. In the end, Butler's troops never really took an active role in the action.

Flag Officer Stringham, on the other hand, became the first naval commander to institute a new and innovative firing maneuver. With his ships sailing before the forts in an elliptical pattern, Stringham's order was to maintain their shelling while moving parallel to the forts. This novel approach of firing from a moving platform was a far cry from the traditional naval tactic of firing only when the ship was in a stationary position. Nevertheless, this maneuver was severely criticized by other navy commanders who claimed the advantage of being a moving target was a poor trade off for the inaccuracy of the shipboard gunners, which they concluded, only tended to waste ammunition and lengthen the engagement.

This first triumph gave the Navy Department a taste of how their future battles would be fought. Over the next four years, relatively few battles would be fought with both navies confronting each other head-to-head on the open sea. Instead, Union ships, in cooperation with army forces, would engage an enemy hidden within seashore fortifications or lurking behind coastal artillery batteries.

The Hatteras Inlet campaign represented not only the first Union naval victory of the Civil War, but also the first noteworthy triumph of any kind for the North. Following the depressing loss on the Manassas battlefield in July and the tragic defeat at Wilson's Creek, Missouri, on August 10, this accomplishment gave the people at home a much needed lift in spirit and pride.

Both Stringham and Butler were beside themselves with excitement over their success, and after leaving the *Monticello*, *Pawnee*, and the tug *Fanny* behind with the occupational force, they literally raced each other back to New York to receive the accolades for a job well done and to be the first to claim bragging rights.

With Hatteras Inlet now safely secured, the immediate concern of the Union commanders was the Confederate troops occupying nearby Roanoke Island. Only 10 miles long, this small island was at the north end of the Sound and separated Pamlico Sound from Albemarle Sound. The Navy Department understood full well that whoever controlled Roanoke Island also controlled the passage through the Sounds, as well as the rivers and communication links to Richmond and Norfolk. It was also known that several ironclads were under construction in the network of adjoining rivers, which made it all the more imperative to gain a foothold in these waters. To rid the North Carolina waters of Confederate presence once and for all, the Union military formed yet another joint venture, with Roanoke Island as its target.

Not able to use the heavier ships of the Home Squadron for this campaign, the Union Navy assembled a fleet of 17 shallow draft vessels, mostly made up of an exotic assortment of river steamers, ferryboats, tugboats, and any other craft capable of carrying large guns. The "gunboats" were under the command of Flag Officer Louis M. Goldsborough, the newly appointed skipper of the North Atlantic Blockading Squadron, an organization formed shortly after Stringham retired in September. A massive man of six feet four inches and over 300 pounds, the red-bearded navy man began his career as a midshipman at the unbelievably tender age of seven. Now at 56, "Old Guts" had spent 49 years in the service of his country. For this operation, Goldsborough's flagship, the *Philadelphia*, was not present for duty, so the *Southfield* was used instead.

Cooperating with the navy was army Gen. Ambrose E. Burnside, a veteran of the Battle of Bull Run fiasco of last July. In preparation for this mission, Burnside had specifically recruited a number of soldiers adept at working with boats, finding them mostly in the New England States, a total of some 12,000 troops that he often referred to as the "Coast Division."

To transport Burnside's troops, equipment, provisions, guns, and ammunition, an enormous fleet of 80 ships was assembled at Fort Monroe. Since the army lacked sufficient skills in ship procurement, the transports under the command of General Burnside were in even worse condition than Goldsborough's. General Burnside himself described the ships as "a motley fleet" of river barges, sailing vessels, passenger steamers, tug boats, and whatever else the army could secure. As bad as the weather was on the outside, living conditions for the troops on board the old ships was even worse. The troops had to sleep with the horses, and were fed nothing but hard, wormy bread, horsemeat boiled in salt water, and rotten pork, all washed down with black coffee.

General Burnside's rickety fleet steamed out of Hampton Roads on January 11, 1862, arriving at Hatteras Inlet two days later. Over the next two days the small armada became caught up in a terrible winter storm. Tossed by heavy swells and gale force winds, the fleet was somehow able to ride it out and miraculously survived none the worse for wear.

Despite horrid weather, over the weeks ahead the combined fleet attempted to cross the sand bar, each ship gingerly inching through water only seven to eight feet deep. Although shallow drafted, many of the vessels were much too heavy when fully loaded and became hung up on the shoals. This only meant further delays for the expedition, as each ship had to be lightened to get them across the bar. By February 4 the entire joint-fleet, now totaling about 65 vessels, had made the passage and were safely anchored in Pamlico Sound.

Finally, on February 5, the weather cleared and the massive fleet was on its way to Roanoke Island, only to be stalled again by another stretch of gale winds and choppy conditions that continually rage in the vicinity of Cape Hatteras.

The Confederate commander on Roanoke Island was none other than former governor Henry A. Wise, the staunch secessionist from Virginia remembered for his mobilization of Southern forces at Harpers Ferry and Norfolk Navy Base last spring. Learning beforehand of the planned attack on his fortifications, Wise decided to impede the advancement of the Union fleet by scuttling a number of old hulks in Croatan Sound, the body of water that separated the Island from the mainland. Also, pilings were placed across the Sound to further discourage Goldsborough from carrying out his attack. The wisdom of ordering the obstructions in Croatan Sound was obvious to General Wise, who knew the forts were grossly inadequate to repel the expected assault and were far from impregnable. On the day of the battle, however, General Wise was in bed at Nag's Head recovering from an illness, leaving his forces under the command of Colonel H. M. Shaw. On Roanoke Island itself, Confederate defenses consisted of three small nondescript forts armed with about 25 guns and garrisoned by some 3,000 troops. Forts Bartow, Blanchard, and Huger were on the northwest side of the island, and a fourth, Fort Forrest, was located directly across Croatan Sound on the mainland. A large swamp, boarded on both sides by seemingly impregnable abatis further enhanced the defenses of the Island's interior. Also, in the Sound were moored nine vessels, seven of which were gunboats.

The attack was set in motion at about 9 a. m. on February 7, 1862, when the Union gunboats opened a heavy barrage on Fort Bartow, the most southerly of the three forts, as well as the Confederate fleet that came out to challenge them. While the fort and the Union ships were thus engaged, at 4 p.m. General Burnside began landing his troops at Ashby's Harbor, several miles south of Fort Bartow. Using a number of launches in a highly coordinated operation, by midnight, 10,000 men were on the beach, along with several pieces of artillery.

The exchange of gunfire lasted throughout the day without any serious damage to the fort or, for that matter, to the Union gunboats. The only loss was nothing less than the entire Confederate fleet. Two of the gunboats, the *Forrest* and the *Curlew*, were disabled early on, but when the rest of the fleet ran out of ammunition, the commander, Commodore William F. Lynch, thought it best to retreat from Roanoke Island and to cross Albermarle Sound to the safety of the fort outside Elizabeth City.

At daybreak of February 8, Burnside's troops began their advance towards the Confederate forts while the Union vessels' covering firepower neutralized the Confederate fortifications, pelting their defenses with a steady barrage of missiles. Following stiff skirmishes with rebel forces and a three-gun battery in the island's interior, around 11 a.m. troops of the 23rd and 27th Massachusetts Infantry began to penetrate the swamp, driving the enemy back into their works. Within moments, as additional Union regiments appeared, the enemy works were easily overwhelmed, trapping the frantic rebel troops inside.

Initially, the obstructions in the Sound were preventing the Union ships from advancing to a more advantageous firing position. Frustrated over this impediment to his forward progress, on the 8th Goldsborough ordered several gunboats to smash through the pilings. Several hours later, nine Union gunboats were positioned to coordinate their firing on the forts with the movements of Burnside's troops.

With their colors now flying briskly on the parapet, the Union forces captured approximately 2,700 Confederate soldiers, General Wise managing to escape with most of his command. A reconnaissance to the mainland found that Fort Forrest was blown up by the evacuating Rebels. Confederate casualty figures were not reported; however, the Union Army listed 47 killed that day, the navy, six.

Historians generally agreed that the capture of Roanoke Island was a classic example of how a joint army-navy operation should be carried out. Each branch was incapable of securing a victory on its own, but working together in a well-coordinated and unselfish manner easily proved to be the winning formula.

Refusing to rest on their laurels, eleven Union gunboats under Cmdr. Stephen C. Rowan immediately pushed off under a full head of steam to pursue the Confederates that escaped to Elizabeth City. Reeling in their anchor at the entrance to the Pasquotank River on the morning of February 10, the Union Navy steamed upriver at full speed toward the only Confederate fort guarding admittance to Elizabeth City. As the Federals approached Fort Cobb, an abandoned four-gun affair presently manned by Confederate crewmen, they suddenly encountered sporadic fire from the gunboats. A brief skirmish ensued and within 30 minutes one Confederate gunboat was captured, while four others were promptly destroyed by their crews. The lone Rebel boat to escape was the *Beaufort*. She steamed off to Norfolk, destined to escort the ironclad *Merrimack* to her infamous battle in the Hampton Roads in March. Witnessing the firepower of the Union vessels firsthand, the crewmembers in the fort quickly abandoned their station, spiking the four guns before they fled into the woods, along with Commodore Lynch. Union forces would soon occupy Elizabeth City, which secured Albemarle Sound for the Federal side.

With nearly all of the Confederate gunboats in North Carolina waters destroyed, the Union fleet virtually controlled both the Albemarle and Pamlico Sounds, with one exception: the approaches to New Bern and Beaufort, at the southern end of Pamlico Sound.

At the urging of President Lincoln and Secretary Welles, in early March Flag Officer Goldsborough was hastily recalled to Newport News. A new Confederate menace, the ironclad CSS *Virginia* (formally the USS *Merrimack*), had destroyed two ships of the admiral's squadron in Hampton Roads. Noting his absence, Secretary Welles blamed Goldsborough for the loss of the two Union warships, remarking that the commander was "purposely and unnecessarily absent, in my [opinion] ... through fear of the Merrimac." Goldsborough was stung by this harsh criticism and was ordered to remain in the Hampton Roads to monitor the movements of the Confederate ironclad to prevent her from interfering with Gen. George B. McClelland's Peninsular Campaign. Cmdr. Stephen C. Rowan, meanwhile, would take charge of the expedition to New Bern.

Focusing their attention on the lower sector of Pamlico Sound, Rowan's gunboats steamed south and, together with Burnside's transports, dropped anchor at the entrance to the Neuse River, 16 miles below New Bern. On March 13, 1862, Burnside's troops, who by now were experts on the intricacies of amphibious landings, went ashore at 6:30 a.m. to prepare for the toughest fight of the campaign. In the pouring rain, eight pieces of artillery were also landed and laboriously hauled along the muddy road. With cooperation from the naval gunboats, Burnside's troops would have to attack and fight their way through pockets of batteries, scattered rifle pits, lines of entrenchments, and a number of garrisoned strongholds, Fort Thompson being the predominant, that lined the river leading into New Bern. In their quest to prevent an offshore attack, the Confederate troops, made up entirely of North Carolinians under Gen. Lawrence O'B. Branch, infested the river with an array of underwater mines, piles, and sunken vessels. In spite of these obstacles, however, the Union fleet managed to follow the troops up the river until nightfall closed the day's action, and the men bedded down in the mud and drenching downpour.

Around eight a.m. of the 14th, the first encounter with the enemy was made. Soon, a general engagement along a three-prong front was underway, supported by the shelling from Rowan's gunboats of the thick woods at the rear of the forts. Over some four hours of extremely hard fighting, a struggle mostly fought in the unrelenting rain, the exhausted soldiers swept through the enemy batteries and drove the Confederates into a retreat along the entire front. By capitalizing on their huge advantage in men and firepower, they overwhelmed the Southern defenders and captured over 300 prisoners. Pvt. Charles Wood of the 23rd Massachusetts Volunteers was there and remembered the brutal fight this way: "I got struck in the back with a piece of shell but it did not hurt me any. It tore a hole in my coat as big as my hand. Capt. Sawyer had one of his legs blown off at the knee joint within two minutes after we got on to the field. The fight lasted about 3 hours and it was a purty tough one too. The fight was yesterday morning and they have not had any time to find out the list of killed and wounded but I guess that our loss was as much as 3 or 4 hundred killed and wounded but we succeeded in driving the dirty buggers. They fled and left the city." In this entire process of securing New Bern, Burnside's casualty figure stood at 470 men, the Confederates, nearly 600.

The next and final objective for the Union's combined force to gain complete control of the North Carolina Sounds was Fort Macon, a battlement built on Bogue Island under the command of Col. Moses J. White. Located 40 miles from New Bern at the most southerly point of Pamlico Sound, it was heavily fortified with a garrison of over 500 men and bristling with 67 guns.

Following a Union reconnaissance of the surrounding area on the 18th of March, the Union troops easily occupied Carolina City, Morehead City, and finally Beaufort on the 25th without a challenge or the loss of a single man. Failing twice to obtain a voluntary surrender from Colonel White, a state of siege was imposed and several batteries of large caliber ordnance were constructed on the island itself within range of the fort.

Following several weeks of backbreaking labor, the guns were finally in place, and on April 25 the Union batteries opened up with three rifled 30-pounders and eight heavy mortars. Supporting the army were three steamers, the *Daylight, State of Georgia,* and *Chippewa,* along with the bark *Gemsbok.* A focused barrage of shot and shell from both the naval vessels and the batteries overwhelmed the Fort Macon garrison, and after ten hours of bombardment the garrison capitulated.

On the Virginia Peninsula, meanwhile, Union Gen. George B. McClellan landed his massive Army of the Potomac at Fort Monroe, and had marched his 100,000 men up the Peninsula to Yorktown on April 5. Assuming he was outmanned, McClellan was unwilling to attack the 17,000-man Confederate force there under Gen. John B. Magruder. Instead, he prepared to place Yorktown under a state of siege. In turn, Gen. Joseph E. Johnston, with the urging of the Confederate government, ordered Magruder to withdraw from Yorktown and to retreat towards the outskirts of Richmond. With Yorktown abandoned to the Union, and McClellan's forces threatening Richmond, it became a military necessity for the Confederates to evacuate the Norfolk Navy Yard, as well as their battery positions at Sewell's Point and Craney Island. Despite pleas from Commodore Forrest that he could defend the base, Secretary Mallory ordered the navy yard destroyed and transferred all infantry units to Richmond to defend the Confederate capital. As a result, on May 9, 1862, the Norfolk Naval Yard was given up to the Union, but not until the dry dock was destroyed and the buildings set on fire.

Within a week Goldsborough sent two of his ironclads, the *Monitor* and the *Galena,* and three wooden steamers on a daring raid to the Confederate capital itself, Richmond. Reaching the menacing batteries of Drewry's Bluff on May 15, 1862, only eight miles below the seat of the Confederate government, the Union vessels were unable to lob their shells to the top of the 200-foot bluff. After four hours of a one-sided confrontation, the Union gunboats, badly beaten, were forced to withdraw, which only provoked even more criticism from the Secretary who wrote that Goldsborough was "inefficient, ... had done nothing effective since the frigates were sunk by the *Merrimac,* nor of himself much before."

Finally, in July Goldsborough was informed that his squadron was being reduced, one third of his vessels going to the newly formed James River Flotilla under Capt. Charles Wilkes. A week later, incensed over this blatant display of dissatisfaction of his leadership and the unfair criticism he was receiving in the press, Goldsborough asked to be relieved from his command. The next day, to show its appreciation for his service to the country, a thankful Congress promoted Goldsborough to permanent rear admiral; and within weeks the James River Flotilla was disbanded, a result some said of Wilkes' incompetence, while others claimed it was because of McClellan's withdrawal from the peninsula, which rendered the flotilla unnecessary.

On September 5, 1862, Acting Rear Admiral Samuel P. Lee, a distant cousin of Confederate Gen. Robert E. Lee, was selected to replace Goldsborough, who was subsequently assigned to administrative duties at the Navy Department for the rest of the war. Although a competent officer who had served with Farragut at New Orleans, some officials in the Navy Department thought Lee lacked the experience necessary for such a high command.

For Lee, the remainder of 1862 saw the North Atlantic Blockading Squadron embarking on occasional clean-up forays along the rivers branching out from the two Sounds. In June, a run was made up the Roanoke River and the town of Plymouth was secured, as was Hamilton the following month. Blackwater River was the site of the next naval expedition in October. This time the small town of Franklin fell into Union hands, and in November it was Washington, on the Pamlico River.

Throughout 1863 and most of 1864 the primary mission of the squadron proved to be a relatively routine affair. With the Union controlling the area encompassing Hampton Roads, Yorktown, and Norfolk in Virginia, as well as the sounds of North Carolina, Confederate activity had dropped off noticeably. Therefore, with the exception of several relatively minor operations (such as Lee's role in the defense of Suffolk, Virginia, on the Nansemond River in April of '63; and ferrying Butler's troops up the James River for his failed attempt to capture Drewry's Bluff in May of '64), the squadron, under Flag Officer Lee, continued to maintain their surveillance of the North Carolina coastline. At times the squadron captured a blockade-runner still intent on going into Wilmington, repelled the occasional Confederate raid, or carried out periodic excursions along the rivers to insure the Union retained control of the North Carolina Sounds.

During this period, information had filtered into Washington that the Confederates had built an ironclad ram at Edward's Ferry on the Roanoke River. Secretary Mallory and his Navy Department was so impressed over the success of their ironclad *Virginia* (*Merrimack*) in the Hampton Roads in March of '62, that they ordered the construction of three additional ironclad rams to destroy the Union's wooden ships in the North Carolina Sounds. Secretary Welles, however, was unable to persuade the Union army to destroy the enemy construction sites, and the first ironclad was launched into the Roanoke River in April of 1864. Called the *Albemarle*, by May 5th she was considered a new and very serious threat to the Union's wooden ships and, in particular, to the control of the North Carolina Sounds. In addition to playing a primary role in the Confederate's recapture of Plymouth, she had already rammed and sunk the *Southfield*, and severely damaged several others vessels, including the *Sassacus*, a large side-wheeler that tried unsuccessfully to sink the ironclad with its three-ton bronze ram.

To counter this real danger to the security of their naval forces, the Union initiated a daring and extremely dangerous clandestine operation. The scheme was devised by Lt. William B. Cushing, a brash daredevil perfect for this bold expedition, and approved by Flag Officer Porter. Two open steam-launches, equipped with spar-torpedoes, would penetrate into enemy water at night-time and sink the Confederate ironclad where she was being repaired at dock-side. The second launch would be nearby to fire canister and to renew the attempt if the attack boat was disabled. Several days after steaming out of the New York Navy Yard for Plymouth, one of the launches was lost around Norfolk while the remaining tiny boat struggled to its destination, arriving in the Roanoke River during the night of October 27, 1864.

Alerted to their presence, a raging bonfire was suddenly lit on shore, exposing the intruding seamen to heavy Confederate musket fire. To the surprise of Lieutenant Cushing, the enemy ironclad was protected by a floating necklace of logs. Undaunted by the Confederate defenses and charging at full steam through a rain of gunfire, Cushing headed directly for the 2-gun *Albemarle*, bounded over the log obstruction, and with the spar fully extended, planted the torpedo squarely under the Confederate ram. Within minutes the ironclad was gone when a tremendous explosion ripped through her bow. Flooded and in a sinking condition by the resultant surge of water, the small Union boat was quickly seized by the Confederates, as was the crew. Of the 15 Union men on the boat, two were killed and only two escaped, one being Lt. Cushing himself. With the CSS *Albemarle* out of the way, three days later a navy flotilla recaptured Plymouth. Soon afterwards, the two remaining ironclads were found in the Neuse River and destroyed by a Federal raiding party as well. On his return to the navy yard, Cushing was treated as a true hero. By direction of the president he was promoted to lieutenant commander; he received a letter of thanks from Secretary Welles; and to demonstrate his gratitude, Admiral Porter assigned his young officer to command his flagship.

Without question, the overwhelming loss of their fortifications and iron-clad gunboats had seriously undermined the Confederate river and coastline defenses. Consequently, now free from any serious challenge from the Confederate Navy, the North Carolina Sounds were once again open. By this time also, the entire Confederate coastline within Flag Officer Lee's cordon had been sealed off to blockade-runners, with the exception, that is, of

Wilmington, North Carolina. The only port still open on the east coast, and the port of choice for blockade-runners from Bermuda and Nassau, Wilmington would be the next objective for the North Atlantic Blockading Squadron.

10

South Atlantic Naval Campaigns: October 1861–December 1862

While Flag Officer Stringham and General Butler were effecting their mission against Confederate land forces at Hatteras Inlet, the Navy Department was thoroughly absorbed in formulating battle plans for a second joint army-navy expedition. This new operation was in response to a recommendation made by the four-member Board of Strategy in August, specifically to seize Port Royal, in South Carolina, for the purpose of establishing a second depot for the Atlantic Blockading Squadron, since reorganized into North and South Blockading Squadrons.

For this critical mission a massive fleet of about 75 vessels, 17 of which were naval warships, was gathered in Hampton Roads, Virginia, on October 27, 1861. Four of the vessels, the *Unadilla*, *Ottawa*, *Pembina*, and *Seneca*, were called "ninety-day gun-boats" in reference to the short construction time specified in their contracts. Also included in the fleet were a hodgepodge of over 30 assorted vessels, ranging from canal and ferry boats to second-hand passenger steamers, all purchased and improvised into transports for carrying everything necessary for the fleet to be self-sustaining. Having departed earlier, 25 sloops, converted into coal tenders, would handle the refueling effort. At the time, this armada represented the largest fleet of ships ever commanded by an American naval officer. A 46-year veteran of the U.S. Navy, Flag Officer Samuel F. DuPont, of the wealthy DuPont gunpowder family, and newly appointed commander of the South Atlantic Blockading Squadron, had the honors of leading the fleet from aboard his steam-frigate flagship, *Wabash*. Cooperating with DuPont were 12,000 troops, including 600 marines, under the command of Gen. Thomas W. Sherman.

Their objective was one of the finest harbors in the South, Port Royal Sound.

The Strategy Board selected this site not only because it was centrally located between Savannah and Charleston, but also because it was a deep-water port capable of accommodating the Union's large vessels. Located near the southern border of South Carolina, like Hatteras Inlet, the channel into Port Royal Sound was protected by a pair of Confederate forts, both commanded by Gen. Thomas F. Drayton. The larger and stronger of the two, Fort Walker, was situated on the northern tip of Hilton Head Island. The other, Fort Beauregard, was located on the southern end of Phillips Island at Bay Point, only two miles across the channel.

With the flagship *Wabash* leading the way, it was an impressive sight indeed as the mammoth fleet sailed out of Hampton Roads towards the open sea. Tuesday, October 29 was a clear and crisp fall day, and the armada could be seen stretched out for miles, their inverted "V" formation moving slowing into the horizon.

Two days later, shortly after the fleet reached the treacherous waters off Cape Hatteras, the "old salts" in the fleet sensed the feel of an approaching storm. As predicted, that afternoon heavy gale winds and extremely rough seas swamped the huge fleet and scattered the ships over a wide area off the coast of Cape Hatteras. Around 10 a.m. of November 1 the storm subsided, but the fleet was so widely dispersed that DuPont decided to delay the expedition until the ships could regroup.

As the ships slowly returned to their position in the formation, DuPont learned that three ships were lost, three were missing, and two disabled. Incredibly, only seven men had died.

Although Secretary Welles took every precaution to maintain the secrecy of this expedition, the inevitable leaks to the British press revealed the ultimate destination of the fleet. This breach of security resulted in a telegram on November 1 from the Confederate Secretary of War, Judah P. Benjamin, which warned Governor Pickens and General Drayton of the imminent attack.

Under a full head of steam, on November 3 the fleet continued its journey south, most arriving outside the entrance to Port Royal Sound in the early morning hours of November 4. At this point DuPont's frustration with the weather was compounded even further when he attempted to navigate the narrow lanes into the harbor. The all-important channel markers were suspiciously missing, which forced the fleet into yet another delay, as much of the day was spent taking soundings and laying buoys to mark the deep-water route through the channel.

On loan from the U.S. Coastal Survey, DuPont had the foresight to include a survey vessel in the fleet for such a contingency. Eager to size-up the strength of the enemy fortifications, however, the lighter boats *Pawnee, Ottawa, Pembina, Curlew,* and *Seneca* slid over the bar to the vicinity of the two looming Confederate strongholds for a quick reconnaissance. Meanwhile, the survey ship went to work placing buoys or guides for the other ships to follow. The soundings continued all afternoon and by nightfall the transports and the smaller ships were anchored safely within the channel.

As the channel was being marked out, a somewhat minor diversion kept several of the Union warships occupied. More of an annoyance than a threat, three small Confederate riverboats conducting hit and run tactics would occasionally venture out to harass the closest Union ships with long-range broadsides. The little vessels, the *Savannah* being the flagship, were under the authority of Commodore Josiah Tattnall, who would later command the ironclad CSS *Virginia* in her final days. The Rebel antagonists would always reconsider their brashness, however, whenever the Union's rifled pivot guns swung their way and returned their fire. Pursued, they would quickly retreat back to safety.

By November 5 the entire fleet was across the bar; the warships being anchored about five miles from the forts, with the supporting vessels secured much farther out. Soon after the *Wabash* anchored, the commanders of the "main line" ships were summoned to the flagship for a meeting with Flag Officer DuPont. At this meeting they were briefed on the battle plan and given their position in the attack formation. Later that day the commanders of the "flanking line" also received their briefing. But, to the disappointment of all on board, the *Wabash* became temporarily grounded, and the heavy seas again delayed the eagerly awaited assault.

The main line consisted of steamers, mostly the larger frigates, sloops-of-war, and gunboats. They would go in first, one ship-length apart, accompanied by a flanking squadron.

Following the 40-gun flagship *Wabash* leading the main line was the 15-gun frigate *Susquehanna,* after which came the sloops *Mohican,* with 6-guns, the *Seminole,* also with 6-guns, and the 8-gun *Pawnee.* Bringing up the rear were the steam gunboats *Unadilla, Ottawa,* and *Pembina,* and finally the disabled sailing sloop *Vandalia,* being towed by the *Isaac Smith.* The flanking ships were the steam gunboats *Bienville, Senaca, Curlew, Penguin,* and *Augusta.* The *Pocahontas* had engine problems and arrived later during the battle. As would be a frequent occurrence in the Civil War where kin opposed kin, the commander of the *Pocahontas,* Cmdr. Percival Drayton, was the brother of the Confederate army commander at Port Royal, Gen. Thomas F. Drayton.

Using a maneuver similar to that originated by Flag Officer Stringham at Hatteras Inlet, the Union warships were ordered to navigate in a counter-clockwise formation in the channel between the two forts. They would then fire broadsides at each of the Confederate works as they passed within 600 to 800 yards. At the end of the first turn the flanking squadron would veer off from the main line to prevent the Confederate riverboats from attacking the ships in the rear of the formation.

Finally, at 9:30 a.m. on November 7, 1861, the Battle of Port Royal began when, at a given signal, the ships began to file through the channel towards the forts. The booming explosions from over a hundred guns were reportedly heard as far away as Fernandina, Florida. With each loud roar a belching cloud of thick smoke hung in the air until the entire field of battle literally reeked with the pungent smell of gunpowder. Armed with Columbiads, heavy howitzers, siege guns, and rifled guns — about 40 pieces of ordnance between them — the Confederate defenders valiantly fought back, and although severely outgunned, were not giving up without a fight.

Following the first left turn after passing Fort Beauregard, the flanking line broke away towards Tattnall's gunboats as directed, while the main line continued on through the first circuit. Approaching Fort Walker the second time, however, in a departure from the battle plan, the last eight ships of the main line veered off and remained in place, firing at the fort, while the *Bienville* assumed a position in the main line behind the *Susquehanna* and the *Wabash* on their pass by Fort Walker and into their third approach to Fort Beauregard.

At that point, however, after three hours of suffering through the heavy barrage of shot and shell, the Southern forces were ready to acknowledge the tremendous disparity in firepower. The defenders of Fort Walker, now out of ammunition and fearful for their lives, were spotted fleeing from their fortifications to transports and to the relative security of a mainland refuge. One Union officer would later describe the furious shelling of Fort Walker "... as fast as a horse's feet beat the ground in a gallop."

Later that afternoon a reconnaissance party was dispatched to investigate Fort Beauregard, which was also found abandoned. As for the Confederate gunboats, when confronted by the guns of the flanking squadron they, too, wisely retreated away from the action. Southern casualties in this brief battle were reported to be 11 men killed and 48 wounded, while the Federal side suffered eight men killed and 23 wounded.

At Fort Walker the national flag was raised amid the wild and celebratory cheers of the victorious crewmen who were threaded into the riggings of their ships. The army transports were soon brought in, pickets thrown out, and the forts garrisoned with Union troops. A week later, on November 15, General Sherman renamed the forts. Fort Walker became Fort Welles, and Fort Beauregard was now Fort Seward.

On the shores of Port Royal Sound a thriving naval station and depot was built that not only benefited the South Atlantic Blockading Squadron but, more

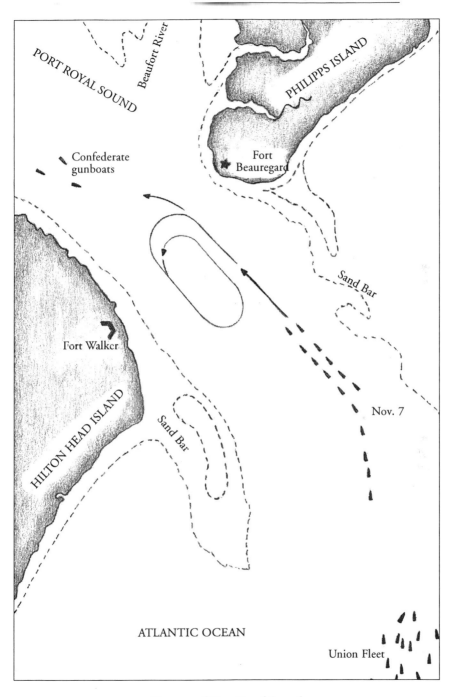

Capture of Port Royal Sound

importantly, secured a strategic foothold on the Confederate coastline between the two major blockade-running ports of Charleston and Savannah. Today, in Port Royal Sound, the U.S. Marine Corps has a training camp at Parris Island.

Like the victory at Hatteras Inlet, Northerners welcomed the news of yet another conquest by the U.S. Navy. Furious and saddened over the most recent bloody fiasco by the army at Ball's Bluff on October 21, many Northerners were gaining a new respect for their maturing navy and were immensely proud of their accomplishments.

When Union troops reconnoitered the vicinity of Port Royal Sound and the nearby coastal sea-islands, they found all the rice and cotton plantations abandoned by their white owners. Deserted also were thousands of slaves who were wandering aimlessly with nowhere to go except to follow behind the Union troops. Taking advantage of their newly found freedom, many of the slaves took to looting the town, the planters' house and barns, and taking special pleasure in destroying the cotton gins. Soon, in a "rehearsal for reconstruction," thousands of slaves on the sea-island plantations were given land and allowed to cultivate crops for themselves to experience their newfound freedom. Soon, Gideonite missionaries and young teachers were hired by the Treasury Department and sent to assist the new freedmen. Called "Gideon's Band," they began to appear on the islands to set up schools and to guide the slaves in the transition from slavery to freedom. As the publicity grew over their efforts, however, so did the number of idealistic Northern politicians and entrepreneurs wanting to take part in the experiment. Gradually, the well-meaning effort to help the former slaves turned into a spectacle of gross exploitation. In the end, much of the abandoned farmland was taken over by the more powerful and influential government officials, as well as Union military officers and cotton businessmen from the North, who in turn employed the freed blacks back on "their" farms for minuscule wages.

Several weeks after occupying Port Royal, DuPont began to consider his next expedition south. Confederate ports along the southern coast of value to blockade-runners still included Savannah, Georgia, as well as Fernandina, and St. Augustine, Florida. Since his attention was now focused on taking down Fort Pulaski, guarding the passageway into Savannah, it was crucial that the Flag Officer know the degree of enemy resistance in his immediate vicinity. Accordingly, over the next two months he dispatched several gunboats on a reconnaissance mission to investigate the strength of the enemy's coastline defenses. Cmdr. John Rodgers took the *Seneca* and the *Paulina* to check out Tybee Island, and Cmdr. Drayton, aboard the *Pawnee*, probed the enemy's waters of St. Helena Sound, while Cmdr. C. R. P. Rodgers examined the area about Ossabaw Sound. They ranged as far north as Beaufort, and as far south as the Ogeechee River, below Savannah.

Meanwhile, concerned over the Union's presence near Port Royal Sound, the Confederate authorities in Richmond in early November selected Gen. Robert E. Lee as the commander in charge of reorganizing the south Atlantic coastal defenses. Taking note of the growing strength of the Union navy and the gross disparity between it and the forces he now inherited, Lee wearily remarked, "There are so many points to attack, and so little means to meet them on water, that there is but little rest." Acting on his veiled displeasure over the Confederate coastal defenses, Lee spent the first weeks of his new assignment withdrawing the many scattered pockets of shoreline troops and yielding much of the coastline to his enemy. He then concentrated the troops at points he considered of prime value and more likely to receive a challenge from the North. Lee particularly focused on strengthening the defenses of Savannah, namely Fort Pulaski, and of the already menacing coastline of Charleston Harbor.

Receiving the reports of his scouts back on his flagship following their fact-finding patrols, DuPont expected a briefing on the location of the enemy, as well as an account on the strength of their fortifications. He learned instead that the Confederates had abandoned all their coastline works south to the shores of Ossabaw Sound. Neighboring towns were also found evacuated, the Confederate troops leaving behind large quantities of rations and thousands of cotton bales, at times left ablaze by the departing soldiers.

Learning also that Commander Rodgers had raised the U.S. flag on Tybee Island, DuPont proudly wired Washington, "I have the honor to inform the Department that the flag of the United States is flying over the territory of the State of Georgia.... The abandonment of Tybee Island ... is due to the terror inspired by the bombardment of Forst Walker and Beauregard, and is a direct fruit of the victory of the 7th."

In the meantime however, DuPont was ordered to downsize his fleet when the navy department recalled many of his remaining ships back on blockade duty. Undaunted, and with this vital information in hand, his some-what smaller fleet headed south along the Georgia coast to the mouth of the Savannah River.

Located off the southern side of the Savannah River entrance and only two miles southeast of Fort Pulaski, Tybee Island was also reconnoitered by General Quincy A. Gillmore, chief engineer of the Expeditionary Corps. Following his recommendations to General Sherman, an occupational force under Col. Rudolph Rosa was led back to the island during the first week of December. Finding no resistance to the presence of his troops, the federal forces, including 2,500 marines, occupied Tybee Island without so much as a shot being fired.

Back in June a scheme was devised by the Strategy Board to block the

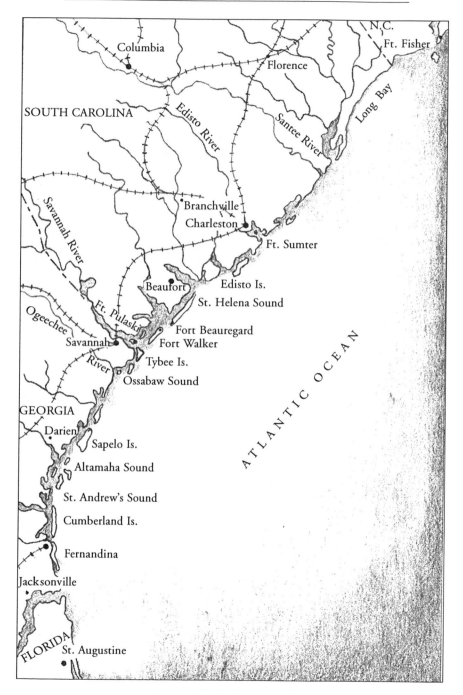

Atlantic Blockading Coastline

entrances to every vital Confederate port used by blockade-runners, Savannah being one of them. Approved by Asst. Secretary Fox, the scheme was to load a number of old ships with tons of stone and rock, and to sink them across the enemy's harbors. Called the "Stone Fleet," the rusted and patched-up hulks, now reinforced to contain the enormous weight, left New Bedford, Massachusetts, on November 20 and dropped anchor outside the Savannah River on December 4. With this large fleet of Union ships gathered outside the harbor, specifically DuPont's vessels, Gillmore's transports, and the "Stone Fleet," the alarmed Confederates presumed a massive attack was about to be launched along the river. Under this erroneous perception, they proceeded to sink three steamers of their own to block the river in order to prevent the supposed Union armada from attacking Savannah. Now that the Confederates had obligingly accomplished the Union's objective, the "Stone Fleet" was no longer needed and, on December 17, 1861, was ordered to Charleston Harbor.

The objective of this expedition, Fort Pulaski, sat just within the entrance to the Savannah River, under the command of Confederate Col. Charles H. Olmstead. Situated on Cockspur Island, the fort was seized by the Southerners on January 3, 1861, two weeks before Georgia officially seceded. The massive fort was a masterpiece of military engineering. Built in 1829, the seemingly impregnable fort was five-sided and built of solid brick walls between seven and eight feet thick and 25 feet high. Although it was designed to contain 140 guns, only about 50 were visible through the casemate, a sign attributed to the high degree of confidence the Confederates had in the fort's strength and its ability to ward off any attack.

Both commanders realized the futility of using their small caliber guns against such a massive structure. In response, General Sherman initiated requests for heavy ordnance, the big weapons he thought necessary to fight against such a fortress as Fort Pulaski.

DuPont and his fleet, meanwhile, continued moving south, leaving behind the army to assemble and man the batteries against Fort Pulaski.

In time, the massive guns began to arrive, such as 10-inch Columbiads, Parrott guns, and 10- and 13-inch siege mortars. It took the army nearly two months of sweat and backbreaking labor to construct the battery emplacements. Working only under cover of darkness, the massive guns (the mortars weighed 17,000 pounds) were mounted on skids and had to be pulled by 250 men from the beach to their intended site. By April of 1862, eleven state-of-art batteries, totaling 34 guns, were built on Tybee Island. The battery sites were painstakingly constructed at varying distances from the fort, ranging from 1,650 to 3,800 yards. Under the command of Gen. Gillmore, each piece was precisely calibrated with Fort Pulaski in their sights.

With a deafening roar, in the early morning hours of April 10, 1862, the barrage was opened on the Confederate fort. Hour after hour the concentrated shower of shell and solid shot took its inevitable toll. The bombardment continued relentlessly throughout the day, never pausing through the night and even into the next day. As each Union battery revealed their position, the garrison meekly fired back, employing only 20 of their guns in a losing cause. Gillmore's batteries, by now, were firing round after round of rifled shells that upon impact bored into the thick walls of the fort, sending up huge clouds of masonry and dirt. Before long the casemate became breached and crumbled to the ground with every blast. With Fort Pulaski in ruins, the garrison of 385 Confederate defenders surrendered on the afternoon of the 11th. A bastion the Chief Engineer of the U.S. Army predicted impossible to capture "in a month's firing with any number of guns of manageable caliber" was taken in just 30 hours.

At long last, the Savannah River was closed to blockade-runners. (The city of Savannah would be occupied by Gen. William T. Sherman in December of 1864 when the Confederate defenders abandoned the city.)

While the batteries were under construction on Tybee Island, DuPont's flagship *Wabash* dropped anchor in St. Andrew's Sound on March 2, 1862. The fleet was located off the Georgia coast just off the northern point of Cumberland Island and about 15 miles north of the small port of Fernandina, Florida. Of particular interest to the navy, and the reason the town was such a choice port to blockade-runners, was the Florida Railroad line, which extended across the state to the Gulf coast of Florida and also connected to the Pensacola & Georgia Railroad line west to Tallahassee. Fernandina had also caught the eye of the Strategy Board, who selected the site "as a depot for coal, [and] as a harbor of refuge, and as a general rendezvous, or headquarters, for that part of the coast." In its recommendation, the Board added, "the naval power that commands the coast of Georgia will command the State of Georgia."

About 25 ships were still left in DuPont's fleet, including the veterans *Mohican, Pawnee, Pocahontas,* and six transports carrying a brigade of marine troops. Here, DuPont split his fleet, sending the lighter gunboats, under Commander Drayton, south through the Cumberland Sound, the stretch of water between the Georgia mainland and Cumberland Island. Drayton fully expected a confrontation with the enemy batteries clearly visible and poised among the dunes. Instead, to his surprise, he found the Confederate defenses on the island were also deserted. Flag Officer DuPont, meanwhile, with the remaining ships of the fleet, moved on to the entrance of Fernandina Harbor. Upon Drayton's return, the entire fleet steamed into the harbor on March 4 and discovered Fort Clinch, the Confederate defensive works protecting this area, also abandoned. In a matter of moments, a Rebel steamer was captured, while the marines secured a railroad bridge. Later that evening the federal banner was hoisted over the fort, and the Confederate fortification occupied by Union troops. To Secretary Welles, DuPont would report, "We captured Port Royal, but Fernandina and Fort Clinch have been given to us."

Flag Officer DuPont and several of his ships moved on, continuing to follow the coastline south. On the night of March 8 the Union ships were outside St. Augustine, staring directly into the lone bastion defending the town, Fort Marion. This time DuPont's men observed a garrison of Southern troops staring in astonishment from the parapet of the fort. The menacing sight of the Union ships was persuasion enough for the Confederate commander to immediately surrender, and once again the Union flag was raised where heretofore waved the Stars and Bars. After leaving a force behind to secure the fort, Flag Officer DuPont began his journey back to Port Royal.

Within a period of eight months, both the North and South Atlantic Blockading Squadrons had accomplished an enormous feat. With the exception of Wilmington and Charleston, by the end of April 1862, while General Grant was in the early phases of his advance through Tennessee and Mississippi, and the Army of the Potomac was just beginning its Peninsular Campaign, every major Confederate port on the Atlantic coast was occupied by federal forces and closed to blockade-runners.

For the remainder of 1862 DuPont's squadron maintained the blockade, supported the occupational forces, and from time to time captured an occasional blockade-runner; but more importantly, the South Atlantic Blockading Squadron was now free to concentrate on Charleston, the "Cradle of the Rebellion."

11

Clash of the Ironclads: April 1861–December 1862

Amid the partially charred buildings in the Gosport Navy Yard, also referred to as the Norfolk Navy Yard, Confederate Lieut. John M. Brooke stood gazing at the remains of the scuttled Union warships. They were the vessels left behind by the federal navy before abandoning the shipyard in the early morning hours of April 21, 1861. Standing before the submerged hull of the steam frigate USS *Merrimack*, Brooke was enthralled over the possibility of raising the waterlogged hulk and of converting her into an ironclad gunboat.

Secretary of the Navy Stephen R. Mallory had summoned Brooke to his office in early June. During this meeting Mallory described his ideas for armored vessels to the Lieutenant, his mind racing wildly over the prospects of such a venture. In these early days of the rebellion, Mallory had no illusions over the chances his young navy would have against the already established U.S. Naval forces. But as they spoke, Mallory's vision looked beyond the numbers of ships, men, and guns to a new technology, and on what he perceived as a tremendous opportunity to gain superiority on the seas. He was also reminded of the ironclad floating battery in Charleston Harbor and of its successes during the Sumter bombardment. Now more than ever, Mallory was intrigued over expanding that technology to his fledgling Navy; and to launch his idea he ordered Brooke to begin work on the design of an ironclad warship incorporating the salvaged hull of the *Merrimack*.

Mallory's excitement over the possibility of commanding the American waterways was adequately demonstrated earlier, on May 11, when he addressed the Confederate Congress. At this meeting he proposed the idea of salvaging the *Merrimack* and refurbishing her into an ironclad, an armored warship that would menace the fleet of the Atlantic Blockading Squadron. Furthermore, Mallory also suggested that a fleet of ironclads could undoubtedly threaten the very survival of the U.S. Navy, not only along the coastal waters but also on the rivers, bayous, and lakes throughout the land. Congress was well aware of the Secretary's enthusiasm regarding ironclads from a letter he wrote to the naval committee a few days earlier. In his letter Mallory evoked a sense of opportunistic urgency, saying, "I regard the possession of an iron-armored ship as a matter of the first necessity. Such a vessel at this time could transverse the entire coast of the United States, prevent all blockades, and encounter, with a fair prospect of success, their entire navy." Continuing on, Mallory wrote, "If we ... follow their [the United States Navy's] ... example and build wooden ships, we shall have to construct several at one time; for one or two ships would fall an easy prey to her comparatively numerous steam frigates. But inequality of numbers may be compensated by invulnerability, and thus not only does economy but naval success, dictate the wisdom and expediency of fighting with iron against wood without regard to first cost." In the end, Congress responded to Mallory's progressive ideas with overwhelming enthusiasm of their own by authorizing several million dollars for the construction or purchase of ironclad gunboats.

A Union naval officer before the war began, Brooke had received some notoriety and was still enjoying a bit of a reputation since the King of Prussia awarded him the Gold Medal of Science in 1860. The award was for his work on depth-sounding devices, specifically his invention of a deep-sea sounding apparatus that could accurately map the topography of the ocean floor.

Mallory had agreed to a recommendation by Brooke to hire naval constructor John L. Porter and Chief Engineer William P. Williamson to assist with the project, and on July 11 the design for the new ironclad was approved and work soon begun. Williamson would repair the engines; Porter was responsible for preparing the *Merrimack*; and Brooke would supervise the construction of the armor and the guns. In all, some 1,500 men worked tirelessly around the clock on this project, although in reality relatively few could be categorized as true craftsmen.

Actually, the concept of an ironclad warship wasn't exactly a new one. The French deserve the credit for coming up with this novel idea in 1858 when they armored the *LaGloire*, a steam-sail frigate, in 4½ inches of iron plate. Even before that, in the Crimean War, the French covered three floating batteries in iron plates in 1855. In fact, it was the success of his floating batteries that prompted Napoleon III to order the construction of ironclad warships. With an iron-armored vessel in their fleet, the French possessed the most powerful navy in the world; and because of this shift in the balance of power, it was considered a definite threat to her neighbors, precipitating a mid–nineteenth century arms race. In 1860 British paranoia over the thought of losing their wooden fleet to the French compelled the English government to ironclad their first ship, a steam frigate called the *Warrior*. The British went one step further than the French by designing the *Warrior* with an iron frame, in addition to plating her in 4½ inches of iron from bow to stern. For this extraordinary engineering effort the English shipbuilders possessed extremely powerful hydraulic presses capable of bending thick iron plates, and equipment that enabled them to shape and punch holes into iron sheets up to six feet wide. The British also used innovative studies to perfect materials and techniques in their designs based on gunnery tests on ironclad mockups at sea.

On May 30, 1861, at the Norfolk Navy Yard, the *Merrimack* was plugged, pumped out, and raised. It was certainly no small task and required Secretary Mallory to part with $6,000 to accomplish this effort. A small price to pay, however, compared to what Mallory would pay for rebuilding the hull, and reconditioning the engines and boilers that were fouled from being submerged in salt water. For that work, Mallory's budget lost nearly a half-million dollars.

Once raised, the 262-foot hull was cut down to her waterline and reconfigured with a so-called "shield," a casemated housing 170 feet long and 20 feet wide, with sloping walls of 35° and two feet thick. Of these two feet, 20 inches were of pine and four inches of solid oak. The shield extended from two feet below the waterline to seven feet above the gun-deck and served as a backing for two layers of iron plates. The plates were made at the Tredegar Iron Works in Richmond by rolling the molten iron from railroad tracks until each eight-inch wide plate was two inches thick. To insure maximum strength, the first layer was bolted on horizontally, the second perpendicular to the first. In addition to the plates, the flat deck was also covered with iron grating and designed with four hatchways and a pilothouse. The pilothouse was located forward of the single funnel, and was itself protected in iron plating. A final touch was a two-foot long cast iron ram. Weighing 1,500 pounds, the wedge-shaped extension was secured to the bow about two feet under water.

Since there were no suitable engines to be found in the South, a decision was made to repair the two salvaged engines from the *Merrimack*. With all the time, effort, and money spent on rebuilding the ship, the salvaged engines proved to be the most unreliable feature of the new ironclad. During one 45-day period as a Union warship, engine breakdowns forced the ship into port for repairs on 32 of those days. Totally appalled with their poor performance, the Union mechanics at Norfolk ultimately condemned the engines.

The all-important firepower consisted of 10 guns. In broadside were six 9-inch Dahlgren smoothbores, of which one on each side was used exclusively for firing hot shot, and two 6-inch Brooke rifles. The pivot guns, fore and aft, were 7-inch Brooke rifles.

During the *Merrimack*'s development, Lieutenant Brooke introduced a new design for the heavy ordnance installed on Southern ships. Called the Brooke rifle, it was a variation of the popular Parrott gun in that the Brooke design used two or sometimes three 3-inch wrought iron reinforcement straps around the breech instead of one. Consequently, from its inception, the Brooke rifled canon was the standard gun for the Confederate Navy. On the other hand, the Union Navy preferred the Dahlgren smoothbores.

Raising the Merrimack and rebuilding her into an ironclad was originally planned to be a highly classified program. As it is even to this day when building a new weapon, particularly one considered a weapon of mass destruction (as the ironclad was thought to be), utmost secrecy was the order of the day. The concept of security, however, wasn't quite realistic in those days, considering the fact that both sides routinely employed networks of spies who could easily infiltrate the enemy's shipbuilding site. Secretary Welles admitted as much when he wrote, "Their efforts to withhold information, though rigid, were not wholly successful, for we contrived to get occasional vague intelligence of the work as it progressed." When the South learned that the Union had ironclads under construction in St. Louis, for instance, the government dispatched mechanics on a clandestine mission to seek work on the ships and to relay back to Richmond such classified information as the ships' specifications, firepower, construction status, and launching schedule. In the case of the *Merrimack* project, the North was well aware of the "secret" work going on at the Norfolk Navy Yard, and as early as October, articles and drawings began to appear in Northern newspapers.

When the Southern government learned of the Union's ironclad program, the Confederates became increasingly apprehensive over the prospect of not completing their ship first. Accordingly, directives were released to accelerate the construction schedule in order to acquire the all important first strike capability. In a way, the intelligence-gathering efforts on both sides seemed to drive their projects. Learning the construction status of the other side always put more pressure on the work teams to double their labors and their energy in order to finish first.

Despite the desire to complete the *Merrimack* as soon as possible, work on the Confederate ironclad progressed very slowly. An ongoing shortage of equipment, material, and labor resources was always a problem in the Confederate navy. Iron stock was constantly in short supply, and delays were a frequent occurrence from the overwhelming demands on the Tredegar Iron Works. Likewise, because adequate supplies of gunpowder were frequently lacking, the Navy Department was compelled to issue new instructions ordering

Southern skippers to use the ram as much as possible. They hoped this would in some small way conserve ammunition. Since an ironclad ate up 3,400 pounds of coal per hour, a shortage of coal was also another huge problem.

After months of struggle, the Southern ironclad was finally completed on February 17, 1862, and re-christened the CSS *Virginia*. (The *Virginia* is still referred to in most instances by her more popular Union name, as I will continue to do.) When the *Merrimack* slid into the water for the first time, her ordnance officer, Lieutenant Catesby ap R. Jones, was there to describe the event: "The iron was put on while the vessel was in dock; and it was supposed that she would float with her ends barely submerged. So great was her buoyancy, however, that it required some 800 tons of pig iron to bring her down to her proper depth.... Now as this iron was put on, the whole structure sunk; and when she was ready for battle, her ends, which extended some fifty feet forward and abaft the shield, were submerged to the depth of several inches and could not be seen."

Her crew of 320, of which about 30 were officers, also included many Confederate infantry soldiers. After interviewing volunteers in army camps at Yorktown, Richmond, and Petersburg, the men selected claimed to have had some experience with boats or with firing large caliber guns, while many of the other seamen picked for this expedition were the crewmen aboard the gunboats that escaped the Goldsborough-Burnside attacks in the sounds of North Carolina.

Mallory was quite proud of his new ironclad, particularly her presumed resistance to Union shells. Of his new ironclad Mallory remarked, "It is believed that thus prepared she will be able to contend successfully against the heaviest of the enemy's ships, and to drive them from Hampton Roads and the ports of Virginia."

The honor of commanding the new ironclad belonged to Capt. Franklin Buchanan from the Border State of Maryland, until recently an officer in the U.S. Navy. In fact, Buchanan was highly influential in selecting the location for the new U.S. Naval Academy in 1845. He was also the institution's prime organizer and served as its first superintendent until 1847. Following a tour in the Mexican War, he held the prestigious post of commandant of the Washington Navy Yard. At the outbreak of hostilities Buchanan was convinced that Maryland would secede from the Union. Acting on this perception, Buchanan resigned his commission to support his home state. However, when it became apparent that Maryland would remain loyal to the Union, Buchanan requested to withdraw his resignation. His plea was rejected, however, and he was dismissed from the U.S. Navy on May 14, 1861; this persuaded him to join the Confederate Navy in September, where he served as Chief of Bureau of Orders and Detail.

In these early days of the war the Confederacy had planned to use their ironclads as offensive weapons. Therefore, Buchanan's first mission aboard the *Merrimack* was twofold. His objectives were to attack and destroy the now obsolete wooden warships tied up at Newport News, ships belonging to Goldborough's blockading fleet in the Hampton Roads, and to threaten Gen. George B. McClellan's invasion of the Virginia peninsula. So high were the expectations for the Southern ironclad, and so confident were the Confederate authorities in her capabilities, that talk was already being bandied about of attacking New York and Washington, and even bombing the White House and the Brooklyn Navy Yard. But as time went by and the Union fleet of ironclads grew and became more dominant, the Confederacy was forced to modify their objectives. From that point on, Southern ironclads were used predominately in a defensive capacity.

With no time left for such incidentals as trial runs and shakedown cruises, at 11 a.m. on March 8, a Saturday, the *Merrimack* steamed out of the Norfolk yard, followed closely by her two escorts, both escapees from the North Carolina Sounds, the *Beaufort* and the *Raleigh*. Chugging along the Elizabeth River at five knots, her maximum speed, the *Merrimack* began her 12 mile voyage to Hampton Roads. As she moved up the Elizabeth River she was saluted by hundreds of Southern spectators who lined the shore to cheer on their newest and deadliest weapon.

Secretary Welles finally broached the subject of ironclads in his report to Congress on July 4, 1861. In his report to the special session Welles said, "Much attention had been given within the last few years to the subject of floating batteries, or iron-clad steamers. Other governments, and particularly France and England, have made it a special object in connection with naval improvement...." In this report Welles also recommended that a board be appointed to "inquire into and report" on this important matter of ironclads. As a result, on August 3 the Congress authorized a three-member Navy Ironclad Board. This board was responsible for reviewing proposed designs of prototype ironclads and for selecting those they favored. Congress also appropriated $1.5 million for the "construction or completion of iron or steel-clad steamers or steam batteries." Unlike the Confederate Congress, however, who appeared to be solidly behind Mallory, the U.S. Senate wasn't exactly enthusiastic about, nor was it totally convinced on the feasibility of, ironclad warships, passing the measure by only two votes.

The Navy Ironclad Board consisted of its chairman, Commodore Joseph Smith, who was the Chief of the Bureau of Yards and Docks; Capt. Hiram Paulding; and Capt. Charles H. Davis, a fleet captain in DuPont's North Atlantic Blockading Squadron. Also unsure about the capabilities of ironclad technology, even this august board wrote: "We do not hesitate to express the opinion, notwithstanding all we have heard or seen written on the subject, that no ship or floating battery, however heavily she may be plated, can cope successfully with a properly constructed fortification of masonry."

From the submissions examined, around 18 or so, only two were selected, and both recommended conventional wooden ships covered in iron plating. One of those chosen by the board was an ironclad called the *Galena*. She was based on a design by Samuel M. Pook and was submitted by her owner, Cornelius S. Bushnell, president of the New Haven, Hartford, & Stonington Railroad. Merrick & Sons, of Philadelphia, was the other winner with their proposal, the *New Ironsides*.

One other ironclad design, however, was not immediately selected by the board, despite the fact that President Lincoln had shown a keen interest in it. The *Monitor*, a name her designer preferred, was the most radical of them all, and, in consequence, forced the board to shy away from accepting it. This design, also submitted to the board by Bushnell, belonged to John Ericsson, a distinguished Swedish-American engineer and inventor. Ericsson was not unknown to the navy, having gained some notoriety in 1841 when Congress authorized funds for his design of a revolutionary screw-propeller steamer. Called the *Princeton*, it was the first in the U.S. Navy.

Informed by Bushnell that the *Monitor* had been rejected, Ericsson, who had a reputation for being an outspoken and egotistical intellectual, decided to confront the board directly and to present the case for his design personally. It turned out to be a wise move, because the stumbling blocks for its initial approval were now explained away at this September 15 meeting, and Ericsson's design was the third and final one to be accepted.

The $275,000 contract for the *Monitor* was issued on October 4. It was, however, written with specific conditions that reflected the government's lingering doubts over this new technology. By signing the contract, Ericsson agreed to construct the *Monitor* in 100 days, and he was somewhat angered over one particular clause that required the builder to guarantee that the ironclad would perform as promised. If not satisfied, the government wouldn't pay a cent.

The design of the *Monitor* was radical indeed. The ship's 172-foot wooden hull was rather conventional, except that its surface was covered with iron plates. Her flat deck, including the one hatchway, was protected with 4½ inches of iron and would ride only several inches above the water, giving the appearance of a raft. The craft was propeller driven and powered by two single-cylinder steam engines capable of supplying five to eight knots. Near the center of the deck sat the most impressive and the most controversial feature of the ship, an innovative rotating gun turret.

A working gun turret was not a new idea, however. An Englishman in the Royal Navy, Capt. Cowper Coles, was also designing ironclad turrets around the same time. The Coles turret was turned by hand and it rotated on roller bearings, while the *Monitor's* turret was moved by steam power and revolved on a central pivot. Ericsson's turret, however, would be the first to be used in battle.

Safeguarded by eight layers of iron plate one inch thick, the 20-foot wide turret contained two 11-inch Dahlgren smoothbores that protruded through ports in its wall. On deck, forward of the smokestack, a tiny pilot-house was built of solid iron blocks, each 12 inches thick and 9 inches high. For pilot visibility, eye slots were formed by placing spacers in the corners of the top two rows of blocks, and the roof was an iron plate one inch thick.

Before long, under the watchful eye of Ericsson and his chief engineer, Alban C. Stimers, construction of the *Monitor* was begun in a shipyard at Greenpoint, New York. On October 25 the keel was laid, and work on the hull continued around the clock. To save production time, Ericsson subcontracted the engine work and the fabrication of the gun turret. Although not quite as serious as experienced in the South, delays were frequent and shortages were many.

As the *Monitor* took shape she was under constant scrutiny, not only from Confederate spies but also by visiting U.S. Naval personnel. Their opinions of the revolutionary new ironclad ran the spectrum from that of Benjamin F. Isherwood, the navy's Chief Engineer, who thought the project was doomed to failure, to that of Capt. David D. Porter. After inspecting the partially constructed ship, Porter said, "Mr. Ericsson has constructed the most remarkable vessel the world has ever seen — one that, if properly handled, can destroy any ship now afloat and whip a dozen wooden ships together." Some of the names given the *Monitor* included "cheese box on a raft," "iron-pot," "Ericsson's folly," "Ericsson's nondescript," and "tin can on a shingle."

On January 30, 1862, the *Monitor* came off the ways, on schedule but not yet completed. After the two guns were installed on February 5, the *Monitor* was turned over to the government on February 20, and commissioned at the Brooklyn Navy Yard five days later.

The commander selected for this important mission was Lt. John L. Worden, a 43-year-old officer who had served as the navy courier during the Fort Pickens episode last April. Fifty-eight handpicked sailors served as the *Monitor's* crew. The volunteers were selected by Worden while visiting the *North Carolina* and the *Sabine* after briefing the two crews on the risks involved in taking part in the expedition.

The long anticipated day finally arrived. On March 6, two days before the *Merrimack* embarked on her mission, the *Monitor* was towed from her berth and steamed off to make history.

The mission for the *Monitor* was to steam up the Elizabeth River to the Norfolk Navy Yard and to destroy the *Merrimack*, which was supposedly still in dry dock. Little did the crew know, however, that at Hampton Roads the *Merrimack* would soon be on the loose, dealing out death and destruction, and that the most historic of all naval battles was waiting for them there.

On their maiden voyage each of the ironclads experienced numerous problems that tested the capabilities of the crews and the resolve of their captains. Both leaked profusely, and both suffered from periodic engine failures. Referring to the *Merrimack*'s troublesome engines, one Confederate officer wrote, "We could not depend on them for six hours at a time." The *Monitor* also had problems with her ventilation system, which in one instance failed and filled the vessel with gas, causing many of the crew to faint. Although the *Merrimack* held the edge in firepower, the Union *Monitor* had several distinct advantages that would soon prove critical. She was faster, more maneuverable, and, most importantly, with only an 11-foot draft she could venture into shallower water where the *Merrimack* could not. In fact, it took the *Merrimack* a half-hour just to make a 180° turn.

On Saturday morning, March 8, some of the first to spot the approaching Confederate ironclad were the soldiers of the 20th Indiana Volunteer Infantry. From their camp guarding Hampton Roads, they sighted the *Merrimack* around 1 p.m., as she rounded Craney Island at the mouth of the Elizabeth River, about six miles away. Caught totally surprised by the sudden appearance of the Southern ironclad, a cry immediately rang out: "The *Merrimack* is coming." Quickly reacting to the alarm, shoreline gun crews hurried to their batteries, and on board the waiting Union ships, instinctive curiosity intermingled with profound fear.

There were several Union warships anchored in the Hampton Roads that sunny and peaceful morning. At Newport News were the 50-gun *Congress* with a crew of 434, and the smaller 30-gun *Cumberland* and her crew of 376 men. Six and a half miles away, near Fort Monroe, the *Minnesota*, of Hatteras Inlet fame, the *Roanoke*, and the *St. Lawrence* bobbed lazily in the early morning current. Like most Saturday mornings in the navy, it was laundry day, and from the riggings aboard the ships at Newport News freshly washed uniforms could be seen hanging out to dry in the cool morning breezes.

Steaming up the Elizabeth River from Norfolk, the *Merrimack* slowly approached the waiting gunners aboard the *Congress*. In a war where brother often fought against brother and father against son, aboard the *Congress* was Lieutenant T. McKeen Buchanan, the brother of the *Merrimack* captain. Around 2 p.m. the silence of a tranquil afternoon was shattered when the *Cumberland* opened fire with her pivot guns as the Confederate ironclad came into range. Passing by the *Congress*, the *Merrimack* unleashed her starboard

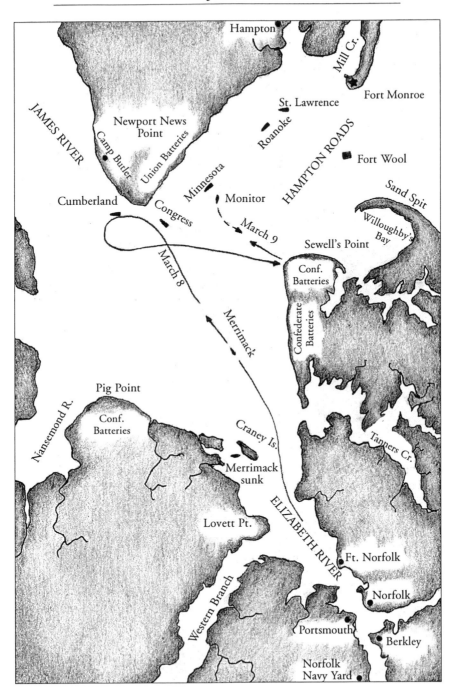

Clash of the Ironclads

broadsides, triggering a thunderous exchange between the two antagonists. Huge clouds of thick smoke rolled over the surface of the water, obscuring both ships as the intense exchange of gunfire echoed through the Roads. This initial skirmish was quickly joined by several gunboats and the shore batteries, which also commenced to bombard the little iron boat. With her crew at their battle stations, the *Cumberland* gunners could only stand by their guns and with enormous trepidation watch as the enemy gunboat slowly approached. One crewmember of the *Cumberland* remembered that scene. "As she came ploughing through the water ... she looked like a huge, half-submerged crocodile. Her sides seemed of solid iron, except where the guns pointed from the narrow ports."

As the *Merrimack* crept closer the *Cumberland* opened up what would have been a deadly volley of canon fire, fatal to any wooden ship. But on this day wooden ships became obsolete. On came the Southern ironclad, totally impervious to the Union cannonading. Direct hits on the *Merrimack*'s casemate merely sent shells pinging off her iron plating, exploding with little damage, or ricocheting harmlessly into the channel "like India rubber balls," as lamented one incredulous Union officer.

Still steering directly for the *Cumberland*, now it was the *Merrimack*'s guns firing round after round into the larger wooden target, killing and wounding scores of the *Cumberland*'s crew. In an instant, the onrushing *Merrimack* rammed head-on into the starboard side of her hapless enemy. The fatal impact shuddered through the doomed wooden ship as the *Merrimack*'s cast iron ram found its mark. The two adversaries were locked together in a death struggle, the *Cumberland* threatening to take the ironclad with her to the bottom of Hampton Roads. Luckily for the *Merrimack*, in her struggle to break free from the sinking ship, the ram was wrenched off and left behind in the gaping hole like the tooth of a killer shark left embedded in its victim. Firing her guns to the very end, the crew of the *Cumberland* went down with their ship; 121 would die. Flag Officer Buchanan later reported, "The crash below water was distinctly heard, and she commenced sinking, gallantly firing her guns as long as they were above water. She went down bravely with her colors flying."

Meanwhile, the 50-gun *Congress* and the shore batteries continued their relentless bombardment on the *Merrimack*, but to no avail. Recognizing the futility of this encounter, and knowing full well that she was next to suffer a similar fate as the *Cumberland*, the *Congress* attempted to escape; but while under tow to more shallow waters she ran aground on a sand bar.

At about this time, three additional Confederate steamers, ships from the James River Squadron, arrived to join forces with the Southern ironclad. The *Patrick Henry*, *Jamestown*, and *Teaser*, evidently seeing the *Congress* in dire straits, proceeded to gang up on the ill-fated vessel, shelling her mercilessly. Witnessing the terrible onslaught, a tugboat captain recalled, "The blood was running from the Congress scuppers on to our deck, like water on a wash-deck morning." After the death of her captain, Lt. Joseph B. Smith, and with the odds overwhelmingly stacked against them, the *Congress* surrendered at 4 p.m.

Observing the white flags, Buchanan ordered the *Beaufort* and the *Raleigh* to assist in the rescue of the wounded men from the *Congress,* to take the officers as prisoners, and to burn the ship. But as the wounded men were being transferred to the Confederate ships, small arms fire from Union coastal defenses raked through the men conducting the rescue effort, killing two Confederates and numerous Union sailors, and wounding many more. Outraged over this apparent breach of military protocol, Buchanan recalled his ships and ordered the *Congress* destroyed immediately by volleys of hot shot. As the *Congress* began to burn, the Union survivors left aboard swam to shore or escaped in small boats. Going topside to direct the operation, Buchanan himself was struck in the thigh by a single shot from a Union sniper, leaving Lt. Catesby ap R. Jones in charge of the mission. Lieutenant Jones was the executive and ordnance officer; and during the construction of the ironclad, he oversaw the armament of the ship.

Earlier, the 40-gun frigate USS *Minnesota*, once the flagship of Commodore Silas H. Stringham, had attempted to enter the fray but was also grounded on a sandbar, helplessly awaiting her fate. Tempting as the *Minnesota* was, with dusk quickly approaching, the *Merrimack* prudently backed away and headed for Sewell's Point. It also became quite imperative that the crew tend to the wounded, particularly Buchanan, and to assess the damage to the iron-clad. She would have to wait until tomorrow to complete her unfinished business. As for the USS *Congress*, at around 1 a.m. the fire reached the magazine, and with a tremendous explosion the ship was totally destroyed.

At Sewell's Point, close inspection revealed major damage to two guns, the smokestack, steam-pipes, and the bow, now leaking very badly from the damage left by the impact with the *Cumberland*. Besides the losses to the *Cumberland* in this historic battle, the *Congress* was reported to have lost at least 136 men, and the *Raleigh* two.

In the morning a telegram was received at the War Department from the commander of Fort Monroe, which disclosed the devastating loss of the two Union warships and their crews, and of the expected destruction of the remaining ships in Hampton Roads. Called to the White House to discuss this latest catastrophe, Lincoln's cabinet experienced a fear they were power-less to prevent. The degree of anxiety was made abundantly clear in comments expressed by Secretary of War Edwin Stanton. "The *Merrimack* will change the whole character of the war; she will destroy every naval vessel; she will lay all the cities on the seaboard under contribution. Likely her first move will be to come up the Potomac and disperse Congress, destroy the Capitol and public buildings ... that the monster was at this moment on her way to Washington.... Not unlikely we shall have a shell or cannon ball from one of her guns in the White House before we leave this room."

Secretary Welles attempted to allay their fears by reassuring them of the *Monitor's* expected arrival at Hampton Roads on that Saturday, and that the Southern ironclad, with a draft of 22 feet, would not be able to get over the shoals in the Potomac River, even if she tried. Despite these assurances, however, Stanton went ahead with his plans to fill some 60 canal boats with stone, and, if necessary, he intended to sink them at the mouth of the Potomac.

The *Monitor* did indeed arrive at Hampton Roads that Saturday, in fact at 9 o'clock that night. She went alongside the *Minnesota*, still firmly mired on the sand bar, and dropped her anchor. The crew, worn out from the exhausting journey from New York, settled down in the ironclad for the night as the *Congress*, burning ferociously a short distance away, lit up the night-time sky.

Around 7 a.m. the following morning, March 9, as if unable to keep their eagerness in check, the *Merrimack* steamed out of Sewell's Point and headed directly for the *Minnesota*. Alongside were her two escorts, the *Yorktown* and the *Patrick Henry*. The Confederate ironclad fired a single round at the *Minnesota* from her forward pivot gun, showing little fear of the iron bodyguard who was now maneuvering ahead of the *Minnesota*. A steady exchange of shots followed as the two iron gunboats slowly circled each other, searching for an opportunity to deliver the fatal blow. By this time, crowds had formed along the opposing shores to witness the historic battle and to cheer on their respective ironclad. The Confederate contingent, protecting the entrance to the Elizabeth River, were at Sewell's Point and Craney Island; and the Union forces lined the shores of the James River at Newport News. Also viewing the contest were the sailors aboard the adjacent ships, their riggings an excellent vantage point to view the spectacle.

As the firing continued, mostly at point blank range, the roar of the blasts swept over the surface of the water, mingling with the metallic echoes of the shells as they bounded off the uncompromising armor. Broadside after broadside was fired, with little noticeable damage to either vessel. But inside both gunboats the scenario was somewhat different. Numerous cases of bloody noses and hearing impairment injuries were reported from the tremendous noise and concussion made by 170-pound shells slamming into the iron walls.

Acknowledging the parity of their defensive armor, both boats moved inside in an attempt to ram the other, directing their movements on damaging the enemy's rudder or propeller. However, the *Merrimack* was difficult to maneuver, and with her bow still damaged from ramming the *Cumberland*, Lieutenant Jones was fearful of opening new leaks. Instead, Jones initiated a new tactic. He ordered his vessel to maneuver alongside the *Monitor* to allow a boarding party quick access to her deck. Once aboard, the turret would be jammed and the *Monitor* captured. Try as they might, however, this tactic proved to be near impossible, and it was quickly abandoned. The Confederates now focused on attacking the small, heavily armored pilothouse where the *Monitor*'s captain was located.

In the pilothouse at that moment, Lieutenant Worden was peering through a viewing slot in the wall when a Confederate shell slammed into the very opening he was looking through. The enormous impact and explosion knocked him sprawling across the pilothouse deck, his face severely burned and his eyes blinded. In spite of his injuries, Worden was able to locate the speaking tube and beckon his 22-year-old executive officer, Lieutenant Samuel D. Greene, to the pilothouse, and to order the pilot to "sheer off."

As Lieutenant Greene was assisting Worden to his quarters, the *Monitor*'s pilot, still following Worden's last order, allowed the ironclad to drift away from the field of battle. During this interval, before Greene could return to the pilothouse to take command, Lieutenant Jones interpreted the *Monitor*'s movements as a withdrawal from the battle, and started for the *Minnesota*. But with the tide now running low, his chances of getting to that area of the channel without grounding were too risky. With the *Merrimack* still leaking profusely, Jones decided to head back to Norfolk for repairs. Following his return to the pilothouse, at about 2 p.m., Lieutenant Greene observed the Confederate vessels moving away towards Norfolk. The *Monitor* then returned to the side of the *Minnesota* and dropped anchor.

After about seven hours, the battle was over. Although neither boat was the first armored vessel to splash off the ways, the meeting of the *Monitor* and the *Merrimack* was the first naval battle between two ironclads. With neither gunboat able to inflict any serious damage to the other, the result was judged a standoff.

The Confederates, however, refused to accept that conclusion, claiming that they won the fight fair and square because the *Monitor* had clearly left the field first. The *Monitor* didn't really leave the battle, the North responded, but was only momentarily delayed while assisting their injured skipper. When Lt. Greene was finally able to regain control of the *Monitor*, the Union side argued, the *Merrimack* was seen retreating back to Norfolk. In their perception of events, the North claimed they had won the battle.

In reality, both sides were unable to continue the fight. The *Monitor* was running out of ammunition, the turret was difficult to control, and her commander was severely injured (Worden lost the permanent use of his left eye). On the Confederate side, with her deep draft the *Merrimack* was in danger of grounding, the wooden backing for the iron plates had fractured in one place, six plates had broken, and the vessel was in danger of capsizing from the leaking bow where the iron ram had broken off the day before.

At Norfolk the *Merrimack*'s bow was repaired and the hull strengthened with additional iron, and a new and heavier ram installed. With a new commander, Capt. Josiah Tattnall, and supported by a flotilla of gunboats from the James River Squadron, the Southern ironclad returned to Hampton Roads on April 11 with a plan to board and capture the Union ironclad. But the *Monitor*'s movements were tightly restricted since the battle of March 9. Until more ironclads were built, President Lincoln did not want to risk the *Monitor* in another confrontation with the *Merrimack*. The *Monitor* stayed put, as did the other Union vessels, even as the flotilla captured three merchant ships and towed them away to Norfolk, unchallenged.

Approximately a month earlier, in mid–March, Gen. George B. McClellan, the commander of the new Army of the Potomac, had transported his 100,000-man army down the Potomac to the Virginia peninsula. Since the devastating loss at Bull Run last July, this was the first major incursion of the eastern army into southern territory. Advancing up the peninsula to Yorktown, McClellan was about to place the town under siege when the Confederate forces evacuated on May 3 and then retreated from Williamsburg two days later to shore up the Richmond defenses. Consequently, with the Union army now in a position to seriously threaten Norfolk, Confederate forces had little choice but to abandon the Norfolk area, including the naval yard. With information from a deserter that the Confederates were about to evacuate, President Lincoln thought the time was right for Union troops to move on Norfolk, and for the navy to remove the threat the *Merrimack* would have on McClelland's drive on Richmond.

On May 8 the *Monitor*, accompanied by the 6-gun ironclad *Galena* and three gunboats, the *Port Royal, Aroostook,* and *Naugatuck,* under Flag Officer Goldsborough, was dispatched to bombard the batteries at Sewell's Point in the hopes of drawing out the *Merrimack* into the open waters where she could be rammed by the heavier steamers. In the meantime, using the navy shelling as a diversion, the army troops would go ashore and advance on Norfolk. Within moments of the Union gunfire, the Confederate ironclad made her appearance and steered directly for her primary antagonist, the *Monitor*. There was a brief exchange of gunfire, but when Goldsborough ordered the ships to withdraw, the *Merrimack* meandered about Hampton Roads for several hours before anchoring below Sewell's Point. Meanwhile, the invading Union troops did indeed find the Norfolk Yard abandoned, the Confederates having shipped everything of value to Richmond before destroying whatever remained.

At that point Tattnall was faced with a serious dilemma. Now that the Norfolk Navy Yard was back in Union hands, as was Sewell's Point, he had nowhere to go. Without a port, he was, in fact, stranded. To compound his problems, Tattnall also knew the *Merrimack* was unable to maneuver in these shallow waters for an escape to Richmond. A decision was made to reach City Point or Harrison's Landing, on the James River, by running the batteries at Newport News. When they finally reached their destination, the plan was to refit the ironclad to assist in the defense of Richmond. First, however, the *Merrimack* had to be lightened. Over the next several hours the crew set to work throwing ballast overboard until two feet of the wooden hull became exposed; but because of additional concerns over low tides and the fear of grounding, the pilots refused to take part in the mission. Now faced with no pilots on board to accept the risks, his vessel now in an unfit condition, and finding no other options available, Tattnall ordered the *Merrimack* run aground on Craney Island on May 11. Set afire, she blew up in a tremendous explosion two hours later.

On May 15, 1862, the *Monitor* ventured out one more time. Now with the *Merrimack* gone, the navy felt free to venture up the James River without troop support and threaten Richmond, only 70 miles away. Working their way around obstructions and up the river, the five Union gunboats steamed by two Confederate batteries with little resistance; but eight miles below Richmond the flotilla reached the last and most strongly defended Confederate fortification on the river, the batteries of Fort Darling at Drewry's Bluff. From their emplacements some 200 feet above the river, the Confederate batteries enjoyed a commanding view of the Union gunboats below. Shortly, the disadvantage of poor field position became clearly obvious to the Union commanders. Unable to elevate her guns sufficiently to lob shells to the top of the bluff, the *Monitor* was forced to retire. Soon the entire Union flotilla was also forced to retreat when the *Galena*, under Cmdr. John Rodgers, ran out of ammunition and caught fire following multiple hits, which severely damaged the thinly armored vessel. The *Galena* lost 13 men that day, and because her armor proved to be too thin, she was subsequently stripped of her plating and served out the remainder of the war as a wooden ship. Several Confederate officers revealed some time later that had Union infantry troops been present in the attack, Fort Darling could have been easily taken, and, there being no further defenses in place, Richmond was there for the taking.

To recognize his gallant service to the Confederacy, in August, Buchanan was promoted to rear admiral and assigned to command the naval forces at Mobile.

The *Monitor* was subsequently assigned to take part in the blockading cordon off the East Coast. Taken under tow by the side-wheel steamer USS *Rhode Island* on December 29, 1862, she was hit by a storm off Cape Hatteras the following night. Overwhelmed by 20-foot waves and 30 mph winds, the *Monitor*, now under the command of Cmdr. J. P. Bankhead, was soon taking on water so rapidly the crew was unable to bail out the flooding ironclad. The sea was pouring into the foundering ship along the 63-foot long joint of the turret. "The water came down under the turret like a waterfall," reported one officer.

Orders were finally given to abandon ship as two launches from the *Rhode Island*, heaving and thrashing in the breaking waves, gingerly approached the sinking craft in the darkness. Despite the obvious risks to their own lives, in two separate attempts the launches were able to rescue the hapless crew of the *Monitor*. Fourteen sailors, however, were lost, many washed out to sea, including several who refused to leave the turret. Finally, at 1 a.m., December 31, the *Monitor* disappeared beneath the waves.

Today the *Monitor* rests in 230 feet of water off Cape Hatteras. Found by a team from Duke University in 1973, the old and rusted relic is resting upside down, encrusted with barnacles, coral, and sponges. Strangely enough, during World War II she was somehow mistaken for an enemy submarine and subsequently damaged by depth charges. Divers rediscovered its location in 1976 and recovered her anchor in 1983.

In June of 1999 the USS *Grasp*, the navy's newest and most technologically advanced salvage ship, anchored over the rusted remains. Over several days, crews descended to the wreck to create a video layout of the site for the National Oceanic and Atmospheric Administration. Hopes are high that the information, pictures, and data will contribute towards the recovery of the turret and the engine before they disintegrate. As of this writing, researchers have recovered the 10-foot propeller and shaft, and several smaller artifacts, including a deck plate, and in July 2001, her steam engine was brought to the surface. It will be on display in Newport News.

12

The Mississippi Flotilla: June 1861–October 1862

Following the secession of South Carolina in 1860, the allegiance of most Kentuckians was torn between providing support to the National flag in the quest to reunite the Union, or to the Confederate cause of States' Rights and southern independence. Increasing signs of political uncertainty were apparent as opposing factions within the state either supported or repudiated secession. In fact, the state was so evenly divided on this issue that the legislature chose to remain neutral and to stay out of the war entirely. Being the birthplace of both Davis and Lincoln, the two presidents were mindful of the backlash they could cause from over-playing their hand for the loyalty of their home state. Both wanted very badly to bring Kentucky into their camp, and have Kentuckians fight for their respective cause, but they were also concerned about interfering in the state's neutrality, which in the long run could cause a possible shift in political sentiment to the other side.

Their concerns were overridden, however, when Gen. Leonidas Polk, acting on his own initiative, invaded Kentucky on September 3, 1861. The Confederate general seized the river town of Columbus, only 20 miles south of Union-held Cairo, Illinois. Strategically located near the junction of the Ohio and Mississippi Rivers, Polk's brash takeover, as predicted, drove Kentucky to the Union side. Polk's move also prompted a Union counteraction. At Cairo, a newly commissioned general, Ulysses S. Grant, was ordered to take two regiments of his 21st Illinois Infantry and to occupy the city of Paducah, 40 miles to the northeast and situated at the mouths of the Tennessee and Cumberland rivers, the super-highways that meandered through Kentucky and Tennessee. Three days later, on September 6, Grant and his troops disembarked at Paducah. With this move, Union forces now commanded the river passage through both States.

In the western theater the primary objective for the Union navy was to gain control of the Mississippi River from the Ohio to the Gulf, and to sever the Confederate supply links from Arkansas, Texas, and Louisiana. To accomplish this goal the strategy of the government depended significantly on conducting joint army/navy operations. Consistent with Gen. Winfield Scott's "Anaconda Plan," these joint actions would be carried out almost simultaneously, one pushing downriver from Cairo and the other driving up the Mississippi from the Gulf of Mexico. The goal was to clear the mighty river of Confederate strongholds and, at the same time, cut the Confederacy in two.

The Union naval presence on the river began in mid–1861 when Secretary Welles, at the request of the War Department, sent Cmdr. John Rodgers to Cincinnati. Rodgers was asked to assist the army in developing a blockade of the Ohio and Mississippi rivers. In June he purchased three wooden gunboats, and by the end of the summer the three steamers were reconditioned, staffed, and provisioned. They were the *Tyler*, sporting six 8-inch Dalhgrens and two 32-pdrs.; the *Lexington*, with four 8-inch Dalhgrens and two 32-pdrs.; and the *Conestoga*, armed with four 32-pdrs. Although staffed with navy officers and crewmen, they were under the jurisdiction of the army.

Named to lead the flotilla was the superintendent of the Brooklyn Navy Yard, Capt. Andrew H. Foote, a Connecticut native who arrived in Cairo on September 12 to take over his new command. With the flotilla under army control, however, Captain Foote soon became embroiled in problems of grade and ego, particularly the many troubling incidents with army generals who insisted on pulling rank on him. To settle his status once and for all, in December Foote requested that Secretary Welles review his appeal and to grant him the title of flag officer, which was the equivalent of major general in the army. Under these unique circumstances Welles agreed to the upgrade, and with his command status finally settled, Flag Officer Foote was ready to take on his new role, albeit still under the control of the army.

Foote immediately began to organize and staff his new command, and the following month the last of seven new vessels arrived, all ironclads, to add to his growing fleet. These seven were the *St. Louis,* later changed to the *Baron de Kalb,* the *Carondelet, Louisville, Pittsburgh, Cairo, Cincinnati,* and *Mound City.* A larger ironclad, the *Essex,* commanded by Capt. William D. Porter, would also join the Union fleet later. Captain Porter, popularly known as "Dirty Bill" because of his less than honorable manner, was the brother of David D. Porter and half-brother to David G. Farragut, both of whom were also serving in the Union navy.

The concept for the seven ironclads came from James B. Eads, a retired naval engineer and millionaire who made his fortune clearing hulks from the Mississippi. His ideas were conveyed to Samuel M. Pook, who came up with the design for the seven boats, thereafter called "Pook Turtles." In August, following the $1.5 million dollar appropriation by Congress to construct ironclads, Eads was awarded the contract to construct the vessels at a cost of nearly $100,000 apiece. The first four ironclads were built near St. Louis, at Carondelet, the latter three at Mound City, near Cairo. Each of the seven ironclads was 175 feet long, carried 13 guns, and employed a steam engine to drive a centrally mounted paddle wheel for speeds of approximately nine knots. The ordnance for the ironclads consisted of four broadside guns on each side, three in the bow, and two aft, all mounted in a slanted casemate protected by iron 2½ inches thick. Their Achilles' heel, however, was that the Eads ironclads were armored only on the bow end of the casemate and only on the sides adjacent to the engines. In spite of this flaw, the seven ironclads would prove to be the premier naval force on the Mississippi River. The *Essex*, a larger and heavier ironclad, was recently converted from the ferryboat *New Era*. Carrying six large caliber guns, she was clad in iron plating 3½ inches thick.

The *St. Louis*, launched on October 12, 1861, was the first of the seven boats delivered, and as such was also the first ironclad gunboat in the U.S. arsenal. Now fully equipped with nearly a dozen gunboats, the Mississippi Flotilla was ready for action.

The first order of business was to join forces with General Grant for a joint, coordinated attack on two Confederate forts. The smaller of the two, Fort Henry, was located in the northwest corner of Tennessee, on the eastern bank of the Tennessee River and a short distance from the Kentucky border. Twelve miles to the east, on the Cumberland River, stood the larger and more heavily fortified Fort Donelson. The two forts had been in the center of the Confederate line of defense, which ran from Polk's encampment at Columbus, Kentucky, to the vicinity of Mill Springs in eastern Kentucky. In January, however, Union troops under Gen. George H. Thomas had broken the Confederates' hold on their eastern line in a battle that saw the Rebel troops retreating south into eastern Tennessee. Capturing the two forts now was calculated to fracture and collapse the western segment of the rebel line as well, and at the same time compromise Polk's position at Columbus. In turn, it would open the way for the navy to begin their push south on the Mississippi, and for Grant's troops to advance down the Tennessee River to the Mississippi border.

The vessels Foote commanded for this mission were three "Pook Turtles," the flagship *Cincinnati*, the *Carondelet*, and the *St. Louis*, as well as the three wooden gunboats *Tyler*, *Lexington*, and *Conestoga*, and the larger gunboat *Essex*.

The plan called for a fleet of transports to ferry Grant's 15,000 troops to within eight miles of Fort Henry on February 5, 1862, while Foote, who had arrived three miles below the fort the day before, would wait for him there. Once landed, Grant and his men would then trek through the woods and attack the fort from the rear while Foote lobbed in shells from the river. Fort Henry, armed with 17 guns, was considered indefensible and a disaster of military engineering. Constructed on a bend close to the waters edge, the fort was partially flooded by the rising river. To the dismay of the forts commander, Gen. Lloyd Tilghman, his guns were now only six feet above the water, which had steadily crept to within a few feet of the magazine. The Confederate general knew he was outmanned and outgunned, so he had previously sent the greater part of his command, about 2,500, on to Fort Donelson. He and the remaining garrison of artillerists stayed behind to delay the Union forces so his men could get a safe head start to the other fort.

On February 6, with Grant's troops delayed by the thick woods and muddy terrain, Foote could wait no longer and decided to proceed with the attack. Just before noon the order was given and the seven gunboats steamed down the Tennessee, the ironclads leading the way, four abreast. Winding their way through the lush growth that overhung the swollen river, the object of their quest was soon discerned through the dense tangle of woods. With the report of a signal-shot from the *Cincinnati*, the peaceful and tranquil scene was transformed into an explosion of missiles as the Columbiads of Fort Henry answered the blasts from the flotilla.

Steaming closer to the fort, the ironclads fired in rapid bursts, sending up clouds of dirt as each round of shell and solid shot found its mark. Advancing through a barrage of returning gunfire, however, the thinly armored ironclads were far from impervious to the tremendous impact delivered by the Confederate guns. Halfway through the battle, a Confederate shell ripped through the *Essex* and slammed into her boiler, scalding to death six crewmen and injuring 18 others. The second mate aboard the *Essex*, James Laning, was there and recorded that tragic scene: "The pilots, who were both in the pilot-house, were scalded to death. Marshall Ford, who was steering when the explosion took place, was found at his post at the wheel, standing erect, his left hand holding the spoke, and his right hand grasping the signal bell-rope. Pilot James McBride had fallen through the open hatchway to the deck below; he was still living, but died soon after. The captain's aid, Mr. S. B. Brittan, Jr., had fallen by the shot as it passed through the gun-deck before entering the boiler. A seaman named James Coffey, who was shot-man to the No. 2 gun, was on his knees in the act of taking a shell from the box to be passed to the loader. The escaping steam and hot water had struck him square in the face, and he met death in that position. Third Master Theo. P. Terry was severely scalded, and died in a few days.... A seaman named Jasper P. Breas, who was badly scalded ... died that night."

Suffering from six direct hits, the *Carondelet's* iron plating could not withstand the tremendous power of the Confederate shells, as one Union officer remembered, "... their heavy shot broke and scattered our iron-plating as if it had been putty, and often passed completely through the casemates." In the struggle, the *Cincinnati* was struck by 32 shells, the *St. Louis*, seven. In fact, before the battle was over, the Confederate guns had inflicted considerable damage to every one of the Union gunboats.

The exchange of gunfire continued for nearly two hours. Finally, to avoid any further loss of life, the Confederate commander gave the order to lower the flag. Gen. Tilghman surrendered the fort (now flooded waist-deep), himself, and the 75 men under his charge. Despite the extensive damage to the Union flotilla, the number of men killed was surprisingly small. The *Cincinnati* had lost only one man, while 10 were listed as killed aboard the *Essex*. The Confederates reportedly placed their loss at five.

About an hour later, around 3 p.m., General Grant and his Army of the Tennessee arrived. Following the general's inspection of Fort Henry, orders were issued for his troops to continue on to Fort Donelson before the Confederate commander in the western theater, Gen. Albert S. Johnston, presently at Bowling Green, sent in reinforcements. Meanwhile, Foote and his gunboats steamed back up the Tennessee and to Cairo for repairs.

The second phase of the campaign against the Confederate forts began on February 13, when around midnight Flag Officer Foote arrived in the vicinity of Fort Donelson with his new flagship, the *St. Louis*, and the gunboats *Louisville, Pittsburgh, Tyler,* and *Conestoga*. The *Carondelet* had arrived the day before, on the 12th, and had unwittingly provided diversionary fire for Grant's army while they moved into their positions in the woods across from the fort. A light snow had fallen, and with the temperature near freezing, the men in Grant's army had to bed down without campfires. Covering themselves with wet leaves for warmth, the Union soldiers tried in vain to sleep through that long and frigid night.

On the morning of the 14th the gunboats went through a form of defensive maintenance. Orders were issued for the decks to be covered with chains, bags of coal, heavy timbers, and anything else able to protect them from the incoming Confederate shells. Foote was well aware that this fight would be much more difficult and certainly more hazardous than the battle at Fort Henry. From that fight he knew the kind of damage the Confederate guns could inflict on his thinly clad gunboats, and he wasn't taking any chances.

Located near Dover, Tennessee, a tiny village populated mainly with a courthouse and tavern, Fort Donelson commanded more than two miles of the Cumberland River, and consisted mostly of four hundred log cabins and other assorted wooden structures. The fort was built on a bluff some 100 feet high, and covered over 80 acres. Surrounded by three miles of rifle pits and abatis, the fort was further protected by two separate levels of batteries dug into the side of the bluff overlooking the river. The first level was about 25 feet from the water, with the other midway to the crest; together they contained a total of one 10-inch Columbiad and twelve 32-pdrs, one of which was rifled.

When all was ready, at 3 p.m. the gunboats began their approach to the fort, located about two miles away. In the same formation used at Fort Henry, the ironclad gunboats proceeded towards the fort four abreast, the wooden boats taking up the rear. Steaming against the fierce current of the river, funnels belching plumes of thick, black smoke, the tiny fleet's mission was to soften up the Confederate works before Grant launched his infantry assault. The guns of the *St. Louis* were the first to challenge the Confederate artillerists, firing repeatedly a mile from their target.

The Confederate gunners, meanwhile, watching intently from their lofty stations, had their guns trained and ready to fire on the approaching Union fleet. From his vantage point in Fort Donelson, Confederate army officer Capt. Jesse Taylor wrote of his reaction to the sight of the Union gunboats. "Seeing the formation of battle I assigned to each gun a particular vessel to which it was to pay its especial compliments, and directed that the guns be kept constantly trained on the approaching boats." Under orders from Taylor, the Union crews found themselves engulfed in terror as Confederate shells and solid shot ripped through Foote's vessels. Union officer Henry Walke was commanding the *Carondelet* and described the effect of the incoming shells: "We heard the deafening crack of the bursting shells, the crash of the solid shot, and the whizzing of fragments of shell and wood as they sped through the vessel. Soon a 128-pounder struck our anchor, smashed it into flying bolts, and bounded over the vessel, taking away a part of our smoke-stack; then another cut away the iron boat-davits as if they were pipe-stems, whereupon the boat dropped into the water. Another ripped up the iron plating and glanced over; another went though the plating and lodged in the heavy casemate; another struck the pilot-house, knocked the plating to pieces, and sent fragments of iron and splinters into the pilots, one of whom fell mortally wounded, and was taken below; another shot took away the remaining boat-davits and the boat with them; and still they came, harder and faster, taking flag-staffs and smoke-stacks, and tearing off the side armor as lightning tears the bark from a tree."

Continuing on with his description of the damage to the *Carondelet*, Walke relates, "Three shots struck the starboard casemating; four struck the port casemating forward of the rifle-gun; one struck on the starboard side, between the water-line and plank-sheer, cutting through the planking; six shots struck the pilot-house, shattering one section into pieces and cutting through the iron casing. The smoke-stacks were riddled.... All four of our boats were shot away and dragging in the water."

Surprisingly, although the *Carondelet* was struck 54 times (the most severe of all the Unions gunboats), she was able to continue fighting and was the last to leave the field. The *St. Louis* and the *Louisville* did not fare as well, however. Direct hits on their steering mechanisms disabled both gunboats, the river's current spinning them helplessly back downriver. Besides disabling the *St. Louis*, the exploding shell sent shrapnel into the ankle of Flag Officer Foote, a wound that would cost him dearly in the months ahead. Moments later, the *Pittsburgh* also had to drop out of the battle, a victim of the Confederates' adept technique of ricocheting their shells off the surface of the water and slamming them into the waterline of the Union vessels.

At the end of a very difficult day the Union gunboats limped back downriver, beaten and battered.

On February 15 the Union seamen held services and buried their 11 dead comrades while General Grant fought off an all-out assault by the Confederate troops to cut an escape path through the Union lines. The Confederates failed in their attempt to escape and were driven back into Fort Donelson after a bloody struggle.

Following a conference among the commanders in the fort that night, the Confederates saw the hopelessness of their situation and elected to capitulate the next day. Before morning, however, several thousand Confederates escaped to the safety of Nashville, either on horseback, as the cavalry did, or on two transports brought up to a remote corner of the fort. Among them were two of the three commanders in the fort, Gen. Gideon J. Pillow, and Gen. John B. Floyd, who was Buchanan's secretary of war and was now under federal indictment. Fearing for their lives if captured, the two generals chose to evacuate with the rest; Gen. Simon B. Buckner, the junior officer, who regarded it as his duty to remain, assumed command. On February 16 Gen. Buckner, on behalf of the 15,000 troops remaining in the fort, accepted Grant's terms of unconditional surrender.

Following the fall of Forts Henry and Donelson, the entire Confederate line across western Kentucky, as predicted, collapsed. General Polk's position at Columbus, now extremely tenuous, compelled him to evacuate his fortifications. Abandoning Columbus on February 20, over next several days Polk's forces were split up, the majority going on to Jackson, Tennessee, the remainder, commanded by Gen. John P. McCown, traveling 45 miles south to Island No. 10, so called because it was the tenth island south of the

Mississippi and Ohio River junction. General Johnston, having moved to Nashville, was also forced to evacuate, ordering all Confederate forces to Corinth, Mississippi.

With Columbus abandoned, the Confederates immediately went to work strengthening their defenses of the river. Through the first two weeks of March, General McCown fortified their hold on the Island with five battery emplacements, 7,000 army troops, and several floating batteries, nearly sixty guns in all. The Island's defenses were also supported by five additional batteries set up along the Tennessee coastline. In fact, these formidable defenses earned Island No. 10 the title of "Gibraltar of the Mississippi." Furthermore, located 12 miles south on the banks of the Mississippi at New Madrid, Missouri, were two additional forts, Fort Thompson and the newly constructed Fort Bankhead. To prepare for an anticipated enemy land movement, General McCown ordered a line of abatis thrown up, and had the two forts reinforced with about seven regiments and several batteries. Commodore George N. Hollins, the commander of a Confederate flotilla tasked with patrolling the Mississippi, was also nearby to help stave off any Union attack.

At Cairo, Flag Officer Foote and his flotilla of "Pook Turtles," transports, and 11 mortar-boats departed for Island No. 10 to challenge the Confederate stronghold. Arriving on March 15, the Union fleet included for the first time the USS *Benton*. Converted from the snag-boat *Submarine*, she was the most powerful ironclad in the fleet, and Foote's new flagship. Constructed with two hulls, the *Benton* had a beam of 75 feet, was 200 feet in length, and was propelled by a huge, steam-driven paddlewheel between the twin hulls. Like the Eads gunboats, she had a slanted casemate, but in this case her iron armor was 3½ inches thick and her ordnance consisted of 16 guns.

The Union mortar-boats were anchored on the Missouri side of the Mississippi, and on signal a continuous bombardment of Island No. 10 commenced. The shelling from both the 13-inch mortars and the gunboats would go on around the clock. After nearly two and a half weeks of constant bombing with little effect, Foote realized that the navy alone would be unable to capture the Island. He needed support from the army troops.

Meanwhile, in early March, Union troops under Gen. John Pope had arrived at Point Pleasant, and also on the outskirts of New Madrid, Missouri, about 12 miles to the south of Island No. 10. On the 12th of March, Pope's forces opened their batteries on the two Confederate forts flanking the city, and continued their bombardment all the next day. Unable to withstand the devastating shelling from Pope's guns, the Confederate forces evacuated both forts during the night, most escaping up the river to Island No. 10, others to the works on the opposite bank and to Fort Pillow, some 80 miles to the South. At Point Pleasant, General Pope intended to assist the navy by crossing the

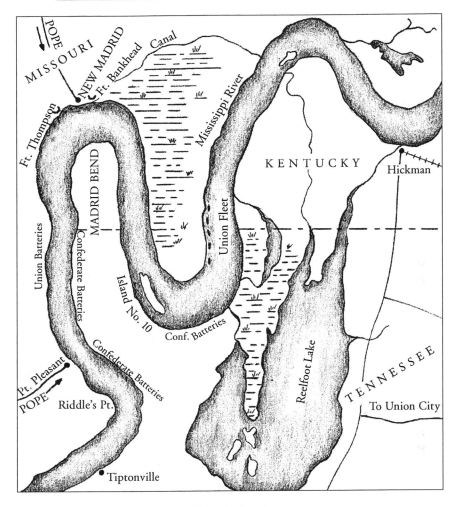

Island No. 10

river and advancing to the opposite side of the peninsula, a distance of four miles. From there his army would attack Island No. 10 from below. First, however, the Confederate batteries across from Point Pleasant had to be destroyed, and his troops had to be protected when they crossed the river. For this he needed gunboats.

At this point Pope made several request for the navy to send gunboats downriver for this purpose, writing to Foote that if the navy were to "... run past the batteries of Island No. 10 with two or three gunboats and reach here, I can cross my whole force and capture every man of the enemy at Island No. 10 and on the mainland." Foote adamantly refused to consider the request, fearing a run by the powerful batteries of the Island too dangerous. He stated it "would result in the sacrifice of the boat, her officers and men, which sacrifice I would not be justified in making." Finally, after several meetings with his commanders, and after the captain of the *Carondelet* volunteered to attempt the run, Foote relented, but with certain conditions. The Union gunboat was reinforced with heavy timbers; chains were draped over the pilot house; and, for extra security, a barge, loaded with coal and bales of hay, was lashed to the port side of the *Carondelet,* the side where there was no plating to protect the magazine. Even the piping for the exhaust steam was redirected to the wheelhouse to dampen the noise it made when it blew out the smokestacks, and hoses were connected to the boilers to scald the enemy if they might attempt to board.

On the stormy night of April 4, 1862, the Union gunboat headed downriver towards the batteries of Island No. 10. Cutting through the heavy rain and choppy waters, the only visibility provided for the passage was the occasional bolt of lightning that flashed its eerie white light, momentarily exposing the Union gunboat to the Confederates manning their batteries. Spotting the intruding vessel, the Confederate gunners were also hampered by the bad visibility, and although several shots were directed towards the Union gunboat, their efforts were futile. The *Carondelet*'s run past the batteries was successful. So much so, in fact, that three nights later the *Pittsburgh* also made the passage and rendezvoused with her sister ship at Point Pleasant. The Confederate batteries were cleared from the shoreline, and Pope's forces, having landed under cover of the two ironclads, prepared to press their advance across Madrid Bend. Recognizing that they were now completely cut off, unable to get reinforcements, and surrounded on both sides by Union troops and naval artillery, the garrison at Island No. 10 surrendered to Flag Officer Foote on April 7.

During all this time Commodore Hollins was below New Madrid with his six wooden gunboats, anxious to do his part. Pope's batteries, however, had disabled several of his boats, and for the most part kept Hollins from entering much of the action. The Commodore and his boats were now en route to New Orleans to help in the defense of that city against the fleet of Flag Officer David G. Farragut. The Union fleet was at present driving up the Mississippi River from the Gulf of Mexico and was threatening to run past the two Confederate forts that guarded the approach to New Orleans.

The upper Mississippi, however, was now under Union control. Not resting on their laurels, Foote's gunboats continued their sweep down the Mississippi River. On April 14 the Mississippi flotilla anchored in the vicinity of Fort Pillow, about 50 miles above Memphis, Tennessee, while General Pope landed his troops preparatory to an attack on the Confederate fort.

Quite suddenly, however, Pope and his army, the Army of the Mississippi, were called to Pittsburg Landing, Tennessee, to join forces with Grant's Army of the Tennessee and Buell's Army of the Ohio. Now without the support of the infantry, over the next several weeks, until May 10, the flotilla remained in place. During this lull the only action upon Fort Pillow was from a single mortar schooner. Tied up at Plum Run Bend each morning under the protection of a gunboat, the schooner resumed her tireless and harassing task of lofting exploding iron into the enemy's works.

Since his injury at Fort Donelson, the strain of his long confinement aboard ship and inadequate treatment had taken its toll on Foote. Finally, unable to effectively command because of failing health, and still suffering terribly from his wound, Flag Officer Foote requested that he be relieved from his duties. Selected as his replacement was Capt. Charles H. Davis, a member of the naval Board of Strategy, and who also served as chief of staff to Flag Officer DuPont at Port Royal. Foote's departure from the Mississippi flotilla on May 9 was emotional in its tributes, as related by an excerpt from a *New York Tribune* article, which read: "When the day was appointed for the Commodore's departure there was quite a stir in the Fleet, and, as he was greatly beloved, his fellow-officers and the sailors generally deeply regretted the loss of their gallant commander. When the hour came for his going up the river, the deck of the Benton was crowded; and as the Flag-officer appeared, supported by Captain Phelps, he was greeted by tremendous huzzas. Old tars swung their hats, and not a few of their eyes moistened when they looked, as they supposed, upon the brave old Commodore for the last time, as indeed they did." In July a grateful government promoted Foote to its newest and highest rank of rear admiral. The following June, Foote was selected to replace Flag Officer DuPont as commander of the South Atlantic Blockading Squadron; however, before he could report to his new command he died in New York from Bright's disease.

Within hours of settling into his new quarters, Flag Officer Davis would confront his first engagement with the enemy. These were the boats of the makeshift Confederates River Defense Fleet, who were preparing to attack the following day.

Established in January by Secretary of War Judah P. Benjamin, the fleet was a naval unit administered by the Confederate army. The vessels of the River Defense Fleet were converted tugboats that were seized and refitted in New Orleans. Transformed into "rams," most of them carried only one or two guns; but their distinguishing feature was a number of thick iron bands bolted across their bows. In addition, the inner bulkheads were filled with compressed cotton, and cotton bales were arranged on the deck of each vessel as a form of armor. Called "cottonclads," they were under the command of Capt.

James E. Montgomery, a veteran officer from the merchant fleet. Of the 14 vessels that made up the fleet, six had stayed in New Orleans to assist in the defense of that city, while the remaining eight traveled up to Memphis to challenge the Union movements down the Mississippi. They were the *Colonel Lovell, General Beauregard, General Bragg, General Sterling Price, General Sumter, General M. Jeff Thompson, General Earl Van Dorn,* and the *Little Rebel.*

On a mission to inflict damage to the Union flotilla, in the early morning of May 10 the eight "cottonclad rams" steamed up the Mississippi. At Plum Run Bend they encountered the Union mortar schooner and her sentry gunboat, the *Cincinnati.* Shots were exchanged as the eight Confederate rams charged directly for the lone Union gunboat. Overwhelmed by the gang of enemy attackers, the *Cincinnati* was soon rammed by the *General Bragg,* spinning her about in the churning waters, and then within moments was mercilessly struck in the fantail by the *General Sumter,* opening her hull, and destroying her rudders and steering mechanism. Severely damaged, the *Cincinnati,* now on the verge of sinking, was rammed a third time by the *Colonel Lovell.* While the Union ironclad floundered in a sinking condition, crewmen spotted on deck, including her commander, were shot dead by Confederate sharpshooters. As the attack on the *Cincinnati* unfolded, the *Carondelet* and the *Mound City* were quickly dispatched to aid the stricken gunboat, as was the *Benton* and the *Pittsburgh.* Fighting frantically to evade the swarming rams, the *Mound City* fired wildly into the circling Confederate boats, at times at point blank range into the tumbling and burning cotton bales, before she too was rammed and sunk by the *Van Dorn.* After one hour, however, all was quiet, and by the time the smoke had cleared, the Confederate cottonclads were gone.

This was the first engagement of the war between the fleets of the two adversaries, and the surprise attack taught the Union a lesson about the inherent risks of not posting picket boats.

Within a week the *Cincinnati* and the *Mound City* were re-floated and sent North for repairs; and to protect the remaining gunboats against similar damage from future encounters with the ram fleet, all the gunboats were reinforced.

Inside Fort Pillow, information had reached the Confederates quartered there that Corinth, Mississippi, was given up to Union forces. With the garrison now left in an indefensible position, several buildings were burned and the magazines blown up before the Confederate troops evacuated the fort on the night of June 4, while the River Defense Fleet, moored nearby, fell back downriver to Memphis.

From the deck of his flagship, Flag Officer Davis saw the thick, black smoke rising above the treetops and heard the explosions erupting from Fort Pillow. Gazing into the distance, he sensed that the commotion was nothing more than the parting sentiments of the evacuating Confederate troops. The next day, as Union forces occupied the fort, Davis continued to push his flotilla farther south, this time to Memphis, for a confrontation with the River Defense Fleet. The flagship *Benton* led the way, followed by the *Louisville*, *Carondelet*, *Cairo*, *St. Louis*, and three mortar boats. About three miles up the coast from the Confederate fleet the Union gunboats dropped anchor.

This time, however, the Union flotilla had several new members, the vessels of the so-called "ram fleet" that had arrived on May 25. Under the command of Col. Charles Ellet Jr., a former Army engineer, the large rams gave Davis the extra muscle he needed to deal with the River Defense Fleet.

In February 1862 Ellet had proposed to Secretary Welles his ideas for converting large steamers into massive rams powerful enough to sink even the ironclads then under the flag of the Confederate Navy. The bows of the vessels would be heavily reinforced, and massive beams would run the entire length of the ship to absorb the impact. The wooden rams, Ellet explained, had one role — incapacitate the enemy by smashing into them. To further focus their singular purpose, the rams would be unarmed, except for a detail of some 50 sharpshooters that would ride as shotgun.

At first, Secretary Welles was not persuaded; but after the *Merrimack* rammed and sank the *Cumberland*, in March he reconsidered the idea and gave Ellet the construction contract, the rank of colonel, and the command of the nine rams. They were called the *Switzerland, Dick Fulton, Lancaster, Lioness, Mingo, Monarch, Queen of the West, Samson*, and *T. D. Horner*. To the annoyance of Davis, however, Ellet's command would also fall under the jurisdiction of the army, completely independent from his control. But following a bitter interservice power struggle, Lincoln intervened and established a compromise in which the navy would control the day-to-day operations, but the overall authority for the fleet would remain under the army, a compromise that pleased nobody.

Arriving at Memphis in the early morning hours of June 6, 1862, the movements of the Union fleet had been picked up earlier by a Confederate picket ship. Forewarned, Montgomery ordered his eight cottonclads into a double line of defense. Reminiscent of a cavalry assault — but on water — the Union vessels charged headlong into the enemy's den, firing their forward guns indiscriminately at the opposing Confederate rams. Montgomery's boats responded with their own barrage, firing repeatedly at the onrushing gunboats, also with no effect. Suddenly, speeding from the rear of the pack, one of Ellet's rams, the *Queen of the West*, raced to the front and slammed full on into the *Colonel Lovell*. As the Confederate boat began to sink, the *Monarch* was upon the Confederate *Beauregard,* who was also rammed. In the swirl of the battling vessels, the *Beauregard* accidentally collided with the *General Price,* forcing her to shore, severely damaged and out of action. Meanwhile, the *Beauregard* and the *Little Rebel* were disabled when Union shells blew up their boilers. Adding insult to injury, the *Little Rebel* was also rammed by the *Monarch,* which propelled her to the shore where she was abandoned. On the northern side, the impact of the initial ramming disabled the *Queen of the West;* and during the battle, Colonel Ellet was shot in the leg, dying on July 21 from his wound.

Panicked and desperate to save themselves, the remaining cottonclads fled downriver, closely pursued by the Union vessels. All this time, thousands of spectators crowded the surrounding bluffs watching the battle unfold before their very eyes.

During the running chase, the *Thompson* was hit and caught on fire. Beached by her crew, she burned fiercely and soon exploded. The *Bragg* and the *Sumter* both ran aground and were abandoned to the Union navy. Only the *Van Dorn* escaped, fleeing to join two other Confederate gunboats at Liverpool Landing on the Yazoo River. Several weeks later, however, the three Confederate gunboats, including the *Van Dorn,* were set ablaze and destroyed as Ellet's rams approached them on the Yazoo.

Meanwhile, as the river battle was playing out off its shores, in Memphis the Confederates were alarmed over the prospect of their new ironclad falling into Union hands. The ironclad gunboat *Tennessee,* still unfinished, was set ablaze and destroyed to prevent her capture. She was one of two ironclad gunboats under construction for the Confederate Navy at Memphis. The *Arkansas,* being the other, was commissioned and dispatched to the Yazoo River in April. Acknowledging that he had little choice, the mayor of Memphis quickly surrendered his city, his only response being, "... the civil authorities have no resources of defense, and by the force of circumstances the city is in your power."

The bloody battles on the upper Mississippi were more or less over. For all intents and purposes, this stretch of the Mississippi was now free of enemy resistance, and Davis now concentrated on the one principal tributary in his sector where Confederate gunboats were still thought to be lurking.

Within a few weeks of the Union occupation of Memphis, Flag Officer Davis ordered an expedition up the White River to destroy any rebel gunboats found there. Dispatched for this mission were the ironclad gunboats *Mound City* and *St. Louis,* and the wooden vessels the *Conestoga* and *Tyler.* Also on hand were troops from an Indiana regiment.

About ninety miles up from the mouth of the river, just north of the town of St. Charles, were four Confederate vessels: two of them remnants of

Hollins' gunboat flotilla, and two transports. Anticipating the Union's incursion up the river, the Confederate commander ordered all but one gunboat scuttled across the river. The artillery from the sunken gunboat, two rifled 32-pdrs. and three Parrott guns, were moved ashore, hidden in the thick brush along the river banks, and manned by the gunners from the boat. Other than the sailors that supported the batteries, Confederate manpower consisted of only 35 men, each one of them armed with only an Enfield rifle.

On June 17, 1862, the Union troops landed below the obstructions and began their advance through the thick tangle of woods towards the hidden Confederates. The Union gunboats, meanwhile, gingerly snaked their way past the half submerged hulks and moved slowly up the river, scanning the riverbanks for the elusive Confederates. Suddenly, explosions of musket fire echoed along the river as the Indiana troops flushed out several Confederate pickets from the dense woods. Instinctively responding to the outburst of gunfire, the Confederate batteries now opened their assault on the approaching Union boats, revealing their position to the navy gunners. Following a short lull, an order was given for the Union troops scattered within the woods to back away to a safer position before the gunboats began shelling the Confederate batteries. Soon a deluge of grape and shell began to pour in from the Union gunboats. During the maddening exchange, however, one Confederate 32-pdr. found its mark. An adept Confederate gunner slammed a shell into the *Mound City*, smashing through the casemate and exploding the steam boiler, always a certain killer. The shell blast killed eight men outright who were manning a gun, and the scalding steam from the ruptured boiler killed many more inside the ironclad. Of the 175 men on board the *Mound City*, only 25 survived relatively unscathed from the disaster. 82 were scalded to death, 43 were drowned or shot after they jumped overboard, and 25 were severely wounded. The Union army commander, Col. Graham N. Fitch, watching this terrible loss of life from the woods, ordered his troops to advance and quickly captured the Confederate works.

The *Mound City* was towed to St. Charles for repairs while the remainder of the expedition continued up the river for about 60 more miles. Finding no sign of Confederate activity, and in danger of grounding in the diminishing water, the Union expedition returned to Memphis.

With the exception of a battle with the ironclad CSS *Arkansas*, which will be covered in the next chapter, Union offensive action north of Vicksburg was somewhat scaled back. Confederate gunboats had been cleared from the upper river, all of the enemy forts were abandoned or destroyed, and overall resistance had dropped considerably. The Mississippi flotilla, having vanquished their enemy, would spend much of their time escorting Union vessels along the upper river and tributaries, and fighting the occasional pockets of Confederate guerrillas — the bands of Southern partisan bushwhackers that hid in the brush to ambush and capture the slow-moving supply boats, disrupted communications and supply lines, and participated in illicit trade.

This relatively low level of activity would remain the norm until October 1862, when a new squadron commander came on board, and when battle plans for Union military forces, both infantry and naval, were coordinated for a joint expedition on Vicksburg.

13

The Gulf Squadrons: May 1861–June 1862

As you may recall, following the reinforcement of Fort Pickens in Pensacola Bay, a 46-year veteran of the U.S. Navy, Capt. William W. McKean, arrived in the Gulf of Mexico aboard the USS *Niagara*. It was May 25, 1861. Under orders from Secretary Welles, McKean had arrived to replace Capt. Henry A. Adams, the senior naval officer on duty in Pensacola Bay. Aboard his flagship that day, McKean began to develop his plans for a blockade of Confederate ports in the Gulf, chiefly Pensacola Bay, Mobile Bay, and Galveston, as well as the mouth of the Mississippi River. As further proof of his resolve, on the 26th he assigned the USS *Powhatan* and the USS *Brooklyn* to monitor the traffic in and out of the Mississippi, specifically at the Southwest Pass and the Pass a l'Outre respectively.

McKean was responding to a directive from Secretary Welles that imposed a blockade of all Southern ports, effective April 19. When informed of McKean's intention to carry out the directive, General Braxton Bragg, who had assumed command of the Confederate forces in Pensacola on March 11, responded, "Your communication … announcing … the blockade of this port, I accept and consider it a virtual acknowledgment of our national existence and independence." The reaction at Fort Morgan, the fortification guarding Mobile Bay, was to taunt the Union blockaders by displaying a huge Confederate flag, below which fluttered the American colors, union side down.

Consistent with the policy established by Secretary Welles for controlling the fleet in the Atlantic, in June the naval forces patrolling the Gulf were organized into the Gulf Blockading Squadron. This step was considered necessary to increase the efficiency and the effectiveness of the rapidly expanding navy cordon.

The commander of the new Gulf Squadron was Flag Officer William Mervine, a septuagenarian who had served 52 years in the military and represented the old, traditional navy in a climate demanding young and aggressive commanders. Scattered throughout the Gulf under Mervine's command were 15 ships: the *Powhatan, Brooklyn, Massachusetts, Colorado, Water Witch, St. Louis, Wyandotte, Niagara, Crusader, Mohawk, Huntsville, Mississippi, Montgomery, South Carolina,* and *R.R. Cuyler.* Although the new commander had the ships to begin his blockading mission, he was faced with one major difficulty. Key West, at the far eastern perimeter of the Gulf, was the only operating base to support his squadron.

With the surrender of the Pensacola Navy Yard, the Union navy lost one of their two supply bases in the Gulf, the other, of course, being at Key West. It was an unfortunate loss for the Union because now, more than ever, the navy desperately needed a second base in the Gulf. The additional base, suitably located, would insure the military readiness of the squadron and would provide the necessary support for future operations already being planned in Washington. Therefore, besides recommending the seizure of ports on the east coast for somewhat similar purposes, the Board of Strategy also recommended seizing a port on the Gulf coast to establish a second naval base there as well. The board selected a tiny piece of barren real estate in the Mississippi Sound. Twelve miles from the mainland, opposite Biloxi, Mississippi, it was called Ship Island. Halfway between New Orleans and Mobile Bay, Ship Island was only 60 miles from the mouth of the Mississippi River, and was an ideal staging site and supply depot for launching an attack on the major Gulf ports.

With Ship Island currently under Confederate occupation, a Union force was formed to drive the Confederates off the island. On September 16, however, Union authorities in Washington were informed that the Confederates had abandoned Ship Island and had also left behind an unfinished fortification. The following day the USS *Massachusetts* brought in an occupational force; and in December, 1900 additional troops under Gen. John W. Phelps were landed to insure Ship Island remained secure.

Within months of Mervine's takeover, the Gulf Squadron was further defined by a decision from one of Welles' earlier strategy meetings, and one specifically motivated by the government's plan to take New Orleans. Effective in October, Welles announced that the Gulf Blockading Squadron would be split into two smaller commands, a West Gulf Blockading Squadron and an East Gulf Blockading Squadron. Captain McKean was retained to command the eastern squadron, which extended from Key West to Pensacola, Florida. The commander of the West Gulf Blockading Squadron, covering the sector from Pensacola, Florida, to the Rio Grande, would be Capt. David G. Farragut.

Although both squadrons appeared in theory to share the surveillance of the Gulf coastline equally, the task of monitoring Confederate movements was actually skewed to the west. Within the jurisdiction of the western squadron were several ports notorious for extensive blockade-runner activity, ports such as Mobile, Galveston, and New Orleans. Considering also the degree of traffic going in and coming out of the Mississippi River, it is only reasonable to conclude that the burden of surveillance over the 600 miles was much more intense for the ships of the western squadron.

Union naval authorities began to impose direct military action in the western Gulf several months after the CSS *Sumter* escaped from the Pass a l'Outre and steamed to Cuba in June of 1861. Following the *Sumter* incident, the Navy Department was stung by a rash of harsh criticism, a rebuke that focused on the opinion that too few ships were assigned to guard the mouth of the Mississippi. Then still under Confederate control, the mighty river was the principal conduit for shipments from New Orleans to and from Nassau and Cuba. However, with only two Union ships to monitor traffic in and out of the many branches or passes, strict surveillance was virtually impossible.

To answer this criticism, in late September four Union vessels gathered together in the Gulf with orders to steam up the Mississippi to the Head of the Passes. Commanded by Capt. John Pope, the tiny combination consisted of the screw sloop-of-war *Richmond*, the steam side-wheel gunboat *Water Witch*, and two sailing sloops-of-war, the *Preble* and the *Vincennes*. (The *Vincennes* held the distinction of being the first U.S. ship to circumnavigate the globe, from 1826 to 1830.)

To appreciate the exact nature of Pope's mission one must first examine the topography of the Mississippi River. The Mississippi did not empty into the Gulf of Mexico directly. Instead, fifteen miles up-river from the Gulf, the broad river split into four smaller branches or Passes that fanned out into the Gulf over a span thirty miles wide, an area called the Mississippi Delta. The common point up-river where the four Passes originated was called the Head of the Passes.

Pope's mission appeared fairly simple. From the Gulf he was ordered to advance up the Mississippi and to occupy the Head of the Passes. Straightforward and logical — whoever controlled that strategic point of the river had a tremendous advantageous. They could intercept any ship heading up or down the river. The Union navy wanted that advantage very badly.

For Captain Pope, however, getting to the Head of the Passes wasn't easy. With a swift current flowing into the Gulf, the two heavier sailing ships, the *Preble* and the *Vincennes*, had to be towed up. Overcoming this problem, the flotilla arrived at the Head of the Passes around October 3, 1861.

But the Confederate Navy also had a presence here on the Mississippi, as the Union vessels quickly discovered. Almost immediately after their arrival, Pope's tiny command began to encounter harassing gunfire from the Rebel gunboats patrolling this section of the river. Stationed in New Orleans, the Southern boats were commanded by Commodore George N. Hollins and consisted of the flagship *McRae*, a captured Mexican revenue steamer, and five converted tugs.

Occasionally the Southern boats would venture down the river and watch the goings-on, or at other times fire randomly in Pope's direction, with no effect. Flex their muscles as they might, however, the Confederates' guns were no match for the firepower carried aboard the Union ships. Carrying over 40 guns, Captain Pope had a superior advantage in weaponry; all six of the Confederate boats combined could only muster about fifteen small guns, seven of which were on the *McRae* alone.

Nevertheless, although the Confederates lacked the ordnance to measure up to the Union boats, one of them did prove quite formidable indeed. She was the converted tug *Manassas*, a boat that was to be operated as a privateer until seized by the Confederate Navy. Now covered in iron three-quarters of an inch thick, she also sported an underwater ram mounted threateningly to her bow. Also included in the Confederate war chest were two fire-rafts, flat boats the Southern seamen would set ablaze and launch into the river to impact Union vessels, hopefully to set them ablaze.

Following days of sporadic skirmishing, an unexpected Confederate attack came in the early morning hours of October 12. It happened around 3 a.m. while the *Richmond* was taking on fuel from her coal-tender. Like a thief in the night, the rebel ironclad silently drifted downriver, hidden by the near pitch-black night. Without a picket ship on station or a lookout to warn the flotilla of the approaching enemy, the ram suddenly appeared and headed directly for the *Richmond*. With an enormous shudder the *Manassas* collided head-on into the side of the Union vessel, puncturing a two-foot hole beneath the waterline. Rapidly taking on water, the crew rushed below to stop-up the gaping wound as sheer terror and mass confusion reigned uncontrollably above deck. In the encounter the *Manassas* herself became momentarily disabled from the tremendous shock that jolted her engines and boilers. Breaking free, however, the *Manassas* quickly disappeared into the blackness.

As the Union crew frantically struggled with the onrushing water, the *Richmond* began to drift down the Southwest Pass in a retreat towards the Gulf; and, likewise, the other vessels of the flotilla followed. But waiting for them at the mouth of the Mississippi was the ever-present and always perilous sand bar. Unable to prevent the inevitable, the *Richmond* and the *Vincennes* struck the bar and became lodged in the riverbed, while the other boats, being lighter, managed to clear it and were safely anchored nearby.

To compound Pope's difficulties, Commodore Hollins and his gunboats suddenly appeared on the scene. Noting the predicament the Union vessels were in, Hollins immediately ordered a long-range gun barrage on the grounded ships. But, luckily for Pope, the small Confederate shells all missed their mark, splashing harmlessly into the river. During the cannonading, the commander of the *Vincennes*, assuming that all was lost, ordered his ship blown up and then appeared on board the *Richmond* wrapped in the American flag. Fortunately, the ship failed to explode; but Captain Pope, outraged over the captain's dramatic display and the blatant disregard for a ship under his command, ordered the *Vincennes's* captain back to defend his ship and the honor of his country.

A couple of hours before noon the Confederate boats withdrew and headed back up the river. For Hollins it was a job well done. In addition to successfully defending the river, the Confederates also captured two tenders left behind at the Head of the Passes.

For the Union, however, "Pope's Run" was a very embarrassing episode. As a result, Pope was stripped of his command, as was the commander of the *Vincennes*. Recalling this chapter in U.S. Naval history, David D. Porter, at that time an admiral, would write, "Put this matter in any light you may, it is the most ridiculous affair that ever took place in the American Navy. There is no instance during the war like it."

Meanwhile, naval operations in the eastern sector were relatively uneventful, dealing chiefly with insuring that the blockade prevented small craft, blockade-runners, and smugglers from entering the Florida coastline from Cuba, Bermuda, and Nassau. One of the few significant engagements under McKean's watch occurred on November 22–23, 1861, and marked the first time since Union losses at Pensacola in January that some retaliatory force was exercised. The flagship *Niagara*, anchored some two miles from Fort McRee, opened up a bombardment of the Confederate positions around Pensacola Bay. Joined by the batteries of Fort Pickens, and supported by the 22-gun screw sloop *Richmond,* the intense cannonading practically destroyed Fort McRee to the point where General Bragg considered evacuating the garrison stationed there. Nothing was actually gained from this exchange, however, except perhaps to demonstrate the firepower of the eastern squadron to the Confederate inhabitants.

The only event of any significance in the eastern sector occurred on May 9, 1862. On this date the Confederate forces burned and ransacked the Pensacola Navy Yard before evacuating the area. Following the occupation of Union forces the next day, the base eventually replaced Ship Island as a depot for the West Gulf Blockading Squadron.

On June 4, 1862, Secretary Welles selected Capt. Theodorus Bailey to relieve Flag Officer McKean. He was given the eastern gulf command, some people opined, as a token of gratitude for his role in the capture of New Orleans two months earlier. Taking on his new responsibility with his customary professionalism, the new flag officer directed his men from his flagship, the frigate *St. Lawrence*, continuing the operations already established by his predecessor. Over the course of Bailey's leadership, some 100 vessels were intercepted, captured, or destroyed in attempts, many at night, to gain access to the many inlets, bays, harbors, and rivers that made up the Florida coastline. Occasionally the East Gulf Blockading Squadron would send expeditions to patrol the many rivers and inlets, and to destroy Confederate blockade-runners at dockside taking on cotton for export. Bailey's squadron also carried out attacks on Confederate salt works. Necessary for the curing and packing of meats, salt was a critical commodity for the Confederacy, with salt production facilities in western Florida becoming prime targets.

For the remainder of the war the sailors of the East Gulf Blockading Squadron diligently performed their thankless role of patrolling the Florida coastline.

14

New Orleans to Vicksburg: December 1861– December 1862

Following the secession of Louisiana on January 26, 1861, the city of New Orleans became the principal center for all Confederate activities in the Gulf. Often referred to as the "Queen City of the South," she was the largest exporting city in the South, catering to privateers and blockade-runners that moved freely out of her docks to the Caribbean and Cuba, bringing back critical supplies to relieve Southern shortages. Secretary Fox had pondered long and hard over the military value of capturing the Queen City, waiting for the most opportune time to set the mission in motion. In September, with Ship Island now in Union hands as a base for the West Gulf Blockading Squadron, the Navy Department pressed forward with a plan that moved away from a mere blockade to an attack and occupation of this vital port. The navy was going to apply the same philosophy for taking New Orleans that was successful at Hatteras Inlet — to shut down the traffic one must close off the highway. Lincoln approved the plan, remarking, "This should have been done sooner. The Mississippi is the backbone of the Rebellion; it is the key to the whole situation."

To conclude their planning efforts, therefore, in December of 1861 Capt. David G. Farragut was selected to command the West Gulf Blockading Squadron; and a month later, in January of 1862, he received his orders for the capture of New Orleans. In the orders the new flag officer was told, "When [the mortars] arrive, and you are completely ready, you will collect such vessels as can be spared from the blockade, and proceed up the Mississippi River, and reduce the defenses which guard the approaches to New Orleans, when you will appear off that city and take possession of it under the guns of your squadron, and hoist the American flag therein, keeping possession until troops can be sent to you. If the Mississippi expedition from Cairo shall not have descended the river, you will take the advantage of the panic to push a strong force up the river to take all their defenses in the rear. You will also reduce the fortifications which defend Mobile Bay and turn them over to the army to hold."

A native of Tennessee, Farragut was 61 years old and had spent nearly his entire life in the navy. Coincidentally, Farragut was the foster brother of David D. Porter, skipper of the USS *Powhatan*, and of William D. Porter, who commanded the gunboat *Essex* during the Fort Henry campaign. Adopted by the Porters when he was five years old, Farragut was exposed to ship-board life since he was eight, when Capt. David Porter, one of America's leading early nineteenth-century naval commanders, took him aboard the original USS *Essex*, on which he traveled the seas for many years. He served in the War of 1812 as a midshipman, and also saw duty in the Mexican War in 1855. His last post was as president of a recently formed board that reviewed and issued officer retirements.

Despite his years of service, the Navy was somewhat reluctant to appoint Farragut to such a high-level position. The fact that he had never directed such a large command was of some concern. Furthermore, considering the mindset of those times, they feared that although he expressed a loyalty to the U.S., as a Southerner who had lived in Virginia with his Southern born wife, any actions against his family or friends could very well influence his decisions and thereby compromise his mission. This fear was particularly worrisome because as a child his father had established the family home in New Orleans. These concerns were put aside, however, because Welles was not only impressed with the captain's credentials, but also believed his loyalty was quite sincere — especially after learning that Farragut had taken up residence in New York when Virginia seceded, and then reported for duty at the Navy Department. In the end, his many years of experience, his fine reputation, his sincerity, and his enthusiasm for the mission had won the day. Graciously accepting the trust placed in him, Farragut prepared to take on his new responsibilities and to lead his command into battle.

Aboard his flagship, the USS *Hartford*, Farragut arrived at Ship Island on February 20, 1862, having been at Key West the previous month working on the initial formation of his squadron. To take New Orleans, the mission was planned as a joint army/navy expedition with a fleet of over 40 vessels. Fifteen warships were assembled for the battle, which included nine sloops-of-war, such as the *Hartford* (carrying 28 guns), the 25-gun *Brooklyn*, and the 22-gun *Richmond*. Six steamers were refitted to tow the heavier ships over the sand bar, and even a survey vessel from the U.S. Coastal Survey was included in the fleet. With over 300 guns on hand, 192 in the main fleet and 110 in the mortar flotilla, the Union firepower was enormous indeed. To provide the heavy firepower, 20 reinforced schooners, commanded by Farragut's brother, David D. Porter, were to be used as a mortar flotilla. His 13-inch mortars and 32-pdrs. were the primary guns of the expedition and expected to batter the defenders of the Mississippi into submission. Leaving no stone unturned, Porter ordered his mortar boats camouflaged with branches of evergreens so they would blend in with the trees on the riverbank, and most of the vessels deployed a blanket of anchor chain over their sides as protection for their engines and boilers against incoming shells. The chains were hung about eight feet above the water and extended about two feet below the waterline. Some captains ordered sand bags stacked on deck and even had their vessels painted mud-color so as to make them less visible during the night.

Farragut's supporting troops were the 6,000 soldiers under Gen. Benjamin F. Butler, a veteran of the battle at Hatteras Inlet in August 1861. The general's responsibility was to provide stability and to keep the peace in the city by moving his occupational troops into New Orleans following her capture. Meanwhile, Flag Officer Andrew H. Foote, presently assisting Grant with the capture of Fort Donelson, was issued orders to advance down the Mississippi and complete a rendezvous with Farragut. If Foote failed to arrive at New Orleans, however, Farragut would continue north to attack any remaining Confederate fortifications on the river with his fleet of ships, ironclads, and mortars.

In December 1861 ground forces in New Orleans consisted of about 8,000 troops under Gen. Mansfield Lovell, a popular figure in these parts and widely known for his superb horsemanship. When information reached the city that month that Ship Island was being occupied by U.S. troops, the citizens and officials of New Orleans were quite apprehensive over the prospect of a Union ground attack. To allay their fears, Lovell spoke of the confidence he had in his forces defending the city by reminding them that the U.S. "could not take New Orleans by a land attack with any force they could bring to bear." Little concern, however, was shown by the city — or by the Confederacy, for that matter — to the possibility of a Union naval offensive. The Confederate War Department assumed the greatest threat of an attack on New Orleans would come from the upper Mississippi. Their letter to General Lovell on February 8 summed up that perception quite clearly: "The President desires that, as soon as possible, on receipt of this letter, you dispatch 5,000 men to Columbus to reinforce that point, sorely threatened by largely superior forces. New Orleans is to be defended from above, by defeating the enemy at Columbus." General Lovell complied with the order but was increasingly concerned that the city's defenses were deteriorating. He said this much in a letter to Confederate Secretary of War Judah P. Benjamin on March 6: "This Department is being completely drained of everything. We have filled requisitions for arms, men and munitions, until New Orleans is about defenseless. In return we get nothing." The only defensive force he had now was the 2,700 troops left behind and the city's militia. Not only were soldiers in short supply but also arms, ammunition, and medical supplies, all of which were sent to other points, chiefly Virginia and Pensacola. By April 1862, not only was General Lovell's command decimated, but most of the Confederate troops in the surrounding area had also disappeared, being shipped off to Corinth, Mississippi, to assist Gen. Albert Johnston. It seems the Confederate general was gathering his forces at Corinth to challenge Grant's army, which had advanced to Pittsburg Landing, Tennessee. In the end, the largest city in the Confederacy was, surprisingly, the least defended.

Nevertheless, to most inhabitants of New Orleans the situation was not all that grim. The reason for their complacency was the confidence they had in two reinforced and strengthened forts, Fort Jackson and Fort St. Philip, located 70 miles below the city. They felt secure, as well, in the knowledge that the navy was also on duty in the river with a number of gunboats; and with the construction of four menacing ironclads underway, the *Arkansas* and *Tennessee* at Memphis, and the *Mississippi* and *Louisiana* in New Orleans, it was fairly certain to most that any Union attack would be easily defeated. What the citizens failed to know, however, was that the Confederacy, owing a million dollars on the construction of the ironclads at New Orleans, was experiencing difficulties with getting credit. Work on the boats, originally scheduled for completion in January, had stalled.

Fort St. Philip was the larger and older of the two and was considered the more formidable. Built by the Spaniards on the east bank of the Mississippi, it was an open fort surrounded by thick brick and stone walls covered with sod, and was defended by some 50 guns. A star-shaped fortification, Fort Jackson was located a half-mile farther south, on the west bank of the river. Mounting over 70 guns, the fort was built of stone and mortar, and was heavily protected with sand bags up to six feet deep. The guns of both forts had a commanding range of the river; and the forts were garrisoned with about 1,100 troops combined, under the overall command of Gen. Johnson K. Duncan.

In addition to the two forts, the Confederates had stationed 14 vessels in the Mississippi under the overall direction of Commodore John K. Mitchell of the Confederate Navy. Somewhat unique, the Southern boats were vessels from three separate commands. Six were from the Confederate Navy, which included the ironclad ram *Manassas* and the gunboat *McRae*, both belonging to Commodore Hollins of "Pope's Run" fame, the unfinished ironclad gun-boat *Louisiana*, as well as the steamer *Jackson* and two launches. Two were gunboats of the Louisiana State Navy, the *Governor Moore* and the *General Quitman*, and six were converted tugboats from the River Defense Fleet. (As you recall from chapter 12, the other nine vessels making up the fleet had been previously dispatched to Memphis.) Converted into "rams," the latter eight gunboats all had a number of thick, flat iron bands bolted across their bows. All together, the entire fleet defending New Orleans carried a force of 40 guns, one-third of which were rifled.

In addition to these defensive measures, the river was obstructed with a necklace of anchored hulks and heavy timber rafts strung together with six heavy chains. Although considerably weakened by severe storms, the barrier was thought adequate enough to delay the Union fleet between the devastating crossfire of the two forts.

Farragut's mission was to blast the two forts into submission with Porter's powerful mortars, which in turn would allow the fleet to advance up the Mississippi to capture New Orleans. With the help of Porter's steamers, which included the *Harriet Lane*, by mid–March of 1862 the heavier vessels and the mortar-schooners had crossed the bar at Pass a l' Outre. A month later the rest of the fleet had arrived at Ship Island, along with General Butler and his troops. By the 15th of April everything was in place, and the order was given to proceed to New Orleans.

Elsewhere, Flag Officer Foote had just won his battle at Island No. 10 on the upper Mississippi; Grant scored a victory at Pittsburg Landing; the ironclads *Monitor* and *Merrimack* were still making history at Hampton Roads; and the Army of the Potomac was slowly advancing up the Virginia peninsula.

The Union survey ship, having traveled up the Mississippi with no resistance from the enemy, had already sounded out the river and, by posting small white flags in the river, identified the most strategic positions for each mortar vessel. Now securely anchored in their battle stations, and within three miles of their target, on April 18 the mortars opened fire on Fort Jackson. The heavy bombing raged on all day and into the night, the 13-inch mortars lobbing massive shells into the fort at a rate of over 200 each hour. This rain of terror continued around the clock for the next five days. By this time, the Union gunners were extremely exhausted and near collapse, particularly from the continuous exposure to the concussion of the mortar blast. In the meantime, on April 20 two heavy steamers were dispatched in an attempt to sever the iron chains stretched across the river. In spite of the heavy fire from Fort Jackson on the two ships, the barricade was broken and the ships safely returned to their lines. At that point Gen. Duncan relayed an urgent message to Commodore Mitchell requesting assistance for the embattled fort, but no aid was forthcoming.

On the same day the Confederate barricade was severed, Farragut conferred with his fleet captains, calling them into conference aboard the flagship. At this meeting the plan was discussed and Farragut announced his decision to attempt the passage of the forts. "The flag-officer," he said, "is of the opinion that whatever is to be done will have to be done quickly, or we shall be again reduced to a blockading squadron, without the means of carrying on the bombardment, as we have nearly expended all the shells and fuses, and material for making cartridges."

Farragut had made it known in the beginning that he did not have confidence in the mortar-fleet, but agreed to their presence only because they were already part of the Navy Department's plan. But, after five days of continuous shelling, the defenders at Fort Jackson were still quite active and Farragut's patience was running thin. "It was plain to him that nothing more would be accomplished by the mortars," wrote Farragut's secretary, so with the mortar-fleet staying behind to provide cover-fire on Fort Jackson, the fleet would attempt the run.

In the early morning darkness of 2 a.m. on April 24, 1862, the fleet steamed through the severed barricade and approached Fort Jackson. The long procession of ships and gunboats chugged up the river in a predetermined order of attack, which divided the fleet into three divisions. The first division consisted of two sloops-of-war and six gunboats led by the *Cayuga*, under Capt. Theodorus Bailey. They were followed, also in single file, by the flagship *Hartford*, and the sloops *Brooklyn* and *Richmond*. Finally, the six gunboats of the third division brought up the rear, while Porter's guns raked Fort Jackson with round after round of shell and canister to minimize the Confederate resistance.

Steaming their way through the persevering shelling from Fort Jackson, the first division began to receive fire from the batteries at Fort St. Philip. Maintaining their forward and steady course through the strong 3½ knot current, the Union vessels returned the fire with devastating broadsides of shell and grape. When safely past Fort St. Philip, the *Cayuga* found herself under attack from a Confederate gunboat sent out to intercept the Union fleet. With help from her mates of the first division, the Confederate boat was soon disabled by the overwhelming firepower of the Union gunboats. All the while the flickering glare of blazing fire-rafts, set adrift into the Union fleet, transformed the smoke-filled darkness into a grotesque panorama and only added to the pandemonium witnessed that night.

Strangely enough, during the height of the battle the Southern naval force failed to support the forts or prevent the passage of Farragut's squadron.

Only three boats, the *Governor Moore*, the *Manassas*, and the *McRae,* were in the thick of the fighting. As the Union fleet approached the end of their passage, around 4:30 a.m., several of the Confederate gunboats were torched and abandoned where they anchored, and others fled towards New Orleans. After ramming the *Brooklyn*, the thinly armored *Manassas* became disabled. Unable to continue fighting in her crippled condition, she was run aground and ordered destroyed by her captain; and without her engines the yet unfinished ironclad gunboat *Louisiana* served only as a floating battery, with only two guns in working order.

Although Farragut's fleet succeeded in the initial phase of their mission, they did not survive unscathed. During the passage the Confederate ram *Governor Moore* had spotted the shadowy silhouette of the Union gunboat *Varuna* as she raced past under a full head of steam. Under pursuit, at 6 a.m., the *Varuna* was nine miles past the forts when caught and rammed by the *Governor Moore*. At this point the *Stonewall Jackson* of the River Defense Fleet, which was fleeing to New Orleans, also rammed the Union gunboat, sinking the *Varuna*. Within moments, the lead vessels of the squadron had arrived on the scene. Under attack from the gunboats of the Union fleet, the *Governor Moore* was soon disabled and ordered burned by her captain, while the *Stonewall Jackson* was also torched and abandoned several miles farther up the river.

Other losses for the Union fleet included three of the slower Union boats at the end of the third division that were so badly damaged they were forced to turn back before they capsized. For the vessels that survived, many suffered varying degrees of damage from the shells of Fort St. Philip and Fort Jackson. The flagship experienced 32 direct hits and was temporarily set ablaze by a colliding fire-raft, while the *Brooklyn* was hit 17 times. One of the mortar-schooners was also lost. In the end, 39 Union seamen perished. The number of Confederate seamen killed is not certain, although it was reported that on the *Governor Moore* alone, 57 men were lost.

On the afternoon of the 25th, as the fleet headed upriver to New Orleans, a Union naval officer carrying a flag of truce entered Fort Jackson to demand the immediate surrender of the fort. The emissary returned to Porter with no assurances from the commander, and within moments the mortars were ordered to resume their bombardment of Fort Jackson. Meanwhile, the weary Confederates inside the fort, now exposed to a renewed downpour of deadly shell and canister, refused to accept their commanders' decision. Instead, they insisted that it was futile to continue their resistance and useless to subject the garrison to further loss of life. Shortly, their pent-up emotions exploded into rage, with many men deserting the fort and others refusing to fight. Guns were spiked in protest, as the men demanded the capitulation of both forts. Try as he may, General Duncan could not persuade the mutinous troops to return to their guns, leaving him no alternative but to surrender the forts on the 28th.

The Confederate officers were ceremoniously escorted aboard the *Harriet Lane* that afternoon to formally surrender the forts to Commander Porter. As the documents were being signed, the ironclad *Louisiana*, set ablaze and cut from her mooring, drifted downriver and was heading straight for the Union gunboats. Warned of the impending collision, Porter insisted the signing continue, remarking to the Rebel officers, "This is sharp practice, but if you can stand the explosion when it comes, we can. We will go on, and finish the capitulation." Luckily, the *Louisiana* exploded before she reached the Union ships. Even the ironclad *Mississippi* was set ablaze to prevent her capture. Of the original 14 Southern vessels, only the *McRae* and one ram, the *Defiance*, survived to surrender.

In May the U.S. Engineer Corps released a report of their inspection of the two forts. The report said, "Fort St. Philip, with one or two slight exceptions, is to-day without a scratch. Fort Jackson was subjected to a torrent of 13-inch and 11-inch shells during 140 hours. To an inexperienced eye it seems as if this work were badly cut up. It is as strong to-day as when the first shell was fired at it."

"Push on to New Orleans," the Flag Officer ordered, and on April 25 the Union fleet pushed on as directed, snaking its way north for 70 more miles. After receiving only mild resistance from a 40-gun battery at Chalmatte, four miles south of New Orleans and the Confederates' last line of defense, the fleet arrived at New Orleans in the early afternoon. With no military opposition to impede their landing, the vessels anchored at the river's edge adjacent to the Custom House.

The scene that greeted the Union men was one of panic, anger, and fear. The city was in chaos. Bales of burning cotton littered the streets, looting was widespread, and despite a pouring rain the squadron was greeted by a taunting mob that lined the levees protesting the presence of the Union invaders. One New Orleans citizen described what he saw that day: "The crowds on the levee howled and screamed with rage. The swarming decks answered never a word; but one old tar on the *Hartford*, standing with lanyard in hand beside a great pivot-gun, so plain to view that you could see him smile, silently patted its big black breach and blandly grinned."

The commander of the first division, and Farragut's second in charge, Capt. Theodorus Bailey, and an aide were soon dispatched to the mayor's office with Farragut's demand for the surrender of the city. At the meeting with the mayor—and General Lovell and his staff—Bailey was told in no uncertain terms that the city would not be given up. Unable to accomplish his objectives, the meeting adjourned and Bailey returned to the fleet to brief his commander. General Lovell, however, returned to his troops and evacuated the city, leaving the fate of New Orleans in the hands of the civilian authorities. Lovell's departure from the city was endorsed by the civilian officials and was meant to remove any vestige of armed resistance. They thought this would prevent Farragut's fleet from opening a bombardment on their fair city.

On the morning of the 26th Bailey returned to the City Hall with an "official" demand for surrender. This time an unruly and threatening mob had formed, which required an armed escort from the City Guard and for Bailey to display his white handkerchief from the tip of a bayonet. Again the mayor refused to surrender the city voluntarily, but, as related by a Union officer, the mayor said, "Come and take the city; we are powerless."

Around noon on April 29, 200 marines and several naval officers were sent ashore to take formal possession of New Orleans. With loaded muskets at the ready and two brass howitzers standing by, the marines formed a cordon around the Union naval officers as they proceeded through the town square to the roof of the Custom House. The New Orleans citizenry stood transfixed in disbelieving silence as the U.S. flag was hoisted up the flagstaff and fluttered broadly in the stiff breeze. From there the Union party went to the City Hall where the State flag was taken down in preparation for the Federal colors which had not yet arrived.

Several days earlier, before the surrender of the city was finalized, an American flag was mysteriously raised over the U.S. Mint. But just as suddenly, a local man had gone to the roof and had torn it down. This incident was not forgotten, however. After taking command, General Butler ordered the man hunted down, and, despite the pleas from his family to spare his life, he was hanged for treason on June 7 for "insulting" the National flag. This was just one of many flagrant abuses of power exercised by Butler. On another occasion during the occupation of New Orleans, this time in May of 1862, he issued his so-called "Woman Order," a proclamation dictating that any Southern woman who insulted or in any way failed to show respect to the federal soldiers would be treated as a common prostitute. This edict sprang from an incident where a woman dumped the contents of a chamber pot from a French Quarter balcony onto Flag Officer Farragut. The order was meant to encourage good behavior, but the Southerners were outraged that an American general was granting his soldiers the freedom to treat Southern refined ladies as common "women of the town," and this would soon earn him the moniker "Beast Butler."

For Farragut, there was still some unfinished business to attend to that left him in somewhat of a quandary. His orders of January 20 had clearly stated that he was to "push a strong force up the river to take all their defenses in the rear." However, Welles also ordered him to "reduce the fortifications which defend Mobile Bay and turn them over to the army to hold." To satisfy both objectives in his orders, Farragut remained in New Orleans until the arrival of Butler and his troops on May 1. He then dispatched the *Oneida* and several gunboats, as an advance division, towards Vicksburg the following day; and to get an early start on the Mobile Bay expedition, Commander Porter and his mortar-schooners were sent back to Ship Island. From there Porter would reconnoiter the Mobile Bay area, organize a naval force, and wait for Farragut's arrival following the expected capitulation of Vicksburg. Farragut also asked Porter to eliminate Confederate resistance on Butler's flank at Lake Pontachartrain.

On May 10 Farragut and 1,400 of Butler's troops under Gen. Thomas Williams landed at Baton Rouge. Without a fight the city had surrendered three days earlier to Cmdr. James S. Palmer aboard the *Iroquois*, as did Natchez on May 12. Shortly after, on the 18th, the *Oneida*, under Cmdr. Samuel P. Lee, arrived at Vicksburg and, faithfully following his orders, demanded the surrender of the city. It was emphatically refused with the reply, "Mississippians don't know, and refuse to learn, how to surrender to an enemy. If Commodore Farragut or Butler can teach them, let them come and try."

Farragut and Williams were already on their way to Vicksburg, arriving three miles below the city on May 24. Peering down from the crest of 200-foot bluffs, the Vicksburg batteries towered menacingly over the Union fleet. A quick reconnoiter soon convinced the flag officer that his guns would never be able to reach the Confederate batteries on the high bluffs. They were useless against such formidable works, he reasoned, and the troops, insufficient in number to begin with, could not land unless the enemy's batteries were silenced. Another problem confronting the expedition was the depth of the river, which was too low for his heavier ships. Having nothing to gain against these odds, Farragut returned to New Orleans on May 30, leaving six gunboats behind outside Vicksburg while the troops were ordered to occupy Baton Rouge. The authorities in Washington, however, had other ideas. They were concerned over reports that because of their deteriorating military position, Confederate troops were escaping across the Mississippi River to Arkansas. Consequently, a message was delivered to Farragut, which stated, "The President of the United States requires you to use your utmost exertions (without a moment's delay, and before any other naval operations shall be permitted to interfere) to open the river Mississippi and effect a juncture with Flag Officer Davis." Without delay, Commander Porter and his mortars were recalled from Ship Island.

With his fleet of ships and ironclad gunboats ready for battle, and with Porter's mortar-schooners in position on both banks of the river, Farragut opened an attack at 4 a.m. on June 28. With the squadron advancing at full steam, a barrage of gunfire was exchanged by both sides as the Union vessels raced past the Vicksburg bluffs, the *Richmond* taking the lead, followed by the *Hartford*, the *Brooklyn*, and the gunboats. Porter's long-range mortars, providing the cover fire, momentarily silenced the Confederate batteries; but, recovering quickly, the Confederates lobbed a continuous shower of missiles through the thick, pungent clouds of smoke onto the passing raiders. As the Union fleet snaked their way up the river, their broadside guns returned the fire, sending their screaming shells and grape into the sides of the lofty bluff. By 6:30 a.m. it was over. Farragut had run the Vicksburg batteries with minimal damage to his fleet. By the same token, the Union guns had made no significant impact on the Vicksburg defensives. Farragut was convinced now, more than ever, that more infantry troops were needed to successfully reduce Vicksburg. He relayed an urgent message to Gen. Henry W. Halleck, at Corinth, Mississippi, asking him to send aid as soon as possible. "I passed up the river this morning, but to no purpose. I am satisfied it is not possible for us to take Vicksburg without an army force of twelve to fifteen thousand men." At Corinth, however, Halleck turned a deaf ear to the flag officer's plea. With over 120,000 troops at Halleck's disposal, Farragut's request was dismissed; reinforcements were not available.

Above Vicksburg, between the city and the Yazoo River, a rendezvous was established on July 1 between Farragut's vessels and several gun and mortar boats from the Mississippi flotilla. At a meeting of the two flag officers, Farragut and Davis, a scheme was devised to dredge a canal across a narrow finger of land formed by the meandering river that was located safely out of range of the Vicksburg batteries. They hoped the canal would provide a bypass route around the Vicksburg batteries. The river, however, gets quite low this time of year, and because Farragut feared of grounding his heavier ships in the shallow water, the partially completed project was called off. To add to his problems, more than half of his men had fallen ill; and with no hope of receiving reinforcements, Farragut decided that, for the moment, Vicksburg was more than he alone could handle. He was going to take his fleet back to New Orleans.

On July 15, however, the Confederates had one more surprise up their sleeve, the formidable ironclad CSS *Arkansas*. The Union commanders had heard reports that the *Arkansas* was somewhere up the Yazoo River, having arrived in April from Memphis where she was built, along with her sistership, the *Tennessee*. Consequently, they decided to investigate the validity of this report by sending three gunboats from their combined naval force on a reconnaissance expedition up the Yazoo. The boats were the unarmed Ellet ram *Queen of the West*, only recently arrived from being repaired; the veteran wooden gunboat *Tyler*; and a "Pook" ironclad gunboat, the *Carondelet*. Winding their way up the river, the Union boats suddenly came upon the *Arkansas* and almost immediately found themselves under attack by the superior Confederate gunboat. Besides being larger and faster, the Southern ironclad was heavier armored and possessed more efficient firepower. Within moments the *Arkansas* began firing aggressively from her two bow guns at the retreating Union vessels. Soon, direct hits on the unprotected stern of the *Carondelet* forced the disabled gunboat to veer off into the shallower water where she ran aground. The *Arkansas*, now under full power, roared out of the Yazoo and steamed straight for the clustered group of Union vessels, some 20 vessels in all. Trading broadsides as she passed through, one Union craft was sunk and several others damaged as the *Arkansas* sped downriver toward Vicksburg.

Highly incensed over this arrogant and bold hit and run tactic, Farragut made plans to strike back at the *Arkansas* as he passed by Vicksburg on the way back to New Orleans later that day. Unfortunately, by the time the Union gunboats were in position opposite Vicksburg, it was much too dark, and the mission failed. Steadfast in their desire to get back at the *Arkansas*, however, another attempt was made on July 22 when Flag Officer Davis dispatched the *Queen of the West* and the *Essex,* still commanded by Capt. William D. Porter, to sink the Confederate gunboat. Charging down the river to Vicksburg with a purpose, the Union boats quickly singled out the *Arkansas* and immediately steamed towards her for the kill. After several attempts to ram the Confederate gunboat failed, only managing to inflict glancing blows, the mission was aborted.

The following month, on August 6, 1862, the *Arkansas* was destroyed by her own crew during an unsuccessful attempt to retake Baton Rouge. While preparing the ironclad for an attack, her engines broke down and caused her to run aground. Not able to use her guns, the captain ordered the *Arkansas* destroyed to prevent her capture.

In the meantime, Farragut and the West Gulf Blockading Squadron resumed their blockading duties on the lower Mississippi and in the Gulf. Porter and his mortar schooners were called to the Hampton Roads to reinforce the James River flotilla; and in December General Butler was sent east, being replaced at New Orleans by Gen. Nathaniel P. Banks.

Without the troops in Farrragut's fleet, forces he had planned to use for himself, Davis saw no point in his remaining at Vicksburg. Instead, he also withdrew, going to Helena, Arkansas. In Washington, meanwhile, Davis was the center of attention. Ever since Flag Officer Davis assumed command of the Mississippi Flotilla, concerns had been mounting at the Navy Department over his capabilities to carry out his growing responsibilities. The success of his naval forces had significantly expanded the role of his command. At the moment, not only was he charged with patrolling the upper Mississippi River, but also the Ohio, the Cumberland, and the Tennessee rivers as well. With plans for a joint army/navy campaign on Vicksburg also in the works, Secretary Welles felt the time was right for a change. These concerns were laid to rest in October of '62 following several meetings between President Lincoln, Secretary Welles, and Asst. Secretary Fox. Commander Porter, having turned his fleet of mortar schooners over to the James River flotilla, was called to Washington where he received the news that he would replace Davis as commander of the newly designated Mississippi Squadron. For Lincoln and the Navy Department, however, Porter's selection placed them in a somewhat troubling position. Although they felt Porter was the right man for this command, his accelerated promotion bypassed a number of senior officers that Welles knew would be bitter and extremely alienated by this action. Meanwhile, Davis was recalled to Washington to head up the Bureau of Navigation.

From Cairo, Illinois, to Memphis, Tennessee, Flag Officers Foote and Davis had swept the upper Mississippi clean, placing it all under Union control. Likewise, except for Port Hudson, Flag Officer Farragut had captured the lower Mississippi from the Gulf of Mexico to Natchez, Tennessee. The four Confederate ironclad gunboats the *Mississippi, Louisiana, Tennessee,* and *Arkansas* were totally destroyed; the remnants of Commodore Hollins' flotilla were no longer a threat; and the rams of the River Defense Fleet had been either captured or eliminated. The army's success in the western theater owed a great deal to the victories and support of the U.S. Navy. Without this support, Union ground forces almost certainly would have had to wage a longer fight, with thousands of additional casualties.

One final piece of business still remained for Farragut, however — the piece of business that would close off the last remaining port in the Gulf to blockade-runners — and that was Mobile Bay.

15

The Mississippi Squadron: October 1862–May 1864

Attired in an admiral's full regalia, Rear Admiral David D. Porter arrived in Cairo on October 15, 1862, to assume command of the Union fleet on the Mississippi, now called the Mississippi Squadron.

One element resulting from this transfer of authority from Davis to Porter was especially pleasing to the new admiral, specifically the news that the War Department agreed to relinquish its role in the operation of the fleet. With the exception of the independent command of Ellet's rams, now led by Lt. Col. Alfred W. Ellet (brother of the late Charles Ellet, Jr.), the Mississippi Squadron was, for the first time, completely under the jurisdiction of the Navy Department. Porter, however, was not totally satisfied and refused to accept the notion of any independent command in his squadron. Now using his new clout as rear admiral, he demanded the rams be transferred to his control also. Following a full Cabinet meeting on November 7, Porter was given full authority over the Ellet rams as well. This was a huge victory for the new admiral because now, without the bureaucratic red tape that Foote and Davis had to contend with, he could manage his squadron as he saw fit. Within days he began to reorganize his new command, bought additional vessels, repaired many others, assigned boats to patrol all the principal waterways, and worked on a myriad of administrative details to improve the operational capabilities of his men and his fleet.

The Mississippi Squadron that Porter inherited still included the original flotilla commanded by Flag Officer Foote back in September of 1861, specifically the three wooden gunboats *Tyler*, *Conestoga*, and *Lexington*. Also included in the original command, and still ready for action, were the seven "Pook Turtles" *Cairo*, *Carondelet*, *Cincinnati*, *Louisville*, *Mound City*, *Baron*

De Kalb (formerly the *St. Louis*), and *Pittsburgh*, all equipped with 13 guns, ranging from 8-inch Dahlgrens to 12-pdr. howitzers. Among the captured vessels seeing duty with the Mississippi Squadron were three rams from the Confederate River Defense fleet, namely the *General Bragg, Little Rebel*, and *General Price*. There was also the *Benton*, carrying seven 32-pdrs., two 9-inch guns, and seven rifled 42-pdrs., and the nine Ellet rams: *Switzerland, Dick Fulton, Lancaster, Lioness, Mingo, Monarch, Queen of the West, Samson*, and *T. D. Horner*. Porter even had a new flagship, the armored steamer *Black Hawk*. One of the more modern vessels of the day, the new admiral's splendid quarters came fully equipped with all the comforts of home.

Flag Officer Porter also made significant additions to the fleet, including five new ironclads. Two of the ironclads were the 8-gun *Lafayette* and the single-turreted *Choctaw*. Huge side-wheel steamers, the two vessels were refitted into ironclad rams in Cincinnati. The *Lafayette* was designed with a sloping casemate, covered in one inch of iron over another inch of India rubber, and carried two 11-inch and four 9-inch Dahlgrens, and two 100-pdr. Parrott guns. The *Choctaw*, on the other hand, was constructed with a stationary turret holding four guns, and was armored with two 1-inch layers of iron over one inch of Indian rubber. Completing this new compliment were the side-wheelers *Chillicothe, Indianola*, and *Tuscumbia*. Constructed in St. Louis with heavier armor, they sported two 11-inch rifled guns and two 9-inch Dahlgrens. The problem with these three vessels, however, was that shoddy construction had made them unreliable and inefficient.

To round out Porter's magnificent fleet, the Mississippi Squadron even boasted of the new "tinclads" as well, among which included such names as the *Brilliant, Rattler, Romeo, Juliet, Marmora*, and *Cricket*, and also the scores of support vessels, tenders, and transports.

The tinclads were the latest and newest breed of vessels introduced into the Union fleet. Stern-wheeled and light-drafted gunboats, they were designed specifically for service on the shallower tributaries of the Mississippi River. With a draft of only two feet, these new vessels were ideal for expeditions on the Yazoo and Red Rivers. There was one drawback, however, and that was the thickness of the iron armor. The metal plates covering the boats were less than an inch thick, hence the name "tinclad." Armed with a battery of powerful howitzers, the vessels were still quite formidable against any of the enemy's river craft willing to take them on.

In contrast, the Southern navy had suffered extensive losses to their Mississippi "fleet." With the loss of their ironclad warships and most of their gunboats, the Confederate naval strength on the Mississippi now consisted primarily of refitted wooden steamships. These losses were further exacerbated by Richmond's inability to maintain the same production capabilities as the

United States. It was no surprise, therefore, that the Southern navy had fallen significantly off the pace and was far from being a serious challenge to Porter's Mississippi Squadron.

Porter had already sent a message to General Grant, the army commander in the western theater, with information that the Mississippi Squadron, at present in an inactive status, was ready and available to cooperate with him in the campaign to take Vicksburg. Lincoln thought the campaign to capture Vicksburg was crucial. "Vicksburg is the key," he said. "The war can never be brought to a close until the key is in our pocket." Vicksburg was indeed the key for controlling the Mississippi, but there was also Port Hudson, some 115 miles downriver, which was still serving as a supply depot for goods coming across the river from Arkansas, Texas, and parts of Louisiana. These states were now the principal sources for much of the provisions sent to the Confederate armies, and Lincoln would like nothing better than to close off this channel.

Recuperating after their battle at Pittsburg Landing, Grant's forces were also inactive and were now bivouacked across the open fields east of Memphis. With both commanders eager to resume the offensive, on December 18, 1862, Grant met with Porter to discuss the final plans for their joint operation. Porter would rendezvous with Gen. William T. Sherman at Memphis, they agreed, and from there, Porter's gunboats and the transports carrying Sherman's troops would depart on December 20 for the Yazoo River, only 12 miles north of Vicksburg. A week before their meeting, as a preparatory measure, Porter had dispatched a small advance force to clear the Yazoo of Confederate batteries and torpedoes and to secure a landing site for Sherman's army to begin their assault. Once the troops were landed, they would attack and overrun the Confederate positions at Chickasaw Bluffs while the navy provided artillery support from their gunboats.

Several days prior to Porter's departure from Memphis, General Grant marched his 40,000 troops south through enemy territory from Tennessee to Granada, Mississippi. To be successful, the plan counted on Grant's ability to draw Confederate forces under Gen. John C. Pemberton out and away from Vicksburg. Once the Confederates moved out to intercept Grant, Sherman would thrust his forces through the rear door of Vicksburg and attack the Confederate stronghold. Unfortunately, the plan failed.

A Philadelphian by birth and an adopted Virginian by marriage, General Pemberton went south at the outbreak of hostilities. The general was not a popular choice for defending what the Southerners perceived as the second most important city in the South, behind Richmond. Despite Pemberton's complete lack of battlefield experience, with one stroke of his pen, President Davis promoted him from his U.S. Army rank of major to a general commanding the Army of Mississippi. E. A. Pollard, editor of the *Richmond Examiner*, was very critical of Pemberton and had several harsh words to say about his fitness for duty. "With armies so intelligent as those of the Confederacy, no man unfitted for command could long maintain their confidence and respect. He might entrench himself with all the forms and parade of the schools; but intelligent soldiers easily penetrated the thin disguise, and distinguished between the pretender and the man of ability. So it was at Vicksburg. Pemberton had already given there [sic] early evidence of his unfitness for command."

Porter's advance unit had arrived at the Yazoo in early December to begin clearing the river before the gunboats and Sherman's army appeared. The tinclads *Marmora* and *Signal* slowly wound their way up the Yazoo River on December 11, along with the ironclad gunboats *Carondelet, Cairo, Baron DeKalb*, and *Pittsburgh*, and the ram *Queen of the West*. The two tinclads spent most of the day detonating the Confederate torpedoes spotted bobbing menacingly in the river, while the gunboats attempted to keep in check the Confederate sharpshooters firing from their rifle-pits. Always innovative, the Confederate mines, or torpedoes, were 5-gallon demijohns filled with gunpowder and fitted with an artillery friction detonator. They were suspended just under the surface of the water by wire that stretched across the river. The following day, about twelve miles up the Yazoo, the *Cairo* struck two of these mines simultaneously, and within minutes she was resting on the bottom of the river, the top of her smokestacks clearly marking her watery grave. Although no one was injured, it was certainly an omen of things to come. (The *Cairo* was salvaged by the National Park Service in 1964 and is now on display at the Vicksburg National Military Park.)

Having successfully lured the Army of Mississippi away from Vicksburg, Grant was fully engaged with Pemberton's forces outside the town of Granada. While this struggle was raging, however, on December 20, 1862, the same day Porter's fleet steamed out from Memphis, Confederate Gen. Earl Van Dorn skillfully led his cavalry troopers around Grant's army and attacked the Union supply depot at Holly Springs. In one fell swoop the Confederate cavalry destroyed all of Grant's supplies, food, and forage. And in a separate attack, a cavalry raid by Gen. Nathan B. Forrest destroyed Grant's telegraph and railroad lines as well. Now isolated in enemy territory without provisions and ammunition, and with no communications to his base, Grant had no choice but to retreat back to Grand Junction, Tennessee.

Three days later, on December 23, Porter arrived at the Yazoo River aboard his flagship *Black Hawk*. Trailing behind were the *Lexington, Benton, Tyler*, and a number of Pook gunboats and tinclads. Sherman and his troops, aboard several transports, soon appeared and anchored alongside the riverbank.

Over the next two days the immediate river was reconnoitered and attempts made, largely unsuccessful, to clear a road for the troops. Not knowing that Grant had aborted his part of the mission, on the 26th Porter and Sherman painstakingly inched their way up the Yazoo River and along the Chickasaw Bayou, fighting off incessant musket fire from hidden Confederate snipers that infested the thick foliage along the river banks. Reaching the base of the Chickasaw Bluffs on December 27, the Union forces were confronted with mosquito infested swamps, flooded bayous, thick, tangled forests, and an impregnable abatis formed from several miles of felled trees, all dominated by towering bluffs where Confederate batteries and rifle-pits commanded the approaches below.

Nevertheless, despite the daunting obstacles, the Union attack began on December 29, with Porter's gunboats providing the cover fire for Sherman's exposed troops as they slogged through the fetid swamps towards the nearest patch of dry land. Attempting to scale the bluffs was near impossible. The difficulties presented by the unforgiving terrain and the withering fire from a well-entrenched foe were only compounded by a thick fog that blanketed the river, and a sudden outbreak of heavy rain.

Meanwhile, Union tinclads and gunboats were also positioned farther up the Yazoo River, shelling the batteries at Haynes Bluff. The Union boats there had bombed the roads leading from Yazoo City to prevent reinforcements from reaching Vicksburg and to confuse the Confederates into believing that Haynes Bluff was the intended point of attack. But nothing worked. Following two hours of horrific gunfire from the Confederate defenders, and suffering terrible losses (Union loss, nearly 2000 men, Confederates, 200), Sherman acknowledged the futility of his assault against such an impregnable position and, hearing news of Grant's withdrawal, ordered a retreat. In a driving rain the expedition headed back to the Mississippi River on January 2, 1863. Grant had failed to seriously consider the topography of the region and the strength and determination of the Confederate resistance. What appeared to be simple in theory was a disaster in reality. One Union soldier summed it all up by saying, "Sherman or Grant or both had made a bad blunder."

Waiting for them at the mouth of the Yazoo was Gen. John A. McClernand. A Lincoln political appointee, he lacked the experience and background to successfully carry out this mission, but as ranking officer he had arrived on January 2 to assume command from Sherman. McClernand had clearly initiated this move behind the scenes in Washington, a move that created waves of resentment and disbelief from General-in-Chief Halleck, Grant, Sherman, and Admiral Porter. Generals Halleck and Grant, however, felt they could not and would not allow McClernand's power grab to succeed.

Although the Union controlled nearly all of the Mississippi, of the four

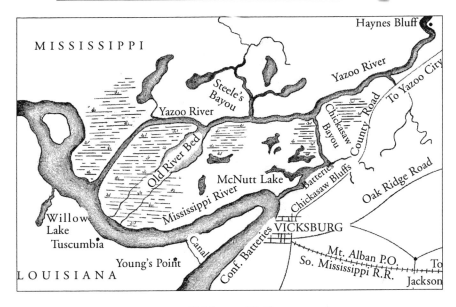

Chickasaw Bluffs

principal rivers that flowed into it below Cairo, two still remained to be reconnoitered and purged of Confederate resistance. They were the Arkansas and the Red rivers. An expedition up the White River had already taken place the previous June, which claimed 150 Union lives from the shelling of the gunboat *Mound City*, and Porter and Sherman had recently experienced the wrath of the Confederate forces on the Yazoo with much greater losses.

In a meeting aboard the *Black Hawk* a plan was proposed to push up the Arkansas, located just south of the White River, and attack Fort Hindman, a Confederate fortification also known as Arkansas Post. A square-shaped fort, it was well constructed, with casemates of heavy oak and armored in iron. The ordnance assembled was also impressive. Fourteen guns were in place, including two Columbiads, a 9-inch Dahlgren, and a number of 6- and 10-pdr. Parrott guns that were mounted in a mile-long ditch that extended from the fort to an adjacent swamp. Located about fifty miles upriver, the Confederate stronghold, commanded by Col. John W. Dunnington, was an important staging site for Confederate raids, and the river was one of the few remaining avenues for shipping supplies to the Southern forces. Commanding approximately 5,000 troops there was Gen. Thomas J. Churchill.

The Union forces, with McClernand now in charge, set their sights on Arkansas Post — not only because Confederate activities there had to be stopped, but also because a successful mission would raise the spirits of the men after their devastating loss at Chickasaw Bluffs. A victory would also help stem the adverse criticism at home over the recent setbacks of both Grant and Sherman in Tennessee.

Porter agreed to support the mission with three ironclad gunboats, which proceeded upriver on January 10, 1863. Shortly before dusk, Porter's ironclads, the *Baron de Kalb*, the *Louisville*, and the *Cincinnati*, positioned some 350 yards from their target, began to pour a torrent of shot and shell into the fort. Directing the operation from a small tugboat, Flag Officer Porter aptly demonstrated the firepower of his gunboats and even called up his flagship *Black Hawk* and the *Lexington* to assist in the bombardment. The next afternoon, Porter's gunboats and two tinclads resumed their merciless shelling of the battered fort, while Sherman's forces, attacking through the woods and swamp from two different directions, overtook and surrounded a contingent of troops commanded by General Churchill. Unable to withstand the humbling firepower any longer, the garrison hoisted their white flag from the parapet around 4:00 p.m. About a half-hour later Dunnington surrendered the fort to Admiral Porter, and Churchill surrendered his army to Sherman.

Although it was a stunning victory for Porter and a great morale booster for his crew, in his reports to Washington, General McClernand took most of the credit for himself. Grant was cool to the attack from the very beginning, and thought the expedition was nothing more than a "wild goose chase."

Grant could not rely on the inexperienced McClernand for such a critical operation as the Vicksburg campaign; with the enormous degree of planning, logistics, and intra-service cooperation that had to be achieved, Grant knew McClernand's inadequacies would compromise the entire mission. Earlier, Grant had written a letter to the War Department stating, "I regard it my duty to state that I found there was not sufficient confidence felt in General McClernand as a commander, either by the Army or Navy, to insure him success." Even Porter had written a letter in which he clearly stated his opinion of McClernand's competency. In the letter to Asst. Secretary Fox he wrote, "I think it is a great misfortune that McClernand should have superseded Sherman who is every inch a soldier, and has the confidence of his men. McClernand is no soldier, and has the confidence of no one, unless it may be two or three of his staff." To settle the matter once and for all, on January 30, 1863, Grant arrived at Young's Point, Louisiana, and took over the command himself.

Over the weeks ahead, both Grant and Sherman took full advantage of Porter's plush living quarters, visiting the admiral frequently on board the *Black Hawk* to discuss various options for getting below Vicksburg. The subject of the unfinished canal was examined, the canal begun by Farragut and Davis last July, as well as the inherent risks of running the Vicksburg batteries. Of all the options bantered about, however, it was quite obvious to everyone that another frontal attack, no matter how well it was planned, would be disastrous. That had already been proven the month before at Chickasaw Bluffs.

It was fairly obvious to everyone also that with the unprecedented rain and flooding taking place, any move down the Mississippi would have to wait until spring. The rain that hampered the expedition on the Chickasaw Bayou was relentless. Flooded rivers, lakes, and bayous continued to overflow their banks. With mud and water everywhere, roads submerged, and high ground at a premium, Union ingenuity was severely tested for finding dry land to bivouac the thousands of troops. In some places the levees were the only places high and dry enough to pitch their tents. In fact, the terrible living conditions took its merciless toll on the army, as hundreds of Grant's men soon died from weather-related diseases.

In the meantime, to keep the men active through the winter, Grant and Porter initiated a number of projects that in some remote way had the prospect of delivering the expeditionary force below Vicksburg without having to run the batteries. Since the mile-long canal through the Young's Point peninsula was intended for that very purpose, the first project decided on was to complete the abandoned short cut. However, when one of the dams gave out, the onrushing water erased much of the work in the canal and nearly drowned the men laboring in it. When the Union soldiers attempted to rebuild the dam, they were so harassed by Confederate snipers that the canal was again abandoned. Admiral Porter had criticized the canal dig as "simply ridiculous, and will never succeed until other steps are taken."

Porter had his own ideas about what those other steps should be, so while the army was dredging out their canal he set out to prove his ideas could work.

Geographically, Vicksburg was located about 12 miles below the point where the southern end of the Yazoo River flowed into the Mississippi. At the northern end, the Yazoo turned into the Tallahatchie River, which then intersected with the Coldwater River and ran back to the Mississippi, a distance of some 200 miles. In effect, the waterway was one continuous river that arched from and flowed back to the Mississippi. The Confederates had built a levee at Yazoo Pass, the stretch of water where the Coldwater joined the Mississippi. The levee, built as a defensive measure, dropped the water level to such a degree that it was impossible for Union gunboats to navigate through that area. Porter wanted to cut through the levee at Yazoo Pass in order to gain entrance to the Tallahatchie. Once through, his gunboats would steam directly for the Confederate transports at Yazoo City and destroy the supply route to Vicksburg. While the navy cut off supplies from Yazoo City, the army would attack Vicksburg from the flank. Grant liked the idea and called for about 20 transports to carry 4,500 troops to support the operation. The ships Porter assigned to this mission included the ironclads *Chillicothe* and *DeKalb*, six tinclads, and the rams *Lioness* and *Fulton*. On February 3, 1863, the final portion of the levee was blasted through, and the onrushing torrent, sweeping everything before it, cut a swath forty yards wide and raised the water level about nine feet.

It took a few days for the water to settle before the Union boats attempted to enter Yazoo Pass, but when they did conditions were far worse than they had bargained for. They found the river clogged with dead trees and rotting branches, and the thick and wild foliage, which flourished along the river-banks, hung heavily over the narrow waterways and caused much damage to the smokestacks and superstructure of the boats. With so many vessels in the expedition, the flotilla moved only about three miles a day, and it wasn't until March 6 before they finally reached the Tallahatchie River. Even the Confederate troops hidden along the river frustrated the procession by felling more trees across the waterway, which created even more delays.

While the navy was meandering slowly through the rivers — rivers only wide enough for two gunboats to run abreast — the Confederates were at work building Fort Pemberton. Consisting only of large mounds of dirt and bales of cotton, the fort was constructed at the junction of the Tallahatchie and the Yazoo. Fully armed with eight guns, and with the old *Star of the West*, of Fort Sumter fame, ineffectually scuttled in the river as an obstruction, the Confederate garrison waited to challenge the approaching naval intruders. When the ironclad *Chillicothe* arrived at the fort on March 11, a stiff exchange of cannon fire nearly disabled the Union vessel and forced her commander to retreat for repairs. The following day, now joined by the *Baron De Kalb*, the *Chillicothe* was again severely damaged by the seemingly accomplished Confederate gunners and was compelled to retreat a second time. It wasn't until the third attempt, on March 13, that the fort's batteries were finally silenced. Instead of assuming the advantage at this most opportune time, however, the Union infantry commander requested a delay in the final assault until his reinforcements arrived. Consequently, by the time the assault was made, it was too late. The Confederates had replenished the ordnance in the fort and reinforcements were manning the rifle pits. In spite of the firepower from the gunboats and pieces of artillery positioned in a small clearing, the attack could not be successful without ground support from the infantry; and there was no place and no way to land the troops without pontoons. Convinced that it was futile to continue, the flotilla retreated back to the Mississippi.

There were other highly imaginative expeditions to find a circuitous route around the batteries of Vicksburg, but like the canal and the Yazoo Pass operation, each one also failed to live up to expectations. Without question,

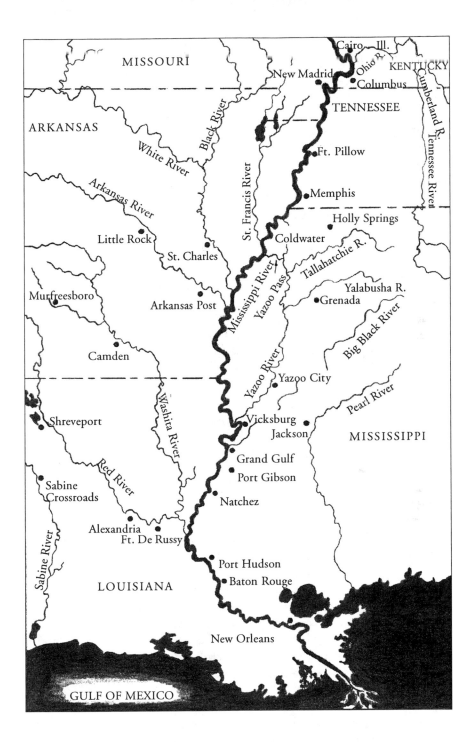

The Western Rivers

Secretary Welles was extremely frustrated. It was difficult to discern what angered him more, the many attempts to find alternate routes to Vicksburg, the failures of these attempts, or both. But one thing was certain: His feelings on these expeditions were quite evident in a somewhat stinging letter he wrote to Porter in which he said, "Rear-Admiral Farragut is below Vicksburg, after a successful and gallant passage of Port Hudson batteries," and that occupying Vicksburg "is of far greater importance than the flanking expeditions. I desire that you consult with Rear-Admiral Farragut and decide how this object can best be obtained."

The "flanking expeditions" alluded to by Welles were not the only incidents that disappointed the Navy Department. Taking advantage of the superior speed of the Ellet rams, in early February Porter dispatched the *Queen of the West*, commanded by 19-year-old Col. Charles R. Ellet, the youngest of the Ellet clan, to run the batteries at Vicksburg. Ellet's specific orders were to ram the Confederate steamer *City of Vicksburg* and to continue south through the only stretch of the Mississippi still controlled by the Confederates, that portion between Vicksburg and Port Hudson. From there he was to steam up the Red River, all the while harassing the Confederate commercial shipping interests along the way.

After permanently disabling the *City of Vicksburg*—and barely escaping herself—the *Queen of the West* made her way down the Mississippi, creating much consternation among Southern officials, as young Ellet managed to capture a number of prizes and a wealth of provisions. Having gone a short distance up the Red River, Ellet was forced to return to the Mississippi to stock up on a fresh supply of coal from a barge Porter had sent adrift down the river. Arriving back at the Red River on February 14, the Union ram confidently puffed her way along the river only to face the 32-pdrs. of Fort De Russy, a small Confederate works built some ten miles below the town of Alexandria. In the ensuing panic to escape the firepower of the fort, the Union ram suddenly became grounded in the shallow water. Now the object of target practice, her steam pipes ruptured by a direct hit, the *Queen of the West,* the leader of the Union charge at Memphis, was quickly abandoned to the Southern forces. Ellet and his crew were picked up by one of their prizes still in the area and returned to the Mississippi, where, on February 15, 1863, outside Natchez, he was joined by the ironclad *Indianola*, also sent down by Porter to join the *Queen of the West* in creating havoc below Vicksburg.

On hearing of the loss of the Union ram, the commander of the *Indianola* made plans to save Ellet's reputation by going to Fort De Russy, where he would not only destroy the fort but also recover the *Queen of the West*. On the night of February 24, however, a pursuing force of four Confederate boats caught up with the *Indianola* in the Mississippi and attacked. The Confederate vessels, under the command of Maj. Joseph L. Brent, were the ram CSS *William H. Webb*, the unarmed steamers *Grand Era* and *Dr. Beatty*, and, ironically, the ram *Queen of the West*. After about an hour of fighting, Brent maneuvered the *Webb* directly behind the rear of the fleeing Union gunboat, a lethal position for the *Indianola* to be in. Knowing the stern of the *Indianola* was unprotected, Brent pressed the *Webb* ahead and slammed into the ironclad with a crushing blow. With the loss of her steering, the *Indianola* drifted towards shore and grounded. Quickly surrounded by Rebel troops, the Union commander had no choice but to surrender his gunboat. Two days later the Confederates blew up the *Indianola* when they mistakenly thought a dummy gunboat Porter sent drifting down the river was a Union recovery vessel on its way to attack them. It was an untimely death for the *Indianola*, the end of her first and only mission.

The *Queen of the West*, now loyal to a different flag, went on to fight another day. A month later she was patrolling Grand Lake, a body of water between the Red River and the Gulf of Mexico. On April 14, during an engagement with a Union side-wheeler, the *Calhoun*, she was hit by a shell from a 30-pdr. Parrott gun. The shell smashed into the roof and exploded, setting her on fire. When the fire reached the magazine, the *Queen of the West* was no more.

The winter had been a disaster for Porter, but with spring in the air the roads were beginning to dry and the commanders became eager to get on with the campaign. In fact, so was Secretary Welles, who telegraphed Porter: "The Department wishes you to occupy the river below Vicksburg, so that Admiral Farragut can return to his station."

It was clear to the commanders that attacking the Confederate stronghold at Chickasaw Bluffs, even with the full strength of the army and Porter's gunboats, was simply out of the question. Instead, once below Vicksburg, Grant would have to cross the river and approach Vicksburg overland from the east while Porter not only shelled the city from the west but also blocked the Confederates' escape route to the river.

To get his entire army of 45,000 men below Vicksburg, Grant ordered the three corps under Generals McClernand, Sherman, and James B. McPherson to march overland down the western side of the Mississippi to the town of Hard Times, a small town north of and across from Grand Gulf, a well fortified Confederate stronghold. While the army moved south along the river, Porter would attempt to run the transports, supplies, and gunboats past the batteries at Vicksburg and rendezvous with the troops. At that point Porter would ferry the men across the Mississippi, where they would capture Grand Gulf, march north to Jackson, the State capital, and shut down the railroad, which transported supplies and reinforcements to Vicksburg. From

Jackson, Grant would methodically march his Army of the Tennessee west along the rail line to Vicksburg.

On March 29 the Army of the Tennessee began their grueling march south through swamps and marshy wetlands; and two week later, on the night of April 16, Porter began his run on the Vicksburg batteries. Porter's flotilla consisted of four Pook gunboats, the *Pittsburgh*, *Carondelet*, *Mound City*, and *Louisville*, and the two new ironclads *Lafayette* and *Tuscumbia*. Also included were the captured steam ram *General Price* and three transports. Leaving the *Black Hawk* behind, the *Benton* would serve as Porter's flagship.

As described in *Land Campaigns of the Civil War*, "As Porter's fleet approached the waiting batteries like a parade of ducks in a shooting gallery, the river was transformed into a blazing panorama of light. Houses and barns were torched along the riverfront, eerily illuminating the passing ships. Citizens poured out of their homes, filling the streets to witness the loud and fiery spectacle. Instantaneously, the shoreline exploded as Confederate artillery, from the base to the crest of Vicksburg's hills, opened their barrage. The constant chatter of muskets added to the deafening scene. On each transport, groups of Union soldiers were stationed below deck. Working feverishly by candlelight, they tried to stop up shell and bullet holes with cotton and gunny sacks. After three hours of continuous gunfire, the fleet got through without a single casualty. Every vessel, however, suffered considerable and varying degrees of damage."

After the success of this first run, on April 22 it was repeated with six more transports and another volunteer crew. Towing barges loaded with provisions and supplies, the transports managed to join their compatriots below Vicksburg, but they lost half of the barges in the process.

Shortly after the passage, while his vessels were being repaired, Porter ordered a reconnaissance of the river before Grand Gulf. At each end of the town, peering down on the river from their lofty perch, were two forts, the defenders of Grand Gulf.

At last the big day had arrived, and on April 29 McClernand's troops boarded the transports for the trip across the Mississippi. Following their landing, the troops would storm Grand Gulf under the cover of Porter's gunboats. Over a period of five hours, however, the gunboats, with the transports following behind, loosened a barrage of iron into the Confederate defenses at Fort Cobun and Fort Wade — with little effect on their resistance to the Union invasion. Both forts were armed with only four guns, but Fort Cobun, constructed about 75 feet above the river, was well protected by a parapet some 40 feet thick. After inflicting only minimal damage to the forts, the frustrated flag officer ordered the transports, with McClernand's troops still aboard, back to the west bank of the river.

Following a meeting between the two commanders on the 30th, McClernand was ordered to march his troops four miles farther down the river, to a town called De Shroon's. In the meantime, Porter would run the transports by Grand Gulf to join the troops downriver. Around 8 p.m. Porter and his gunboats weighed anchor at Hard Times, followed obediently by the line of empty transports. The next day, at De Shroon, the transfer of McClernand's troops went as planned, and after months of struggle Grant's army were landed on the east bank of the Mississippi, at Bruinsburg, a small town some nine miles below Grand Gulf. The transports would continue to ferry the troops across the river until the entire Army of the Tennessee was safely across the Mississippi.

The Confederates during this time were becoming increasingly concerned over the close proximity of their enemy. So as not to be trapped between the growing number of Union troops on their flank and Porter's gunboats in the river, the Southern forces at Grand Gulf, commanded by Gen. John S. Bowen, evacuated their works on May 3, as did the garrison at Port Gibson. Three days later the Army of the Tennessee, now back to full strength, marched towards Jackson, leaving the Mississippi Squadron in the river below Vicksburg.

While Grant's forces moved inland on their circuitous route to Vicksburg, Porter's attention now focused on the Red River and capturing the Confederate steamers that may be found there, particularly the *Webb* and the *Queen of the West*. (The *Queen* had already been destroyed in April of '63. In the last Confederate action on the Mississippi, the *Webb* will be run aground and burned by her captain on April 24, 1865, while attempting to break through the blockade at New Orleans.) Leaving four gunboats behind at Vicksburg, Porter headed south with the *Benton, General Price, Pittsburgh, Lafayette*, and a captured tug, *Ivy*. At this time, Farragut's flagship, the USS *Hartford*, and several gunboats were anchored in the Mississippi and had been blockading the mouth of the Red River for about two weeks. After conferring with Farragut, Admiral Porter and several gunboats entered the Red River, inspected the abandoned Fort De Russy, routinely swept the river of any remaining Southern vessels, and seized Alexandria, Louisiana.

Leaving Cmdr. Henry Walke and the gunboats behind to patrol the Red River, on the 20th of May the *De Kald, Choctaw*, and four tinclads were dispatched on a reconnaissance mission up the Yazoo River. This time, as they snaked their way through the obstructions, the batteries at Hynes Bluff were found abandoned, as was also the case with the Confederate works at Yazoo City and a number of other smaller forts scattered along the river.

As the Army of the Tennessee slowly and methodically advanced west from Jackson to Vicksburg, six mortar boats and several gunboats of the

Mississippi Squadron maintained a continuous and destructive shelling of the city. The intense barrage went on around the clock and at times was so intense that the citizens of Vicksburg were forced to live in the some 500 caves scattered throughout the city. The batteries defending Vicksburg, however, were just as persistent and continued to exchange fire with the gunboats. The resonating pings of the Minie balls and shells that ricocheted off the iron armor was a frequent reminder of the awesome firepower that towered over the vessels. In fact, the tenacious Confederate gunners, always resolute in their purpose, managed to sink the Pook gunboat *Cincinnati*, as a torpedo would also do to the *De Kalb* in July in the waters of the Yazoo River.

Unable to penetrate the strong and determined defenses of Vicksburg, on May 22 General Grant placed the city under siege. And to increase the firepower of Grant's siege line, Porter graciously transferred about 13 heavy naval guns, 8-inch and 9-inch howitzers, from his squadron to the army, and the crews to man them as well. General Sherman commanded the forces positioned on the right flank, McPherson's corps was in the center, and McClernand was on the left. With the Mississippi Squadron in the river below, the investment was complete.

By July, the inhabitants of Vicksburg were desperate. With little food to eat, the people had little choice but to depend on the Confederate army defending the city and to wait for assistance from Confederate Gen. Joseph E. Johnston, whose army of about 12,000 men was approaching from the northeast. But General Pemberton's emaciated and ragged troops were also in a grave and seemingly hopeless position. Now forced into eating rats, and with no chance for an orderly retreat, Pemberton was persuaded to surrender his forces — and the city — on July 4. Early that morning General Grant sent a message off to Washington: "The enemy has accepted in the main my terms of capitulation, and will surrender the city, works, and garrison at 10 a.m."

In the meantime, the besieged Confederate army at Port Hudson, starving and surrounded by the forces under General Nathaniel P. Banks and the guns of Rear Admiral Farragut, were now isolated from the rest of the Southern armies. Five days later they also surrendered, unconditionally.

At last the Mississippi River was won and back in Union hands. The great river was now completely open from Cairo, Illinois, to the Gulf of Mexico, and, militarily, the Confederacy was split in two.

For his unselfish and close cooperation with the Union army, Grant had high praise for Porter. Commenting later, Grant said, "The navy, under Porter, was all it could be, during the entire campaign. Without its assistance the campaign could not have been successfully made with twice the number of men engaged. It could not have been made at all, with any number of men, without such assistance. The most perfect harmony reigned between the two arms of the service. There never was a request made, that I am aware of, either of the flag officer or any of his subordinates, that was not promptly complied with." Porter was also given the thanks of Congress and was elevated to the rank of permanent rear admiral.

Following the surrender of Vicksburg and Port Hudson in July, General Grant traveled to New Orleans to consult with Flag Officer Farragut. At this meeting they discussed a proposal, which both commanders enthusiastically supported, for a joint army-navy campaign against Mobile, Alabama. At the conclusion of their talks, the commanders were in full agreement that now was the best time to attack. The railroad lines from Mobile extended throughout the South, and once the army secured them for Union use they could provide needed reinforcement and provisions to the Army of the Cumberland in their drive against Gen. Braxton Bragg in Chattanooga. At the same time, by capturing three Confederate forts guarding the entrance to Mobile, the navy would effectively shutdown Mobile Bay, a highly prized harbor that attracted scores of blockade-runners. The Union forces for this expedition would be the ground troops of the Army of the Gulf, commanded by Gen. Nathaniel P. Banks, out of New Orleans, supported by Farragut's gunboats of the West Gulf Blockading Squadron.

During the month of August, communications from the two Commanders were exchanged with the War Department, requesting approval of the mission. Lincoln's attention was focused elsewhere, however, and in telegraphed messages to New Orleans he denied the requests.

The Lincoln administration had been receiving reports on Napoleon III of France, more specifically, on his attempt to gain a foothold in Mexico. President Lincoln was very much concerned over this development and wanted desperately to "plant the flag at some point in Texas." Consequently, instead of marching to Mobile, General Banks was ordered to take his troops west. As Halleck would explain, the campaign "was undertaken less for military reasons than as a matter of state policy."

After two unimpressive expeditions by Banks to the Sabine Pass in September, and along the Texas coast near the Rio Grande, he finally managed to plant the flag in Brownsville and Corpus Christi in November of 1863. Still persuaded however, that Texas was more advantageous than Mobile, General Halleck ordered Banks to the Red River for a drive through eastern Texas via Shreveport, Louisiana. To assist Banks, a frustrated Grant was pressured by the War Department to loan 10,000 troops, under Gen. A. J. Smith, from Sherman's army for 30 days, troops Grant sorely needed for his still-planned Mobile expedition. The Red River campaign would to be a combined army-navy affair, with Porter's Mississippi Squadron supplying the gunboat support. To the chagrin of Flag Officer Farragut, however, the campaign reeked with the aroma of Washington politics, the goal being to gain control of the political influence in that part of the South by clearing the Confederates out of Arkansas and Louisiana and seizing the enormous quantities of Confederate cotton there. Meanwhile, Grant, Farragut, and their venture to Mobile would have to wait.

Admiral Porter was very concerned about participating in this mission. He was troubled because the Red River was quite low for this time of year, and this would only make the journey more treacherous for his fleet.

On March 10, 1864, a somewhat reluctant Porter arrived at the mouth of the Red River, his banner whipping briskly high above his flagship *Black Hawk*. Assembled there, as well, were an assortment of 19 ironclad and tinclad gunboats from the Mississippi Squadron. The following day General Smith arrived on schedule with the 10,000 infantrymen aboard five transports, while General Banks, marching his troops overland, had promised to rendezvous with Porter at Alexandria, Louisiana.

As predicted, the river was unusually low and the problems to navigate its length would plague Porter's entire expedition. Departing on March 12, the fleet and Smith's transports managed to slowly snake their way up the river until about eight miles below Confederate-held Fort DeRussy, where a tangle of trees in the river impeded their forward progress. After returning to garrison the abandoned fort, the forewarned Confederates had built what amounted to an enormous floating abatis that extended across the entire width of the river. Not wanting to delay the attack on Fort DeRussy any longer than necessary, Porter divided his fleet, ordering four of his gunboats to clear the obstruction while the rest of the expedition steamed up the Atchatalaya River and landed the troops at Simmesport. After twelve hours of grueling effort, the obstruction was finally breached and the way cleared for the four gunboats to join General Smith, who had arrived at Fort DeRussy around 4 p.m. In the river outside the fort, however, Porter's gunboats were unable to take part in the assault for fear of endangering the troops that were advancing towards the Confederate stronghold. After two hours of heavy musketry between Smith's men and the fort's defenders, Porter and his fleet appeared on the scene just as the U.S. flag was raised above the parapet.

Continuing to press their movement up the river, on March 16 nine of Porter's light-drafted gunboats reached Alexandria and waited there until General Smith's forces arrived two days later, followed by General Banks on the 25th. Pushing on, and with barely enough water to float Porter's gunboats and the transports carrying the army troops, the combined fleet arrived at Springfield Landing, 30 miles from Shreveport, on April 10. Here Porter was told that Banks' forces, which had advanced overland from Alexandria to reunite with the navy at Shreveport, were in full retreat. Having encountered Gen. Richard Taylor's Confederates at Sabine Crossroads, only about 30 miles from Shreveport, the Army of the Gulf was severely beaten and driven back on April 8. Highly incensed over Banks' incompetence, and with the water falling rapidly, Porter was forced to return his fleet to the Mississippi, arriving on May 21, 1864, with nothing accomplished. Even more frustrating was that Porter's fleet suffered the loss of one ironclad and two tinclads from mishaps while negotiating the treacherous river on the way back, and 120 casualties from skirmishes encountered with pockets of Confederate troops that ranged along the riverbanks. General Grant was also disturbed over this loss, telling Halleck, "General Banks, by his failure, has absorbed 10,000 veteran troops that should now be with General Sherman and 30,000 of his own that would have been moving toward Mobile, and this without accomplishing any good result."

For the Union, the mission was a total disaster. As Porter would remark later, "That the expedition was unwise and unmilitary no one now hesitates to assert, for all can see what was seen then by many, that it should never have been undertaken at all."

Despite calls for his dismissal following the Red River fiasco, the politically popular Banks was replaced by Gen. Edward R. S. Canby, a fifty-year-old Kentuckian, and spent the rest of the war confined to administrative duties. For the navy, the war on the Mississippi River had just about played itself out. The "Ole Miss" was back in Union hands again and the routines of the seamen were more or less back to normal. All that remained for the fleet of the Mississippi Squadron was to return to their stations to patrol the miles of rivers under their watch. Admiral Porter, however, would still have another battle to fight on the coast of North Carolina.

16

Gunboats at Mobile Bay: August 1863–December 1864

From Pensacola to the Rio Grande, the ships of the West Gulf Blockading Squadron continued to maintain an around the clock vigilance against the ever-present blockade-runners. Following the surrender of Port Hudson, the main focus of their surveillance was the area in and around Mobile Bay, a superb harbor mid-way between Florida and Texas. With the exception of New Orleans, Mobile Bay was reputedly the most important source for cotton exports, and a choice port for blockade-runners. The attraction for the enterprising blockade-runners were the vital railroads at Mobile, about 30 miles from the entrance of the Bay, that branched out through the South and helped to furnish the Confederacy with their necessities of war and life.

As you recall, Admiral Farragut was still under orders from Secretary Welles, the very same orders issued on January 20, 1862, that directed him to take not only New Orleans but also Mobile Bay. These orders stated, in part, "You will also reduce the fortifications which defend Mobile Bay and turn them over to the army to hold."

In August of 1863 an attempt was made by Farragut and General Grant to persuade Washington that the time was right to attack the fortifications in Mobile Bay with the combined forces of General Banks and the West Gulf fleet. The admiral knew the Confederates were constructing ironclads up the river from Mobile, at Selma Alabama, and wanted desperately to control the bay before the gunboats were completed. Because of Napoleon III's foray into Mexico, however, a diversion that directed Lincoln's attention away from the Gulf, General Banks was sent to Texas instead, and Farragut's campaign against Mobile was put on hold. In the meantime, the fleet maintained its blockade in the Gulf, an expanse of some 600 miles of coastline and a task somewhat complicated by the many inlets that populated that region. It was during this lull that Farragut took his flagship *Hartford* to New York for badly needed repairs, a little rest, and to spend some time in Washington conferring with his superiors. While in New York, the flag officer was given a hero's welcome. He was wined and dined, and for his successes on the Mississippi, the grateful New Yorkers gave him a gift of $50,000.

The Confederates were well aware that an attack on Mobile Bay was a confrontation waiting to happen. After General Banks was ordered to Texas, they spent much of their time improving their defensive works to a point where the security of the bay was even more assured.

The principal access to Mobile Bay was through a narrow channel between two islands, Dauphine Island on the left and Mobile Point on the right. Located on the channel side of each of the islands was a Confederate fort. With a number of high caliber guns, they closely guarded the entrance to the bay. Fort Morgan, the larger bastion, carried 48 guns and was located on Mobile Point; and Fort Gaines, mounting 21 guns, loomed only three miles to the west on the end of Dauphine Island. Several miles inside the bay, situated on a sand bar, was a third, but smaller, stronghold, Fort Powell, which not only commanded the channel to the city of Mobile, but also guarded an alternate route into Mobile Bay called Grant Pass. To further impede the passage into the bay, the Confederates had placed a line of pilings across the channel from Fort Gaines half way towards Fort Morgan. As an extra measure of security, extending east from the last piling was a field of torpedoes, or mines, that the Confederates had strung out in the channel as well. Most were tin containers filled with powder and fitted with percussion caps. Others consisted of beer kegs with small tubes of fulminate extending from its sides. Tethered to the bottom of the channel, the submerged torpedo field was carefully identified by a number of black buoys, the easternmost, however, being red. The result of these obstructions was to force incoming vessels through a narrow passage about 500 yards wide that crossed directly in front of the guns of Fort Morgan.

Built of brick, dirt, and sand bags, Fort Morgan was by far the strongest of the three forts. Nestled within three tiers of embrasures were eleven 32-pdrs, twenty-four 24-pdrs, seven 10-inch Columbiads, three 10-inch mortars, two Blakley rifles, and one 8-inch smoothbore. Across the channel Fort Gaines was armed with fifteen 32-pounders, five 24-pounders, and one 10-inch Columbiad. Besides keeping the Union vessels out, these defenses also protected the blockade-runners who found the safe refuge of Mobile Bay a welcomed sanctuary.

The Confederates had also built a naval base along the Alabama River at Selma, where several new ironclad rams were being built, among them the

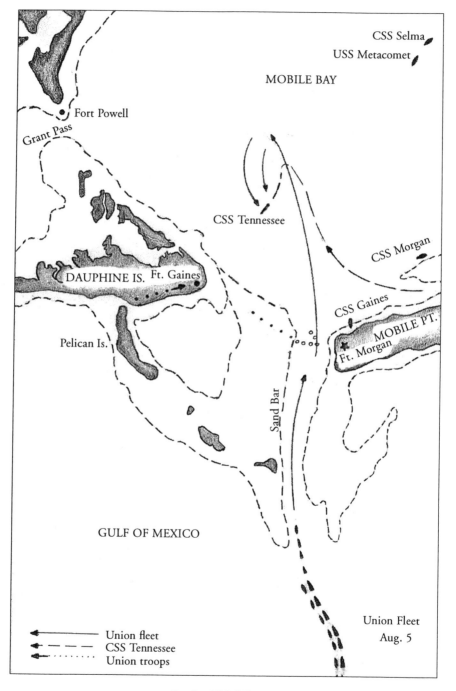

Battle of Mobile Bay

second *Tennessee*, the *Tuscaloosa*, and the *Huntsville*. The first one completed was the CSS *Tennessee*. Launched in February of 1863, the ram was constructed with a wooden casemate nearly two feet thick and covered in three layers of 2-inch iron plates, each plate being 21 feet long and 7 inches wide. Her awesome display of ordnance was installed under the direction of Commander Catesby ap Roger Jones, of *Merrimack* fame, and consisted of four 6-inch Brooke rifles in broadside, and two 7-inch Brooke rifles in pivot. An army officer aboard the *Hartford* later wrote that the *Tennessee* "was then considered the strongest and most powerful iron-clad ever put afloat." As the flagship of Adm. Franklin Buchanan, the famed commander of the Confederate ironclad *Merrimack*, she would soon be added to the defenses of Mobile Bay. The other ironclad rams, however, would not be ready in time to join Buchanan's small flotilla of wooden gunboats, the *Selma, Morgan*, and *Gaines*, each equipped with two 9-inch Dahlgren smoothbores and, in pivot, one 6-inch rifle and one 8-inch smoothbore.

Farragut's vessels, on the other hand, the ships of the West Gulf Blockading Squadron, were all wooden steamers. From his experience with the CSS *Arkansas* in July of 1862, Farragut was extremely concerned that without an ironclad or two, his fleet would be decimated in a fight against the Confederate ram if that occasion should arise. To gain some form of parity, Farragut began to ask the Navy Department to furnish his squadron with ironclad gunboats from the many stationed in the Mississippi River or from those in the James River. Considering the firepower of the forts, the hazards of the torpedoes, and the seemingly impregnable defenses of the *Tennessee* against wooden boats, the campaign seemed suicidal to most observers. The 63-year-old Farragut, however, known as "the old Salamander," was determined not only to carry out his orders, with or without the ironclads, but also to win.

In early January of 1864, while the *Hartford* was still under repair and Farragut was in Washington, a telegraph message came in to the Navy Department that the *Tennessee* was maneuvering down the river towards Mobile Bay. Rumors were also circulating that Buchanan was planning to take the Southern ironclad through the blockade and attack Pensacola, Fort Pickens, and perhaps even retake New Orleans. Suddenly jolted into action with this latest intelligence, the Navy directed Flag Officer Farragut to prepare his squadron for the long delayed attack on Mobile Bay, and he was also assured that plans for obtaining infantry support would be completed by the time he was ready. Finally armed with the go-ahead orders, Farragut traveled to New York, boarded the *Hartford*, and arrived at Pensacola on January 17, 1864. Three days later he reconnoitered Mobile Bay and the two forts to determine for himself the exact conditions he would have to face during his assault. From a safe distance of some three miles, Farragut saw that the *Tennessee* had yet to arrive and was able to examine the forts and the extent of the pilings through his field glass. He was quite satisfied that they were indeed as formidable as he was led to believe. Again, the Union admiral asked for ironclads to supplement the power of his squadron against the daunting defenses he expected to face. The reply from Washington was always the same: The delays were attributed to problems with the contractors building the ironclads. To which Farragut responded, "I ... deeply regret that the department has not been able to give me one of the many iron-clads that are off Charleston and in the Mississippi. I have always looked for the latter, but it appears that it takes us twice as long to build an iron-clad as any one else. It looks as if the contractors and fates were against us. While the rebels are bending their whole energies to the war, our people are expecting the war to close by default; and, if they do not awake to the sense of their danger soon, it will be so."

A short time later Farragut received a wire that reported the movements of the Southern ironclad down the Alabama River. The CSS *Tennessee* had, in fact, come down the river, the report stated, but was stalled on a sand bar, eight miles up the bay, and would remain there until massive floats were attached to get her clear. Farragut saw this opportunity as an ideal time to try out a scheme he had been planning. By possessing Fort Powell, he reasoned, not only would he have easy access into the bay through Grant Pass, but he could also destroy the Confederate ironclad while she was on the sand bar; and by his forces being inside the bay he could keep other vessels from delivering reinforcements to the two forts.

Putting his plan into action, a number of ships from the Union blockading squadron moved into position about 4,000 yards from the fort. With their long-range 13-inch mortars, the ships maintained a steady bombardment of Fort Powell from February 22 to March 2. Incredibly, the barrage failed to achieve its objective. One Confederate remarked, "The bombardment was steadily kept up ... without making any serious impression whatever on the fort; not a single gun had been dismounted, not a single traverse had been seriously damaged, nor had the parapet and bombproof lost any of their strength; all damage done by the exploding shells being at once repaired by throwing sand-bags into the open craters."

Admiral Buchanan had indeed planned to attack Pensacola and Fort Pickens, but the operation was meant to catch the Union forces by surprise. The Southern ironclad, however, had drawn so much attention getting over the sand bar that Buchanan knew the element of surprise had been lost. Consequently, he called off the operation, and his new strategy was to wait for the fleet to enter the bay and approach Fort Morgan. At this point, while they were in the narrow channel, he would attack in concert with the guns of the fort.

The *Tennessee* was eventually freed from the sand bar and, on or about May 23, anchored in Mobile Bay close to Fort Morgan, where she was closely observed during a second reconnaissance by the Union admiral. Somewhat alarmed over the impressive superiority of the ironclad ram, Farragut repeated his demand for additional ships, including ironclads, and 5,000 troops to assist his campaign. This time, however, learning that the *Tennessee* was actually in the bay, the Navy Department was persuaded that the Confederate ram was indeed a serious threat to the success of the operation. Yielding to the Flag Officer's request, two ironclads of the monitor class were ordered for Farragut, the *Manhattan* from New York, and the *Tecumseh* from the James River. Each of them bore two 15-inch guns mounted inside a single turret. In addition, two river monitors were dispatched from Admiral Porter's fleet in the Mississippi. Armed with four 11-inch guns, the twin-turreted monitors were called the *Winnebago* and the *Chickasaw*. The army, meanwhile, was still in New Orleans.

The *Manhattan* arrived on July 26, 1864, and over the next nine days the *Winnebago*, *Chickasaw*, and *Tecumseh* also reported on station. On the western flank of the Bay, meanwhile, a division of troops under Gen. Gordon Granger disembarked on the western tip of Dauphine Island. Once his men were landed, Granger prepared for the long awaited assault on Fort Gaines. Even a detachment of army signal officers were distributed among the Union vessels to insure effective communications between the commanders during the height of the battle, and to establish a communications link with the army after the attack.

Shortly after the *Tecumseh* arrived on August 4, a meeting was held on the flagship to inform the commanders that the attack on Mobile Bay would commence early the next morning. Instructions were also given to each captain on his position in the line. For this attack, the Union fleet of 18 vessels consisted of four ironclads, seven sloops, and seven gunboats, with the ironclads leading the way. Immediately behind the ironclads, the wooden ships would follow, each large sloop paired with a smaller gunboat that was lashed to her side with cable, seven pairs in all. The USS *Brooklyn* would be in the lead pair, selected because she alone possessed the necessary equipment for picking up torpedoes.

The Union sloops were stripped of all non-essential equipment, their decks were covered in sand bags to absorb the plunging fire, and iron chains were draped over the sides to protect the engines. The vessels that made up the attacking line were the ironclads *Tecumseh*, *Manhattan*, *Winnebago*, and *Chickasaw*, in that order. They were followed by the sloop-gunboat pairs *Brooklyn-Octorara*, *Hartford-Metacomet*, *Richmond-Port Royal*, *Lackawanna-Seminole*, *Monongahela-Kennebec*, *Ossipee-Itasca*, and *Oneida-Galena*.

At 7 a.m. on August 5, 1864, as the thick morning fog began to lift, the fleet filed within range of Fort Morgan. Within the hour both the fleet and the guns of the fort were heavily engaged. When they reached Fort Morgan, however, the commander of the lead ironclad spied the *Tennessee* moving in the distance. Obeying his orders to pursue her, the *Tecumseh* suddenly veered off to the left towards the Confederate ironclad and inadvertently steamed within the red buoy and into the torpedo field. In an instant, an enormous explosion rippled across the bay as the wayward ironclad heaved violently in the churning waters. Before the men had time to escape, the ironclad sank, with 93 of her 114 crewmen lost. Assuming there were additional torpedoes in his path, the captain of the *Brooklyn* ordered the ship stopped, causing the rest of the vessels in line to close up on each other until the entire procession had come to a halt. Confused over why the *Brooklyn* had stalled, Farragut signaled for the ships to resume their advance, but the lead ship, the *Brooklyn*, remained in place. Meanwhile, the flagship *Hartford* and the other paired vessels began to receive the full wrath of the fort's guns. Scores of Union crewmen were killed as round after round of shot and shell rained upon the sitting ducks before Fort Morgan. One observer on the *Hartford* described the terrible carnage this way: "Shot after shot came through the side, mowing down the men, deluging the decks with blood, and scattering mangled fragments of humanity so thickly that it was difficult to stand on the deck, so slippery was it." Farragut ordered the signal officer to send a second order to the *Brooklyn*, and still the order was ignored.

Earlier, to gain a better vantage point to view the battle over the huge clouds of smoke, Admiral Farragut had climbed high into the ship's rigging. Percival Drayton, the ship's captain, recognized the admiral's form threaded into the ropes high above the deck and became concerned that in the heat of battle a simple slip would prove fatal. He immediately directed a crewman to tie the admiral to the rigging to insure that he was firmly secured to his lofty perch.

Infuriated that his fleet had stalled before Fort Morgan and was being used for target practice, Farragut ordered the *Hartford* ahead, saying, "I will take the lead."

It was around this time that the famous words attributed to Farragut were supposedly yelled from high in the rigging and over the roar of a raging gun battle. In response to a warning from the commander of the *Brooklyn* as the flagship passed by, Admiral Farragut shouted back, "Damn the torpedoes, full steam ahead!"

In maneuvering around the *Brooklyn*, Farragut knew he would have to enter the same mine-infested waters where the *Tecumseh* had just met her fate, and that the rest of the squadron would follow. But he took the risk, and the gamble paid off. As the *Hartford* steamed ahead, the remainder of the fleet began to follow, as did the three Confederate gunboats that now joined in the fray, raking the fleet as they passed by. At that moment, the *Tennessee* came back into view. She was steaming at full speed directly for the midsection of the *Hartford*, a collision that meant certain death for the Union flagship and the men aboard her. At the last minute, however, the Confederate ironclad altered her course and headed straight for the rest of the fleet instead, most still crowded together before Fort Morgan. Confidently challenging the Union ships, the onrushing *Tennessee* sent two shells blasting into the *Brooklyn*, causing the ship to shudder violently, all the while ignoring the Union solid shot that ricocheted harmlessly off her armor. Recognizing that their shells were useless against the thick iron plates, attempts were made to ram the *Tennessee* as two more Confederate shells ripped into a second Union vessel, the *Oneida*, at point-blank range. After many futile attempts to sink the *Tennessee* by ramming had failed, as did the continuous volley of broadsides, the Southern menace suddenly steamed away and disappeared behind Fort Morgan.

In the meantime, several of the Union gunboats had severed the cables that bound them and were free to join in the battle. The gunboats *Metacomet* and *Itasca* gave chase as the *Selma* and the *Morgan* attempted to escape to Mobile, while the *Gaines*, disabled and leaking badly from a shot from the *Hartford*, headed for Fort Morgan in a sinking condition. Finally, three miles up the bay, the *Hartford* dropped anchor, eventually followed by the rest of the squadron.

The peaceful respite from the smoke, noise, and carnage was greatly appreciated by the crew, in spite of the unpleasant task they now faced of washing the blood and flesh from the decks and collecting the mangled bodies under canvas covers. Halfway through this stomach-wrenching chore, a cry was heard: "The ram is coming." The *Tennessee*, supremely confident in its ability to destroy the Union fleet, was clearly visible against the blue morning sky churning directly for Farragut's armada.

By this time, Farragut had concluded that his ironclads were much too slow to have any significant advantage over the Confederate ram. No longer relying on his armored vessels, he ordered two of his fastest gunboats to meet the challenge of the enemy ironclad. The *Lackawanna* and the *Monongahela* responded quickly to the order, both ramming the *Tennessee*, with no damage inflicted except to the Union gunboats themselves. Ignoring the Union boats that came out to harass her, the *Tennessee* set her sights on the flagship instead, singling out the *Hartford* as her first victim.

The two adversaries, one a wooden warship and one an iron gunboat, began their duel for the possession of Mobile Bay. Maneuvering into position, the two ships charged each other head on but struck only glancing blows. As the *Tennessee* turned for another run at the *Hartford*, she became trapped by the swarming Union gunboats that surrounded her. The *Chickasaw* trained her guns on the enemy's unprotected stern. The *Ossipee*, *Monongahela*, and *Lackawanna* also joined in, directing their guns towards the doomed prey. The Union gunboats, four wooden and three monitors, continually rammed the *Tennessee* and opened a flurry of broadsides, pelting the ironclad with everything they had. Soon the continuous pounding from the *Manhattan*'s 15-inch gun began to take its toll on the outnumbered Confederate warrior, as pieces of fractured iron began to fly off into the thrashing water of Mobile Bay, as did the smokestack and the flagstaff. In the course of this cannonading a shot smashed full into the rudder-chain and paralyzed the *Tennessee*. The Southern ironclad's Achilles heel had been hit.

Although the *Tennessee*'s armor on the outside was able to withstand the tremendous impact of the solid shot, on the inside of the gunboat the same impact usually sent the washers and nuts of the plate bolts, or splinters of iron, screaming through the compartment like shrapnel. After one such impact, Admiral Buchanan's leg was shattered by this shrapnel, and was later amputated. Too injured to continue, Buchanan turned the command over to Cmdr. James D. Johnston. It soon became apparent to the new commander that without the rudder his ability to direct his guns was lost. Not being able to defend the *Tennessee* and his men inside, Johnston went below and briefed Buchanan on the status of their predicament, at which the admiral replied, "Well, Johnston, if you cannot do them any further damage you had better surrender." For the CSS *Tennessee*, at 10 a.m. the war was over.

As for the three Confederate gunboats, the *Gaines* had been disabled in a duel with the *Hartford*. Run aground near Fort Morgan, she was blown up by her crew. The *Selma* was chased down and captured by the *Metacomet*; and the *Morgan*, temporarily grounded, escaped to Mobile that night.

When the dead were counted, the Union killed stood at 145, including the 93 in the *Tecumseh* and 25 from the *Hartford*. Several days after the battle, four addition Union sailors were killed as they collected torpedoes from the bay. The Confederate loss was a modest 12 killed, two of which were on the *Tennessee*, eight from the *Selma*, and two on board the *Gaines*.

Fort Powell was the first of the three forts to concede. On the night of August 5, following the capture of the *Tennessee*, the small garrison ignited slow fuses to the magazine and evacuated to the mainland. Within moments, the fort was destroyed.

General Granger's troops, in the meantime, had crept up to the rear of Fort Gaines on August 5. With his artillery in place, a general bombardment commenced, with assistance from the *Chickasaw*, who began shelling the fort on August 6. The following morning a white flag appeared. Whipping broadly in the stiff ocean breeze, it was unceremoniously carried to the flagship, where terms for surrender were requested and duly carried out unconditionally the following day.

On August 9 Granger's troops landed on Mobile Point. Over the next several days siege lines were constructed and by the 21st the army had approached to within 200 yards of Fort Morgan. On the morning of the 22nd, troop reinforcements were all in position, and the 25 guns and 16 mortars were set and primed to bomb the fort into submission. During all this time, Union sharpshooters were a constant harassment for the Confederate gunners who by now were beginning to feel the strain from the daily diet of incoming gunfire. The Union fleet also surrounded the fort, bombarding it throughout the day in concert with Granger's heavy artillery, but Gen. R. L. Page and his 400 men refused to surrender as long as they had the means to fight. Finally, surrounded by forces on the land and sea, with the fort's casemate about to be breached, all but two guns useless, the powder in the magazine destroyed, the wooden buildings burned, and no means to defend the garrison, General Page surrendered Fort Morgan at 6 a.m. on August 23, 1864.

The city of Mobile was taken in April of 1865 after a successful joint expedition by Flag Officer Henry K. Thatcher, then commander of the West Gulf Blockading Squadron, and Gen. Edward R. S. Canby. Following the capture of four Confederate forts defending Mobile, the mayor surrendered the city on April 12. During this campaign, the partially completed ironclads *Tuscaloosa* and *Huntsville* were sunk, and the Confederate gunboat *Morgan* was captured.

The significance of capturing Mobile Bay was stated rather admirably by Admiral Porter, who wrote: "The days of blockade-runners were over. No more would those snug-looking clippers slip into the bay at night in spite of a most watchful blockade, and, carrying their welcome cargoes into the port of Mobile, supply the Confederacy with food, clothing and munitions of war. The steam locomotive no longer blew its shrillest whistle as it started from Mobile with a rich load of provisions and arms for the city of Richmond, to enable their brave and desperate soldiers to sustain the lost cause by a few spasmodic efforts that could be of no service to them."

The Southern press, principally the *Richmond Examiner*, downplayed the whole episode as much ado about nothing. After all, they remarked, "The capture of the forts did not give the city of Mobile to the enemy, or even give him a practicable water basis for operations against it.... It was a most unequal contest in which our gallant little navy was engaged, and we lost the battle; but our ensign went down in a blaze of glory."

News from Mobile Bay greatly excited the administrators at the Navy

Department. With the exception of the operation against Mobile itself, the Navy turned its attention back to the east coast, specifically Cape Fear, North Carolina. It was here that the Confederate defenses, primarily Fort Fisher, had enabled Wilmington to remain a leading haven for blockade-runners since the beginning of the war. Unable to secure the necessary land forces to support a campaign until now, the Navy saw this moment as an opportunity to take care of business.

The commander of the North Atlantic Blockading Squadron at that time was Rear-Admiral Samuel P. Lee, an officer of notable credentials but relatively inexperienced for this type of joint operation. Secretary Welles was greatly concerned over Lee's inexperience and seized this opportunity to replace him with Farragut as the squadron commander. Once the decision was made, Farragut was ordered to report to Beaufort, North Carolina, by September 1864. Farragut, however, highly resented this appointment because he felt the plan to attack Fort Fisher was unsuitable and he should have been consulted first. In the end, because of ill health, he refused to accept it, choosing to retire from command of the blockading squadron instead. Capt. James S. Palmer would replace Farragut, but in February of 1865 Capt. Henry K. Thatcher took over the reins of the West Gulf Blockading Squadron.

On December 22, 1864, a thankful Congress bestowed Farragut with the rank of Vice Admiral, a rank created specifically for him, and in July of 1866 he was promoted again, this time to full admiral, the first in the U.S. Navy. Farragut then went on to serve as commander of the European Squadron.

17

"Cradle of the Rebellion": December 1861– February 1865

With the opening of the Mississippi and the closing of Mobile Bay, the unrelenting grip of General Scott's anaconda was nearly complete. Along the entire 3,500 miles of coastline, only two Confederate strongholds remained to be taken. Defiant in their brashness, secure in their defenses, the Carolina sisters flaunted their determination and challenged the Union's military might. These two remaining Confederate ports were, of course, Charleston, South Carolina, and Wilmington, North Carolina.

Called the "Cradle of the Rebellion," Charleston was the one Southern city the Northern people, the Government, and the Union troops wanted to punish. This was where it all began, they argued, and as a consequence they wanted the city to pay. In military terms, capturing Charleston would not have ended the war. It would, however, be a tremendous boost for the Union and a devastating defeat for the morale of the Confederacy. But, as they soon would learn, bringing down Charleston was far easier said than done. To the people of the South, Charleston represented the birthplace of the Confederacy, a sacred ground they were determined to defend to the last.

In December of 1861, ships of the South Atlantic Blockading Squadron were moored outside the entrance to the Savannah River with a scheme to sink a number of old ships across the channel. Its success would effectively close the river to Confederate blockade-runners coming in and leaving the port city of Savannah. Called the "Stone Fleet," the decrepit old ships were loaded with tons of stone and rock. When the Confederates themselves blocked the river, however, the "Stone Fleet" was no longer needed and was promptly dispatched to Charleston Harbor on December 17. The Union plan was simply to sink the old ships in the main channel to discourage the blockade-runners from their nighttime sprints into Charleston. In the early morning of December 20, 1861, the old vessels arrived at the main channel, and within hours the seacocks were opened. The old wrecks, laden with tons of stone, were sunk in a scattered pattern in the hope that the blockade-runners would find it impossible to navigate around them in the dark. Ironically, however, the scuttled ships only created a form of breakwater, or jetty, the current of which formed an even deeper channel than before. Soon the business of running the blockade was back in full swing, and Charleston continued to flourish as a prime importer of European goods and munitions of war. Nevertheless, the Charleston authorities were incensed over this blatant display, as were England and France, calling the act "indefensibly barbaric." Even Gen. Robert E. Lee, who was at the time organizing Atlantic coastal defenses, denounced the action, writing, "This achievement, so unworthy any nation, is the abortive expression of the malice and revenge of a people which it wishes to perpetuate by rendering more memorable a day hateful in their calendar."

Flush from their successful campaigns from Port Royal to St. Augustine, the entire inventory of the South Atlantic Blockading Squadron was again at sea, maintaining the blockade and supporting the occupational forces along the southern coastline.

In the fall of 1862, Rear Admiral Samuel F. DuPont, commander of the South Atlantic Blockading Squadron, first suggested his plans to the Navy Department for a joint venture to attack the batteries in Charleston Harbor, knowing full well that the navy alone could not succeed. The naval authorities as well opined that a combined expedition was absolutely critical for a campaign as perilous as this was predicted to be. DuPont's expedition was dashed, however, when he requested 25,000 infantry troops to support the mission, troops the War Department said they could not spare. But, with public pressure clamoring for action against Charleston, the navy felt compelled to move as soon as possible, even if it meant going in alone against the awesome Confederate defenses. Gaining full and enthusiastic support from Asst. Secretary of the Navy Gustavus V. Fox, DuPont's daring objective would have to wait, however, until nine ironclad gunboats promised by Fox were delivered to Port Royal.

The Confederate commander at Charleston was Gen. G. T. Beauregard, who had relieved Gen. John C. Pemberton as commander of the Department of South Carolina and Georgia in August of 1862. Soon after arriving in Charleston, Beauregard's first order of business was to improve the defenses in and around the harbor against an anticipated Union naval attack. The battered walls of Fort Sumter were reinforced, and heavier caliber ordinance was mounted in the embrasures, doubling the firepower, as was done also at Fort Moultrie. Fort Johnson, on James Island, was re-equipped; more batteries were constructed along the beaches and near the city; and additional torpedoes were hidden in the channels. Two ironclad rams were also in Charleston Harbor, the *Palmetto State* and the *Chicora*, and two additional rams, the *Charleston* and *Columbia*, had yet to be completed.

With his two ironclads, Beauregard thought the time was ripe for a preemptive strike against DuPont's wooden steamers observed daily silhouetted against the horizon. It would be to his advantage, mused Beauregard, if he attacked now, before DuPont received his new gunboats. Although his boats were much too heavy, too slow, and lacked adequate firepower, Beauregard still believed his ironclad rams had an obvious and distinct advantage over the wooden ships of the blockading squadron.

On January 31, 1863, the Southern gunboats, under Commodore Duncan N. Ingraham, steamed out from Charleston and attacked the unsuspecting Feds. Outside the harbor at 4 a.m. the blockading fleet was caught completely off guard, detached from the moment by another dark and cold morning of yet another routine day at sea. The steamers assigned to blockade Charleston Harbor were the *Powhatan, Keystone State, Memphis, Canandaigua, Ottawa, Stettin, Flag, Housatonic, Mercedita, Quaker State, Augusta,* and *Unadilla*. Of this fleet, however, the *Powhatan* and the *Canandaigua* were at Port Royal replenishing their coal supplies.

The *Mercedita*, which had just returned from investigating an unknown ship, was the first victim of the Confederate rams. Attacked by the *Palmetto State*, she quickly surrendered after losing 20 men, most scalded to death when a shell punctured her boiler and exploded a huge hole in her port side. Within moments, an officer from the stricken ship boarded the Rebel gunboat, where he received a parole for the officers and crew. Hurrying off in search of their next conquest, the Southerners failed to take possession of the *Mercedita*, which was quickly towed away by several other Union ships.

Continuing on with their seemingly unchallenged assault, the rams pounced on the *Keystone State*. With his ship severely damaged from a dreadful onslaught of gunfire and a shot through her boiler, the captain lowered her flag to signal the surrender of the crippled craft. In their eagerness to resume their destruction, however, the Confederates failed to notice the capitulation of the *Keystone State*; and, as a result, the captain ordered the flag returned to her mast and likewise was towed from the field. The two ironclad rams continued their patrol until the first light of dawn. With no Union ships in sight, they returned to port.

Within hours the Confederate Government filed an official appeal to the British consul in Charleston, stating that because the blockading ships had left their picket line, the blockade was no longer effective and, therefore, under international law, should be lifted. If the Confederates were able to convince the British that the blockade was ineffective and therefore illegal, they would in turn attempt to persuade the British to provide warships to protect their trade agreements and, in effect, recognize the Confederacy. However, when the captain of the *Housatonic* presented his log at the hearings, it provided clear and convincing evidence that a Union ship was indeed still on duty, and, in fact, had fired on the departing rams. In the end, the blockade continued, and was strengthen even more when the *New Ironsides,* just commissioned last August, arrived for patrol duty outside Charleston Harbor on February 1.

The entrance to Charleston Harbor was the span of water between Sullivan's Island on the north and Morris Island on the south, a distance of about one and a half miles. Due to the sand bars and shoals, however, the entrance was reduced to four narrow navigable lanes — three smaller channels running through the northern half, by Sullivan's Island, and the main shipping channel, flowing through the center. Fort Sumter was located about four miles inside the harbor on the southern edge of the main channel, and about three miles from the city of Charleston.

The Confederate defenses were quite formidable indeed, and practically guaranteed that no wooden warship would ever survive once within range of its point-blank power. They began with the outer line of works, specifically the batteries along the coast of Morris Island at Fort Wagner, and Battery Gregg at Cumming's Point. Across the harbor entrance, on Sullivan's Island, were the batteries of Fort Moultrie, Battery Bee, and the battery at Fort Beauregard. Just across from Fort Moultrie the big guns of Fort Sumter stood waiting, and farther down the channel were the batteries of Fort Johnson, Fort Ripley, and the firepower of Castle Pinckney, not to mention the many smaller gun emplacements scattered around the harbor's perimeter and along the city's waterfront. In all, the Confederates estimated that some 385 pieces of ordnance were poised and primed to defend Charleston from any direction. In fact, no other city in the South was as defended as she was. In the harbor, beside the two Confederate ironclad gunboats, there was also a floating rope obstruction between Forts Sumter and Moultrie, and numerous torpedoes lurking farther down the channel.

With the last of his new monitors delivered in March of 1863, DuPont's fleet consisted of his flagship *New Ironsides*, one of the three original ironclads and boasting of firepower from no less than 16 smoothbores, and seven monitors. DuPont's new monitors were the *Montauk, Weehawken, Passaic, Patapsco, Catskill, Nantucket,* and *Nahant.* Called the Passaic class of warships, they were constructed under a contract issued in April of 1862 for new

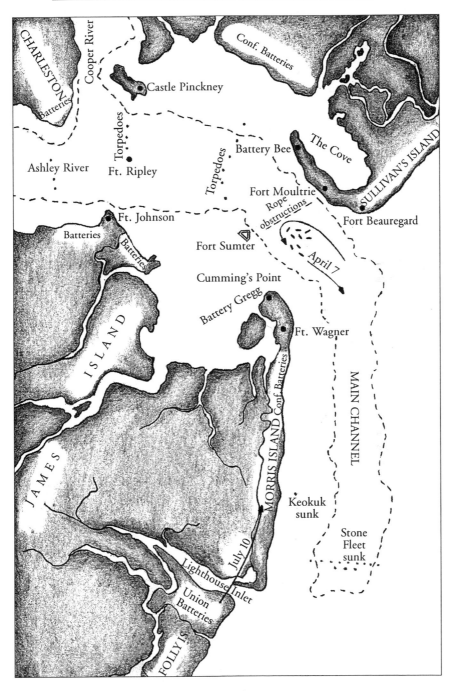

Charleston Harbor — 1863

and improved versions of the ironclad USS *Monitor*. Each of the monitors was single-turreted, with side armor five inches thick, bolted on three feet of oak. Each turret was constructed with 11 layers of iron plating one-inch thick and housed two guns, a 15-inch and an 11-inch Dahlgren smoothbore. Also on hand was the *Keokuk*, a larger, experimental vessel constructed with twin stationary towers firing two 11-inch smoothbores from each tower. She was armored in horizontal iron bars only two inches thick, mounted alternately with strips of wood.

DuPont was also slated to receive the latest in Union underwater technology, a submersible called the *Alligator*. Designed by the Frenchman Brutus de Villerio, the 45-foot, hand-cranked craft was launched in Philadelphia in July of 1862. Following additional sea trials and improvements, the USS *Sumter* was taking the *Alligator* under tow to Port Royal. When the vessels were caught in a storm off Cape Hatteras, the *Sumter*'s crew cut the tow lines and sent the Union's first submarine to the bottom on April 2, 1863.

Admiral DuPont felt fairly confident that his new ironclads could survive Beauregard's batteries, but he wasn't entirely convinced about their offensive firepower. To demonstrate their effectiveness, he decided to test the capabilities of their armor, their guns, and the mechanical efficiency of their turrets before committing his squadron to the Charleston batteries. For this trial, on March 3 he dispatched the *Passaic*, the *Patapsco*, and the *Nahant* to instigate a raid on Fort McAllister, a small 6-gun earth and sand bag fort on the Ogeechee River. After eight hours of trading shells, little damage was done to either the ironclads or the fort. Evidently DuPont was not impressed with the offensive performance of his ironclads, writing to the War Department, "whatever degree of impenetrability they might have, there was no corresponding quality of destructiveness as against forts." Assistant Secretary Fox, on the other hand, thought highly of the monitors and confidently reassured DuPont that the ironclads were quite capable of performing the mission.

DuPont's plan was to take his column of ironclads down the main channel of the harbor and attack the northwest side of Fort Sumter. Following the fort's surrender, the fleet would then attack the batteries on Morris Island.

Venturing into the harbor in the early afternoon of April 7, 1863, the Union column filed along the main channel towards Fort Sumter. Not a shot was fired, nor any other resistance made to the Union fleet as they snaked their way past the Confederate batteries. Continuing on through the channel, the steering of the *New Ironsides* became difficult in the swift current and forced the pilot to struggle repeatedly to maintain a steady forward course. Then, around 3 p.m., DuPont's lead gunboat, the *Weehawken*, commanded by Capt. John Rodgers, came upon the channel obstructions and veered off from the planned route, attacking the northeast face of Fort Sumter instead, from a distance of about 800 yards. This abrupt change in course by the *Weehawken* created much confusion in the column and forced several vessels to close up with the others and some to fall out of formation. At this point, with the Union ironclads in disarray, the barrage from Fort Sumter was opened in earnest and was nothing short of devastating. Armed with high caliber Brooke rifles, Dahlgrens, and Columbiads, it wasn't long before the Southern artillerists were getting the upper hand over the invading gunboats. Soon, despite the valiant effort to fight back, the fleet was trapped in a horrific crossfire between the guns of Batteries Bee, Beauregard, and Wagner, as well as shelling from Cumming's Point and Forts Sumter and Moultrie. Confederate reports later estimated their firepower at 76 rifled and smooth-bore guns firing at DuPont's ironclads tightly grouped within the throat of the harbor.

During the course of the fighting, DuPont learned it was 5 p.m., and ordered his fleet to retire for the night, saying, "It is too late to fight this battle to-night; we will renew it early in the morning." At the time, DuPont was unaware that his fleet of ironclads had suffered a severe mauling. Aboard his flagship that night, however, after receiving the reports from his commanders on the conditions of their ships, DuPont called off resuming the attack. Five of his nine ironclads were so disabled, he said, that if he resumed the attack, instead of this setback, he would have a naval disaster on his hands. The five ironclads most damaged were hit an average of 67 times each from the hundreds of shells raining down on the fleet. Under this battering, turrets and port shutters became jammed on many of the gunboats, while others had guns disabled or iron plates fractured. Again, one of the major concerns was the shrapnel injuries from the nuts and bolts that flew off inside the turret after the armor was hit. Most had suffered severe damage from numerous direct hits, and all of it coming from just the outer line of the Charleston defenses. The following morning the thinly armored *Keokuk* sank off the coast of Morris Island from the effects of her damage.

In contrast, the Confederates reported that Fort Sumter received only about 55 direct hits out of an estimated 125 shots fired, a fault some would blame on the Union's 15-inch turret guns. They were too slow, the critics would claim, taking up to ten minutes to load and fire, while the smaller caliber 11-inch guns were more efficient, being able to fire one round every 60 seconds. In the end, it was a victory of old fashioned defensive land tactics over a budding naval technology.

The authorities in Washington were greatly distressed over the fact that so many of the navy's premier fighting machines, the latest state-of-the-art monitors, had been repulsed. Union Gen. Quincy A. Gillmore, the officer who would soon command the army troops at Charleston, would later write,

"The disheartening fact was that the iron-clads had conspicuously failed in the very work for which they had been supposed to be peculiarly fit, and the country had nothing whatever to take their place." Even Secretary Welles himself was quite critical of the expedition and DuPont's refusal to renew the battle. But DuPont knew from the start that without the support of infantry troops the expedition would be very difficult, if not impossible, and although the admiral felt he had no choice but to retreat with so many crippled vessels, the authorities in Washington still thought otherwise. Hearing the talk about censure, and expecting the worse, in a letter to Secretary Welles on April 16 DuPont wrote: "... I have to request that the Department will not hesitate to relieve me by an officer, who, in its opinion, is more able to execute that service in which I have had the misfortune to fail — the capture of Charleston. No consideration for an individual officer, whatever his loyalty and length of service, should weigh an instant if the cause of his country can be advanced by his removal." Criticized and humiliated, DuPont retired three months later, on July 6, 1863.

Secretary Welles had originally selected Rear Admiral Andrew H. Foote to replace DuPont. The rear admiral, however, who had served with distinction as commander of the Mississippi flotilla, died shortly before assuming his new command. The next choice was Flag Officer John A. Dahlgren, the navy's resident expert on heavy ordnance and the developer of the popular smoothbore that bore his name.

The Lincoln war office refused to accept DuPont's withdrawal from Charleston Harbor as a defeat and was more determined than ever to renew the effort. Even before DuPont's retirement became official, plans were being put together with General Gillmore, and strategies discussed over the next expedition to Charleston Harbor. This time the assault would be a joint venture, but the army would be the primary player and General Gillmore, the commander of the forces that destroyed Fort Pulaski a year ago, would be in charge. From the lessons learned in April, the consensus was that eliminating Fort Sumter was the key to a successful campaign. With the firepower of Sumter removed from the equation, the fleet could easily skirt along the southern edge of the main channel, keeping a relatively safe distance from Fort Moultrie and the other batteries lining Sullivan's Island. But first Morris Island had to be occupied by Gillmore's troops, and batteries set up for the aerial attack on Fort Sumter.

Since early April, the Union occupied Folly Island, a piece of real estate adjacent to Lighthouse Inlet and opposite the southern tip of Morris Island. A base of operations was established on the island, which would serve as a staging area for the planned attack. Gillmore's campaign strategy called for his troops on Folly Island, using the cover of their own battery fire, to invade the southern end of Morris Island. The infantry forces of about 10,000 men, backed up by artillery units and four ironclad monitors, would then march up the peninsula and reduce and capture Fort Wagner, commanded by Gen. William B. Taliaferro, as well as the batteries at Cumming's Point. The Union's rifled batteries would then focus their shelling on the destruction of Fort Sumter before Admiral Dahlgren's fleet steamed down the channel to Charleston.

While plans to return to Charleston Harbor were being discussed, intelligence reports on the completion of a new Confederate ironclad had spurred the Navy Department into action. For months, sporadic reports had been filtering into the department concerning a steamer called the *Fingal*. These reports revealed that the *Fingal* had slipped by the blockade into Savannah in November of 1861; but shortly afterwards, with DuPont's fleet blocking the river mouth around Tybee Island, she was unable to return to England. Eager for an opportunity to increase the fighting capacity of their navy, southern authorities promptly dispatched the steamer to a local shipyard where she was converted into an ironclad warship. Christened the CSS *Atlanta*, she was constructed with a casemate of 3-inch oak over 15 inches of pine. The wooden casemate was then covered with 4 inches of iron plating and armed with 4 Brooke rifles and a spar torpedo. With the *Atlanta* reported to be in the waters around Savannah, and a definite threat to the wooden ships of the blockading fleet, the monitors *Weehawken* and *Nahant* were ordered to seek out and destroy the Confederate ironclad.

Under the command of Capt. William A. Webb, the new ironclad was poised to attack in the early morning of June 17, 1863. Detecting the presence of the Union monitors in the pitch-black waters of the Wilmington River, the supremely confident crew of the *Atlanta* charged at full steam towards their enemy. In his eagerness to pounce on the *Weehawken*, however, the *Atlanta*'s commander diverted away from the narrow channel and within moments became grounded. With the Confederate ironclad a virtual sitting duck on the sandbar, Captain John Rodgers of the *Weehawken* quickly moved in for the kill firing his huge Dahlgrens nearly point-blank into the doomed ironclad. After only 15 minutes, Captain Webb was forced to surrender his battered warship. While Webb and his crew spent several months in a Union prison, the CSS *Atlanta* became the USS *Atlanta*, serving duty on the James River.

With the final orders for the Charleston Harbor mission released, in the early morning hours of July 10, 1863, six days after Vicksburg capitulated to Grant and Gettysburg fell to Meade, nearly 50 field and siege guns, and four ironclads, stood poised to support the invasion of Morris Island. To eliminate the problem of flying shrapnel, Dahlgren had the engineers install iron shields inside the turrets. Following two hours of continuous shelling, and a diversionary demonstration on James Island, Gen. George C. Strong led the first wave of troops across Lighthouse Inlet in forty launches and stormed ashore to initiate the attack. Within a few hours, Strong's forces overran the Confederate defenses, capturing eleven pieces of artillery. By 9 a.m. the Union forces were in control of three-quarters of Morris Island, up to the southern perimeter of Fort Wagner.

As the troops advanced towards Fort Wagner on July 11, the navy fleet, specifically the *New Ironsides, Catskill, Montauk, Nahant,* and *Weehawken,* lent their support with a day-long barrage of the fort to soften up the Confederate works. The army's assault on the fort, however, in the face of deadly concentrations of grape and canister, was unsuccessful, failing again on July 18 with over a thousand men killed, including General Strong.

Even though General Beauregard suspected the attack would be directed towards Morris Island, he dreaded the thought that there was a possibility James Island would be selected instead. He disclosed this fear when he wrote, "It was, in reality, the gateway to the avenue which would have almost assuredly led into the heart of Charleston. The enemy had preferred breaking in through the window, and I certainly had no cause to regret it. He was held in check there, and never got in until we finally opened the gate ourselves toward the end of the war."

The two devastating defeats in front of Fort Wagner, an earthworks mounting high caliber guns and protected by mines and rifle pits, and the continuing destructive shelling from the fort itself, forced the Union command to pull back and reassess their strategy. A state of siege was imposed, and while the generals returned to their maps, Dahlgren's ironclad monitors maintained their bombardment of the formidable Confederate fort and the batteries on Cumming's Point.

An abrupt change in tactics saw the Union army shifting their assault priorities away from Fort Wagner to the bombing of Fort Sumter instead. To accomplish this new objective, it became necessary to move the heavy rifled ordnance back several miles so as to fire over Fort Wagner. From this point the shelling of Fort Sumter was opened and continued around the clock. Beginning on August 17 and lasting a full week, sixteen Parrott rifles and two Whitworth rifles launched some 450 shells a day into the battered and crumbling Sumter. Following the shelling, General Gillmore described the condition of the fort by writing, "The seven days' service of the breaching batteries, ending August 23d, left Fort Sumter in the condition of a mere infantry outpost, without the power to fire a gun heavier than a musket, alike incapable of annoying our approaches to Battery Wagner, or of inflicting injury upon the fleet."

One monstrous gun, an 8-inch rifled Parrott weighing over 10,000 pounds, took two weeks to set up. So massive was its weight in the soft mud of the surrounding marshes that it took 450 men to put the gun in place on a platform built of 13,000 sandbags. Called the "Swamp Angel," the gun was positioned to bombard the city of Charleston itself some five miles away. Although some damage was done to the city by the impact of its 200-pound shells, the gun fired only 36 rounds before it burst at the breech.

Still encountering extreme resistance from the feisty Confederate garrison in Fort Wagner, on September 5, 1863, the Union forces were determined to bring the fort and its inhabitants to their knees. Assembled within range of the fort, 17 siege mortars, 10 siege rifles, 14 Parrott rifles, and the eight broadsides of the *New Ironsides* began an unrelenting and merciless barrage of Fort Wagner. The destructive bombardment lasted for 42 hours straight, every day and every night. Finally, outnumbered by superior forces and overwhelmed by the Union's firepower, the Confederates evacuated both the fort and Cumming's Point on the night of September 6. Escaping aboard the ironclad *Chicora* and a number of barges, the Confederate troops abandoned Morris Island and concentrated their forces on James Island. Within moments of the Confederate withdrawal, Gillmore's troops moved into the abandoned fort, finding 18 pieces of heavy artillery. At Cumming's Point, seven additional guns were captured; but more important, however, was that now the city of Charleston could be plainly seen in the distance.

Fort Sumter, once the magnificent, new, state-of-the-art fortress, was now a huge pile of rubble. It was indeed the grand irony. The U.S. Government had destroyed the very same fort they struggled to defend two and a half years earlier as a symbol of Federal authority over States' Rights, and for the very same reason. The editor of the *Richmond Examiner*, however, saw the damage to Fort Sumter in a different light: "Fort Sumter had, indeed, been severely injured; but it was in one respect stronger than ever; for the battering down of the upper walls had rendered the casemated base impregnable, and the immense volume of stone and debris which protected it, was not at all affected by the enemy's artillery."

Within the walls of battered bricks and mortar the garrison still held on, their Confederate flag still flying smartly above the ruins. Under a white flag of truce, on September 7, 1863, Admiral Dahlgren sent a note to Beauregard demanding that he surrender the fort, but was promptly refused. Beauregard's reply was that Dahlgren "must take it and hold it if he can." With that said, the next day Dahlgren sent a landing party of about 500 marines and sailors to take Fort Sumter by force. It was a tragic mistake, however, because the Confederates were laying in wait for the party to land. The first wave of onrushing marines were met with a deadly storm of musketry and hand grenades, which sent them scurrying for cover among the refuse surrounding the fort. Within minutes, the surprised marines approaching the fort in a second assault quickly retreated back towards their ships, abandoning those still cowering among the mountains of debris. It was revealed some time later that the Confederates had found a signal book in the *Keokuk* back in April, and with this information had been intercepting messages relating to the attack; as a consequence, the defenders knew it was coming that day and were ready. The Union navy paid another terrible price in its fight for Fort Sumter. With the exception of four marines killed, every Union trooper left on the island, over a hundred, was quickly captured.

Following this incident, the two sides settled into a relatively routine standoff that would last for over a year. In the meantime, with the exception of Dahlgren's gunboats playing a standby role in the army's unsuccessful campaign in Florida in February 1864, the Union monitors spent their time on picket duty along the blockade line, while the Confederates kept a vigilant watch from behind their fortifications. At Fort Sumter, most of the remaining heavy artillery in working condition was removed to strengthen the interior defenses, while chevaux-de-frise and wire entrapments were placed along the perimeter of the fort to discourage invasion from enemy landing parties.

Meanwhile, always the innovators in times of adversity, the Southerners were secretly experimenting with a new type of vessel, a 35-foot submersible built from an old boiler. It was powered by a propeller-tipped shaft, hand-cranked by a crew of eight sitting four abreast along its interior while one man steered. The business end of the submarine was a twenty-foot pole extending from the bow. Attached to the end of the pole was a torpedo that would, upon impact, become imbedded in the wooden hull of an enemy ship.

The new craft was the third generation of the so-called Pioneer class of submarines, following two earlier and unsuccessful attempts at New Orleans and at Mobile. Called the *R. L. Hunley* after its builder, the new craft was transported to Charleston from Mobile. During the course of her sea trials, the Confederates met with fatal results when on two occasions the craft went down, drowning the crews each time, including Hunley himself. In time, the new technology was improved upon, and soon the *Hunley*'s unique ability to submerge and resurface was perfected.

On the night of February 17, 1864, the *Hunley* ventured out of Charleston Harbor in quest of her first target, the wooden sloop-of-war USS *Housatonic*. In a daring raid, the torpedo struck just as the Union crew realized they were under attack. The resulting explosion occurred when an attached lanyard detonated the imbedded torpedo as the *Hunley* backed away. Within minutes the two-year-old *Housatonic* went down, killing five crewmen, the first warship ever sunk by an enemy submarine. Unfortunately, the *Hunley* became an unwitting victim of its own cunning. Never resurfacing, the Confederate submarine was lost, along with her nine-man crew.

In 1995 a team of divers from the National Underwater and Marine Agency, in partnership with the South Carolina Institute of Anthropology and Archaeology, discovered the *Hunley* in 28 feet of water four miles off Sullivan's Island. Finally, after 136 years, she was raised from her watery grave on August 8, 2000. Following conservation efforts, which are expected to take about seven years, she will go on display at the Charleston Museum.

Frustrated over the Union's inability to penetrate the Charleston defenses, General Gillmore received a requested transfer to a new command in May of 1864. Taking his place on May 26 was Gen. John G. Foster, who on July 3 made an unsuccessful attempt to capture Fort Johnson. Instead, 140 Union officers and men were taken prisoner in the failed assault.

In December 1864 General William T. Sherman had completed his famous "March to the Sea," captured Fort McAllister, and was occupying Savannah, Georgia. From Savannah, Sherman began his march north through the Carolinas in January 1865, the plan being to join forces with Gen. George G. Meade's Army of the Potomac in Virginia. With Sherman's army marching to the rear of Charleston and all communications severed to the rest of the Confederacy, the Confederate troops evacuated the city on February 18, 1865.

Within days, Admiral Dahlgren and his monitors of the South Atlantic Blockading Squadron steamed into the harbor and captured the ironclad ram CSS *Columbia*. The other three gunboats were found destroyed, blown up by the departing Confederates, as was the city of Charleston, now a raging inferno. Warehouses full of cotton were ablaze, as was supply depots and arsenals, the winds casting hot embers into the air and igniting nearby structures. Four city blocks were leveled when a large quantity of gunpowder exploded at the rail depot, setting off a firestorm. Remarked one Southern citizen after the war, "Charleston came into the enemy's possession a scarred and mutilated city. It had made a heroic defense for nearly four years; for blocks not a building could be found that was exempt from the marks of shot and shell; what were once fine houses, presented great gaping holes in the sides and roof, or were blackened by fire; at almost every step were to be found evidences of destruction and ruin wrought by the enemy."

18

The Capture of Fort Fisher: September 1864– January 1865

It was a massive fleet indeed. As far as the eye could see, nearly 100 Union ships and gunboats of the North Atlantic Blockading Squadron were strewn over the sea in a polka-dotted mosaic. They included the new monitors *Canonicus, Mahopac, Monadnock,* and *Saugas,* and the largest of the Union frigates, the *Minnesota, Colorado,* and *Wabash.* Also present for duty was the ironclad *New Ironsides,* the last of the three original ironclads still in service. Built in Philadelphia, she was equipped with 16 eleven-inch Dahlgrens, and was by far the most powerful of the Union ironclads. She had served her country with distinction, fighting in both squadrons of the Atlantic Blockading fleet, most recently in Charleston Harbor. It was 1864, and, assembled in the early morning December twilight, the newly arrived armada anchored in sight of their objective, the infamous Fort Fisher. Named after Charles F. Fisher, a native of North Carolina who was killed at the First Battle of Bull Run (or First Manassas, in the Confederate vernacular), its huge expanse of batteries guarded the entrance to the Cape Fear River.

Since 1862 Secretary Welles had patiently waited for this opportunity to attack the South's most formidable fort. Fort Fisher provided the security for the city of Wilmington, located only 20 miles up the Cape Fear River, and made Wilmington the port of choice for blockade-runners ferrying supplies from abroad. Leading from the city were the vital railroad links that provided Charleston and Richmond with the goods and supplies they so desperately depended on, and the Army of Northern Virginia with the materials to fuel its war effort. Not only was Wilmington protected by the batteries of the fort,

but the fresh water swamps, sand dunes, and shallow waters of the river provided the city with natural defenses that restricted the Union navy to the
ocean-side perimeter of the river mouth. The treacherous channels and sand
bars kept the heavier and less maneuverable Union ships at bay, only able to
picket the blockade lines in hopes of intercepting a prize. On the other hand,
the Confederate blockade-runners, enjoying the benefits of speed and shallow draft, could dart in and out of the river with relative ease in the pitch-
black shroud of night.

With the focus on Wilmington growing, squadron commander Samuel
P. Lee had devised a three-tier system of patrolling the waters off Cape Fear.
The blockading ships were positioned along three semi-circular arcs, about
20 ships to each line, with the outer line 130 miles from the coast. The navy's
strategy maintained that their surveillance in this configuration increased the
chances of capturing a blockade-runner because any craft that outran a
blockading ship, either entering or departing, would be picked up by the next
tier of Union vessels. To some extent, this strategy proved quite successful —
but not totally, at least not until the Union ships could actually patrol the
Cape Fear River itself. Until then, supplies continued to get into port, albeit
at a diminished rate, and millions of dollars worth of cotton were slipping
out to Europe.

When Welles first proposed a joint attack on Fort Fisher, it was a much
smaller works and would have been a relatively routine confrontation. At the
time, however, the war was raging from the Mississippi to Virginia and, as a
consequence, an attack on the defenses of the Cape Fear River was a low priority for the army. Steadfast in their purpose, the War Department refused
to allocate any troops for the expedition, insisting the men could not be spared
from other, more pressing land campaigns.

In the intervening years the Confederates extended Fort Fisher, strengthening its defensive posture to 44 heavy guns and three mortars, and stretch-
ing its battery emplacements for over a mile along the North Carolina
coastline. Built on a flat, narrow finger of sand, the fort was an "L" shaped
bastion, extending some 1,300 yards along the seacoast and 480 yards across
the peninsula. Constructed of log frames covered by sand and thick layers of
coarse marsh grass, the 25-foot-thick inclined walls were designed to absorb
the force of the incoming shells instead of being destroyed by their impact.
Defensive systems were also in place against an enemy infantry assault. These
deterrents included scores of torpedoes scattered about the perimeter of the
fort, and a palisade of sharpened logs nine feet high. With some help from
the Governor of North Carolina, who pleaded for reinforcements for Fort
Fisher, the original garrison of some 700 men was eventually increased to
over 1,500 troops, including 350 from Fort Buchanan. The Confederates by

this time were aware of an imminent Union assault, and at the direction of the fort's commander, Col. William Lamb, the garrison was well prepared to receive the attack.

To prepare for this campaign, the navy had only their past experience to rely on; and although they had been tested by the defensive fortresses outside New Orleans, Port Royal, and Hatteras Inlet, they knew that Fort Fisher was something more to be reckoned with. Two years after Welles first proposed his plan, he still considered a joint army/navy expedition necessary; but now, to successfully attack and capture the strengthened Confederate fortification, the assault had to be conducted on a grand scale.

With Grant and the Army of the Potomac in Virginia trying to outmaneuver Gen. Robert E. Lee, the shrewdest strategist of them all, the War Department suddenly became more receptive towards eliminating Wilmington as a port of call for blockade-runners. The only remaining Confederate port receiving goods and munitions of war, Wilmington was Lee's principal conduit for supplies, and it was instrumental in sustaining the Army of Northern Virginia. It was now to General Grant's advantage to attack Fort Fisher, shut down Wilmington to blockade-runners, and remove Lee's main source of materials and equipment. In light of this scenario, the army became increasingly amenable towards providing troops for the campaign.

As plans progressed for the attack, on September 22, 1864, Welles sent a dispatch to Admiral Porter ordering him to Beaufort, North Carolina. Earlier, on the 5th, Secretary Welles had appointed Admiral Farragut to command the North Atlantic Blockading Squadron as a preparatory step for the Fort Fisher campaign. This communication to Porter was in response to Farragut's refusal to accept the command, and it read, in part: "You will, ... on the receipt of this order, consider yourself detached from the command of the Mississippi squadron, and you will turn over the command, temporarily, to Captain A. M. Pennock. As soon as the transfer can be made, proceed to Beaufort, N. C., and relieve Acting-Rear-Admiral S. P. Lee, in command of the North Atlantic Blockading Squadron." The command of the Mississippi Squadron would then be turned over to Lee.

Soon after Porter arrived at his new command on October 12, a meeting was held at City Point, Virginia. Attended by Grant, Assistant Secretary Fox, and Porter, the high-level conference was held to fine tune the final plans for the Fort Fisher campaign and to discuss such matters as the number of troops Grant would provide, the logistics of transporting the men, and who would command the land forces. From past experiences at New Orleans, the navy was not pleased with the prospect of working with Gen. Benjamin F. Butler. As Commander of the Army of the James, however, Butler still held the Cape Fear area under his jurisdiction, specifically the Department of

Virginia and North Carolina, and Grant was obligated to put Butler in over-all command, with Gen. Godfrey Weitzel in direct charge of the assaulting troops.

Following Porter's meeting with General Grant, several months went by without any movement from Butler's troops. During this lull, nearly 100 vessels were assembled in Hampton Roads, vessels of all classes — from sloops-of-war to ironclads to coal tenders, from frigates to tugboats — all to support the navy's role in the upcoming battle. While waiting for General Weitzel and his troops to arrive, the crewmen drilled each day in the fine art of gunnery, and the commanders became acquainted with the plan of battle, the position of their ship, and the role they had to play.

As the weeks went by, Secretary Welles grew increasingly frustrated. His patience was wearing thin over the delay in getting Weitzel's troops in place. In writing for Lincoln's intervention, Welles revealed his dissatisfaction by saying, "The importance of closing Wilmington is so well understood by you, that I refrain from presenting any new arguments. I am aware of the anxiety of yourself and of the disposition of the War Department to render all the aid in its power. The cause of the delay is not from the want of a proper conception of the importance of the subject, but the season for naval coast operations will soon be gone. The public expects this attack, and the country will be distressed if it is not made. To procrastinate much longer will be to peril its success."

In the latter half of November, General Butler, accompanied by General Weitzel, finally made his appearance aboard Porter's flagship, the *Malvern*. At this meeting in Hampton Roads, Butler announced his grand plan to destroy Fort Fisher in one stroke. The Confederate fortification would suffer enormous damage, he confidently predicted, by anchoring an old steamer close to the fort and detonating nearly 200 tons of gunpowder stowed on board. Following the massive explosion, the fleet would commence a shelling barrage while the troops stormed ashore. All concerned went along with the plan, as grandiose as it sounded. Even General Grant, who approved it, admitted later, "I had no confidence in the success of the scheme, and so expressed myself; but as no serious harm could come of the experiment, and the authorities at Washington seemed desirous to have it tried, I permitted it." At this point the navy thought any plan to get the expedition underway was better than none, even though few had little faith in its success.

At last the campaign to close down Wilmington was underway. Butler's transports finally sailed from Hampton Roads on December 16 to assemble at Masonboro Inlet, 30 miles from Wilmington. Porter's fleet had arrived on December 20 and were scattered some 20 miles offshore from Fort Fisher.

At the appointed hour on December 23, an old gunboat, the *Louisiana*, carefully loaded with tons of powder, was towed by the steamer *Wilderness* up the darkened channel and anchored as close to the fort as possible, about a half-mile distant. Fuses timed to detonate in one and a half hours were lit, and the Union sailors scrambled overboard to row to the *Wilderness* waiting some distance away. At 1:30 in the morning of December 24 the nighttime sky was suddenly illuminated by a blast that scarcely drew the attention of the Confederate garrison. As darkness quickly returned to embrace the fort, it became apparent to the men of the Union fleet that, in spite of Butler's predictions, the fort had suffered no damage whatsoever. In fact, the Confederate troops thought the blast was merely a boiler exploding on a Union gunboat.

At dawn the army troops had yet to appear, and despite the failure of the explosion to damage the fort, at a given signal the fleet got underway and formed their line of battle. Besides the frigates *Minnesota*, *Colorado*, and *Wabash*, the formation also included old battle proven warships like the screw-sloops *Mohican* and *Brooklyn*, and the veteran side-wheel steamer *Powhatan*. About noon the Union ships took their place on the firing line, with the *New Ironsides* leading the way, followed by the four new monitors, all five positioned three-quarters of a mile from the fort. Next in formation were the large wooden ships, which lined up one mile out behind the monitors, their broadside guns trained on the enemy batteries lining the coastline; the rest of the fleet, the reserves, likewise took their places in front of Fort Fisher.

It was an impressive sight indeed as over 60 ships opened fire with a thundering roar, a huge sheet of flame, and billowing clouds of smoke. Signals from the flagship to control the movements of the ships were useless in the poor visibility and forced Porter to use a tugboat to relay his orders, as he had done in January of 1863 battling Arkansas Post. The unrelenting shelling continued throughout the afternoon, but after only an hour the guns of Fort Fisher fell silent, an obvious indication to the Union gunners that the garrison had fled to the refuge of their bombproof shelters. Nevertheless, the one-sided barrage of shot and shell, estimated to be 115 rounds per minute, was maintained for five long hours. At sunset, to the relief of the weary gun crews, the welcomed order to retire was given, and the ships filed back to their previous anchorage. Fatalities for that day were somewhat surprising, the Confederates reporting only one man killed, while the Union lost 22, the result of five guns exploding.

The following day, at 7 a.m. the fleet resumed their positions off the coast of Fort Fisher. Butler's 6,500 troops, having arrived the previous day during the naval bombardment, began their amphibious landing on the beach around two o'clock that Christmas afternoon under the watchful eye of Porter's gunboats. But when the first wave of troops, about 1,500, stormed the beach five miles from the fort, the firepower from the fleet was noticeably diminished. Porter's ammunition was running low, forcing his cannonading to be sporadic and slow.

Dispersing his forces along the beach, General Weitzel directed his troops towards the fort, encountering stubborn resistance from two Confederate batteries. In their sweep to the fort, the Union troops overran both batteries and captured nearly 300 men before it became evident to General Butler that Fort Fisher was more than his men and equipment could handle. Informed by Weitzel that Confederate gunfire was as heavy as ever, and learning that the approaches to the fort were laced with mines, Butler concluded that further attempts to take the fort by direct assault would be futile. After only three hours, Butler ordered his troops back to the transports.

The general had been quite irate that morning because Porter exploded the *Louisiana* before he arrived, and now he was even more upset at the admiral for failing to soften up the enemy garrison for his troops. Before leaving, therefore, he sent a parting remark to Porter's flagship that read, "Upon landing the troops and making a thorough reconnaissance of Fort Fisher, both General Weitzel and myself are fully of the opinion that the place could not be carried by assault, as it was left substantially uninjured as a defensive work by the Navy fire." At that point, 20 transports steamed off to Hampton Roads, stranding hundreds of troops still under fire in rifle pits.

Incensed over Butler's sudden withdrawal from the campaign, a disappointed Porter ordered the abandoned troops picked up off the beach, and the fleet steamed off to Beaufort to restock their fuel and ammunition. Still fuming over the army's desertion and perhaps Butler's stinging assertion that his ships failed to damage Fort Fisher, Porter sent off a flurry of letters to Welles venting his anger and asking for the return of the troops, and adamantly insisting on a new commander. Ironically, reports written by the Confederate commander, Colonel Lamb, more or less supported Butler's claim. Lamb revealed that at least a third of the shells had fallen into the river or the surrounding marshes, and that no significant damage was sustained to the magazines or the bomb proofs. Although some of the wooden buildings were burned, in spite of tons of Union iron pouring down on the fort, only eight guns were disabled.

General Grant was also taken aback by Butler's failure to follow his instructions. Grant's orders to him were rather explicit, informing Butler that if he should make a landing, "the foothold must not be relinquished." For failing to follow his orders, Butler was sent home to Massachusetts and Gen. Alfred Terry, a 37-year-old lawyer, assumed command of the Army of the James.

Grant assured Admiral Porter that the troops would be returned, and requested that he maintain his force at Beaufort until their arrival from Fort Monroe. True to his word, on January 8, 1865, General Terry and 8,000 troops disembarked at Beaufort and the campaign was back on track. Meeting during a snowstorm to discuss plans for the assault, the two commanders found they were both of one mind and spirit, which afforded a most congenial relationship, so vital for a joint expedition to succeed. Four days later the weather had improved and the combined force departed for Fort Fisher.

On January 13, 1865, the army troops were landed on the river-side of the fort in an enormous amphibious operation. In something of a presage to the D-Day invasion at Normandy many years later, 200 small boats ferried 8,000 troops to within five miles of the fort where they waded ashore and entrenched for the upcoming assault. Protected by the gunboats of Porter's fleet, the landing took four hours.

As the troop landing was underway, the monitors had resumed their shelling of the fort. Positioned much closer for this engagement, at about 700 yards, they were instructed to concentrate their fire on disabling the fort's guns. Around 2 p.m., after the last of the troops had been delivered to the beach, the big guns of the fleet opened their barrage as well. With these ships also firing from a much closer range, Porter's intent was to increase the efficiency of the bombardment, "to lodge the shell in the parapets, and tear away the traverses under which the bombproofs are located." The massive shelling would continue relentlessly for two days and two nights. At sunset of each day the bigger ships were ordered to retire while the monitors maintained their fire throughout the night. Colonel Lamb, meanwhile, concerned by what he saw developing along the beach, wired General Bragg asking for reinforcements that never came.

On the morning of the 15th the entire fleet was on station preparing for an all-out bombardment as a prelude to the storming of the fort by Terry's men later in the afternoon. Porter, however, was determined to have his men take part in the assault as well. Assembling some 2,000 volunteers from the various ships of the fleet, 400 of them marines, the naval force landed about 800 yards down the beach. Porter's plan called for the sailors to charge down the beach under cover from the marines and attack the ocean-side face of the fort at the same time the army troops charged towards the land-side of the fort. The minefield, unknown to Porter, was destroyed in the bombardment, and would not be a factor in the attack. Problems occurred, however, when the sailors began their advance earlier than expected. Armed with only handguns and cutlasses, and with no experience in close combat, their advance down the beach caused the Confederates to assume the main assault was underway. Accordingly, Colonel Lamb quickly shifted his manpower to the ocean-side of the fort to confront the onrushing threat. Charging down the

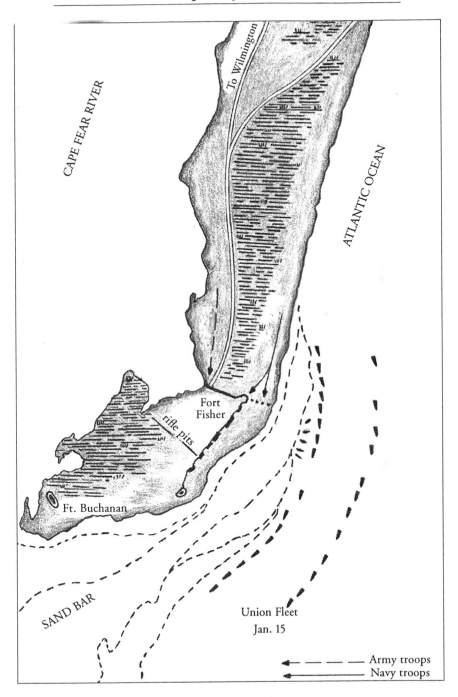

Attack on Fort Fisher

beach, stumbling over the bodies of their fallen shipmates, the sailors dashed towards the fort, many seeking protection among the dunes from the near point-blank fire. One Union officer hidden in the sandy mounds before the fort recalled, "Oh, such a fire as we were under. Sailors and officers were dropping all around me." Soon, upon reaching the palisade that blocked their way, the advance force halted. A small group managed to scale the obstruction, but with the charging mass of men arriving from the rear, everyone was now stacked up "like sheep in a pen." Only 40 yards away, the Confederates took this opportunity to fire into the crowded throng as they herded together on the beach. Suddenly, as the slaughter continued, by some unheard signal, the sailors at the rear broke and retreated in a wild stampede, quickly followed by the remaining men on the beach.

During this episode, around 3:30 p.m., the army invasion troops were storming the opposite side of the fort. Taking advantage of the shift in Confederate resistance to the ocean-side, Terry's men found it relatively easy to breach the fort and gain a foothold within the compound. After several hours of close and intense hand-to-hand fighting, the Fort Fisher garrison surrendered. The fort's commander, Colonel Lamb, later wrote, "Had there been no fleet to assist the army at Fort Fisher the Federal infantry could not have dared assault it until its land defenses had been destroyed by gradual approaches."

Many Confederates put the blame for the fort's demise squarely on the shoulders of Gen. Braxton Bragg, commander in charge of the defenses at Wilmington, for not sending reinforcements. As Mary Chestnut, the Southern diarist remarked, "He knew what was coming.... He remained in gunshot with ten thousand men, when one thousand would have saved Fort Fisher."

Terry's army reported nearly 700 troops killed, wounded, and missing that day, two hundred of that number occurring after the battle when they inadvertently entered the fort's magazine with a lighted torch and set off about 12,000 pounds of gunpowder. But the real loss was on the navy side, with 390 sailors killed in there misguided but gallant effort. The defenders of Fort Fisher, on the other hand, estimated that 500 men were killed and wounded in their fight to save the last vestige of Southern resistance.

For the Army of Northern Virginia, and the Southern cause, Fort Fisher was indeed the last lifeline in their long struggle. Three months later, the war was over.

Glossary

Abatis: a barricade of felled trees, with branches pointed towards the enemy. Used as a defensive weapon to impede enemy cavalry or an invading infantry force.

Aft: at, near, or toward the stern of a ship

Bark: a three-masted vessel with its two forward masts square-rigged and its rear mast rigged fore and aft.

Battery: a grouping of four to six field guns.

Blakely: British heavy artillery. Blakely rifled canon came in various calibers with barrels made of cast iron strengthened with steel.

Bow: the front part of a ship or boat; prow.

Breach: to break into or open a hole in something. A force might *breach* the casemate of a fort with artillery shells, or a defensive line with charging troops.

Breech: the back end of the barrel of a gun, the part of a breech-loading cannon behind the barrel where the shell is inserted.

Brooke rifled gun: a Confederate cannon developed by Lt. John M. Brooke. Essentially a version of the Parrott gun, modified with two or three wrought iron reinforcement straps around the cast iron breech.

Bulkhead: a partition dividing a ship into separate watertight compartments.

Casemate: a shellproof or armored enclosure or room with openings for guns, as in a fortress or on a warship.

Cheval-de-frise (pl. **chevaux-de-frise**): an obstacle, usually wooden spikes secured to a casemate or erected around the perimeter of a fort used to discourage onrushing enemy infantry.

Columbiad: a large caliber smoothbore siege gun capable of firing a large projectile at high elevations over great distances. Three calibers were used, the 8-inch, 10-inch, and the massive 15-inch, which weighed 50,000 pounds. Named after the Columbia Foundry in Washington, D.C., where they were manufactured.

Conscription: compulsory service in the armed forces; a military draft.

Contingent: a group of troops.

Contraband: a black slave who fled to, was smuggled, or was found behind the Union lines.

Corvette: a sailing warship larger than a sloop but smaller than a frigate.

Cottonclads: Confederate gunboats that were "armored" with compressed cotton bales for protection against enemy fire.

Cutwater: the foremost part of a ship's bow that cleaves the water.

Dahlgren: heavy artillery made of cast iron but otherwise similar to the Columbiad. It was a standard U.S. Navy artillery piece named after its designer, John A. Dahlgren.

Demijohn: a large bottle of glass or earthenware with a narrow neck and a wicker casing.

Draft: the depth of water that a vessel draws, or needs, in order to float, especially when loaded.

Earthworks: an embankment made by piling up earth as a fortification.

Embrasure: an opening in a casemate or parapet with the sides slanting outward to increase the angle of a gun.

Enfield rifle: an English made rifled musket used extensively by both sides throughout the war.

Fantail: the part of the main deck, or overhanging portion of the stern on some ships.

Fire-raft: a name applied to a boat, usually a wooden flat boat, filled with combustibles or explosive materials. Set afire, it would be launched in the current towards the enemy ship in the hope of setting it on fire.

Flag Officer: a naval commander above the rank of captain entitled to display a special flag from a ship's mast indicating his rank.

Flagship: the ship that carries the flag officer of a fleet or other large naval unit and displays his flag.

Flotilla: a small fleet of ships.

Frigate: a fast, medium sized three-masted warship, which usually carried from 30 to 50 guns.

Fulminate: an explosive salt of fulminic acid used in detonators and percussion caps.

Galley: a kitchen of a ship or boat.

Gangway: an opening in a vessel's railing that allows passage on or off the ship.

Garrison: troops assigned to service in a fort or fortified place.

Grape: small iron balls which, when bound together, formed a stand of grapeshot. Usually fired from artillery in close range combat against charging enemy forces, with the same effect as a large shotgun.

Grog: alcoholic liquor, usually rum, diluted with water.

Gunboat: a small, armed vessel of shallow draft. Designed principally for use on rivers.

Gunny-sack: a sack made of a coarse cloth, usually made from jute.

Hardtack: hard, unleavened cracker, measuring nearly three inches square.

Hot shot: a solid shot projectile that was heated white or red hot in a specially constructed furnace. Its primary purpose was to set fire to wooden ships or wooden buildings.

Howitzer: a short-barreled weapon with a large powder chamber, capable of lobbing a shell with low muzzle velocity but high trajectory.

Ironclad: a warship armored with iron plating.

Landsman: inexperience sailor, a recruit.

Letters of Marque: a license or permit sanctioned by the Confederate Government allowing privately owned vessels to attack and capture U.S. merchant vessels at sea.

Limber: a two-wheeled, detachable front part of a gun carriage, usually supporting an ammunition chest.

Magazine: a safe storage area in which ammunition and explosives are stored.

Master: a highly skilled craftsman qualified to follow his trade independently and, usually, to supervise the work of others.

Mess: the term applied to a meal or place where a group of people of similar rank regularly have their meals together.

Monitor: name applied to a class of Union ironclad gunboats. Modeled after the USS *Monitor*, they were distinguished by employing either a single or a double revolving gun turret.

Mortar: a short, heavy piece of artillery that fired large projectiles over a high trajectory. Mortar shells usually exploded while high in the air and rained shrapnel down on fortifications and enemy personnel.

Mortar boat: vessel carrying a short-barreled cannon (mortar).

Palisade: a row of large pointed stakes set in the ground, upright or oblique, as a defensive weapon.

Palmetto flag: State flag of South Carolina displaying the palmetto palm.

Parapet: a wall used to screen troops from frontal enemy fire, usually seven feet high.

Parrott gun: a smoothbore or rifled cast-iron cannon that employed a heavy wrought iron band shrunk around its breech for extra strength. Named after its designer, Robert P. Parrott.

Pdr.: an abbreviation for pounder, a term generally used to distinguish one piece of artillery from another by noting the weight of its projectile in pounds, as in 32-pdr.

Percussion cap: a small brass "cap" that contained a small amount of fulminate of mercury. It was placed on a cone or "nipple" mounted on the firearm adjacent to the chamber containing a charge of gunpowder and the bullet. The fulminate exploded when struck by the hammer, sending a flame through a hole in the cone into the powder charge and firing the bullet.

Pickets: a group of soldiers or ships, usually positioned along the perimeter of an encampment or fleet, to guard against surprise attack.

Port: the left side of a ship.

Powder monkey: a naval term for a boy who passed powder cartridges to the guns. It was a position calling for sailors of small stature. In some cases nine-year-old boys were accepted for this task.

Prize: a captured merchant ship and its cargo taken by force and later sold to the highest bidder.

Ram: name applied to a warship equipped with a metal projection attached to the bow, usually below the waterline. Intended to pierce and sink wooden enemy vessels on impact.

Ransom-bond: a document issued to a captured merchant ship carrying cargoes belonging to foreign nationals stating that the value of the ship would be paid to the Confederacy at the end of the war.

Receiving ship: an old ship that was stripped of its guns and used as a holding vessel or for training seamen recruits in basic seamanship.

Refit: to make fit for use again.

Revenue cutter: a small, armed sailing vessel used by the U.S. Revenue Service and authorized to pursue smugglers.

Rifled: cut spiral grooves in the bore of a cannon that causes the shell to spin for greater stability, accuracy, and penetration.

Regiment: in the Civil War, a military unit usually consisting of about 1,000 men.

Rigging: the ropes, chains, and other gear used to support, position, and control the masts, sails, etc. of a vessel.

Schooner: a sailing ship with two or more masts, rigged fore and aft.

Scuppers: openings in a ship's side to allow water to run off the deck.

Scuttled: to make or open holes in a ship below water level in order to sink it, as by opening a seacock.

Seacock: a valve below the waterline in the hull of a ship, used to control the intake of seawater.

Sheer: to turn aside sharply from a course; swerve.

Shell: a hollow projectile of cast iron containing a bursting charge, which was ignited by means of a fuse.

Shoal: a sand bar or piece of rising ground forming a shallow place that is a danger to navigation.

Side-wheeler: a steam-driven vessel having a paddle wheel on each side.

Sloop: a small fore-and-aft-rigged single-masted sailing vessel.

Sloop-of-War: a sloop armed with its main broadside battery on one deck only.

Snag-boat: a heavy steamboat used for clearing obstructions from waterways.

Solid shot: a solid iron projectile cast without a powder chamber or fuse hole.

Spiking: to make a cannon unusable by driving a spike into the touchhole, the hole in the breech through which the charge is touched off.

Starboard: the right side of a ship or boat.

Steamers: a ship powered by a steam engine.

Sutler: a person following a military unit to sell food, liquor, and personal items to its soldiers or sailors.

Tender: a small vessel used to transport passengers, goods, fuel, etc. from or to a larger ship.

Tin-clads: light-drafted ironclad gunboats designed for use on shallow rivers. Usually armored in iron less than one inch thick.

Traverse: a parapet or wall of earth protecting troops or a battery in a trench.

Ways: the wooden structure over which a ship moves when being launched.

Bibliography

Anderson, Bern. *By Sea and by River: The Naval History of the Civil War.* New York: Knopf, 1962.

Catton, Bruce. *The Coming Fury.* New York: Doubleday, 1961.

Davis, William C., and Bell Irvin Wiley, eds. *The Civil War Times Illustrated Photographic History of the Civil War.* 2 vols. New York: Black Dog and Leventhal, 1994.

Eisenschiml, Otto, and Ralph Newman, eds. *The Civil War: The American Iliad, as Told by Those Who Lived It.* 1947. New York: Mallard, 1991.

Gosnell, H. Allen. *Guns of the Western Waters: The Story of River Gunboats in the Civil War.* Baton Rouge: Louisiana State University Press, 1949.

Hearn, Chester G. *Admiral David Dixon Porter: The Civil War Years.* Annapolis, Md.: Naval Institute Press, 1996.

Holland, J. G. *The Life of Abraham Lincoln.* Springfield, Mass.: Gurdon Bill, 1866.

Johnson, Robert U., and Clarence C. Buel, eds. *Battles and Leaders of the Civil War.* 4 vols. Edison, New Jersey: Castle, 1884.

Katcher, Philip. *The Civil War Source Book.* New York: Facts on File, 1982.

Kirchberger, Joe H. *Eyewitness History of the Civil War.* New York: Facts on File, 1991.

Kunhardt, Philip B., Jr., Philip B. Kunhardt III, and Peter W. Kunhardt. *Lincoln: An Illustrated Biography.* New York: Knopf, 1992.

Pollard, E. A., ed. *The Lost Cause.* 1886. New York: Gramercy Books, 1994.

Porter, David D., Admiral. *The Naval History of the Civil War.* 1886. New York: Dover, 1998.

Rye, Scott. *Men & Ships of the Civil War.* Stamford, Connecticut: Longmeadow Press, 1995.

Stern, Philip Van Doren. *The Confederate Navy: A Pictorial History.* New York: Da Capo Press, 1962.

Still, William N., Jr., John M. Taylor, and Norman C. Delaney. *Raiders and Blockaders: The American Civil War Afloat.* Washington Brassey's, Inc., 1998.

Wideman, John C. *Civil War Chronicles, Naval Warfare, Courage and Combat on the Water.* New York: Friedman, 1997.

Index

223